School Reform and the
School Library Media Specialist

Recent Titles in Principles and Practice Series

School Reform and the School Library Media Specialist

Sandra Hughes-Hassell and Violet H. Harada

Principles and Practice Series

LIBRARIES UNLIMITED

A Member of the Greenwood Publishing Group

Westport, Connecticut • London

Library of Congress Cataloging-in-Publication Data

Hughes-Hassell, Sandra.
 School reform and the school library media specialist / Sandra
Hughes-Hassell and Violet H. Harada.
 p. cm. — (Principles and practice series)
 Includes index.
 ISBN 978–1–59158–427–8 (alk. paper)
 1. School libraries. 2. Educational change. I. Harada, Violet H.
II. Title.
 Z675.S3H74 2007
 027.8—dc22   2007016437

British Library Cataloguing in Publication Data is available.

Library of Congress Catalog Card Number: 2007016437
ISBN-13: 978–1–59158–427–8

First published in 2007

Libraries Unlimited, 88 Post Road West, Westport, CT 06881
A Member of the Greenwood Publishing Group, Inc.
www.lu.com

Printed in the United States of America

The paper used in this book complies with the
Permanent Paper Standard issued by the National
Information Standards Organization (Z39.48–1984).

10 9 8 7 6 5 4 3 2 1

Contents

Illustrations

FIGURES

TABLES

Foreword

The pioneers of the school library movement in the early twentieth century, including C. C. Certain, Mary P. Hall, Mary Peacock Douglas, Frances Henne, and Mary Gaver, envisioned a place in the school far beyond a repository of books. They saw the school library as distinct from the public library because its central focus was teaching.

Today, we have both books and technology systems in school libraries. Having stuff and hooking technology up and turning it on, however, does not fulfill the dreams of the early pioneers. Neither does it fulfill the dreams of the authors represented in this book. We look for an active, not passive, role the school library can play in teaching, and by extension, in learning. In fact, as information and technology have expanded to become the new real environment of our society, this new role takes on even more significance. Early behavior indications from our learners indicate that there is an easy way to deal with the information environment: simply cut and paste into worksheets and reports something easily located from digital databanks. Such behavior worries school library professionals as they try to take responsibility as an active teaching entity.

Not only are there challenges with technology today, but other pressures have changed the nature of many schools. Schools now have children with even more diverse backgrounds and abilities than ever before. There are pressures from the government to score high on standardized tests. Everyone seems to feel that the responsibility to produce results revolves around a sole teacher in a lone classroom. Teachers are feeling frustrated, isolated, and threatened. They lock their doors, crying, "Let me alone! I have too much to cover!" To our school librarians, this resistance comes at a time when we have more to offer than ever before.

The authors represented in this book provide substantive recommendations about the role of the school library in the 21st century. The book is a cry for administrators, teachers, and parents to take note: "Hey you (y'all)! We are here! We can help! We know how! Let us strut our stuff!" Reading the essays herein demonstrates that just as the information and technology world has evolved, so have the skills and abilities needed to extend the impact the library has in the school. So while the vision of our early pioneers has not changed, the set of skills needed to fulfill that vision have expanded. We need our current professionals to retool; our new crop to innovate; we need a new dawn of relevance both to our students and teachers. The authors represented in this excellent collection of essays see that new vision, or more precisely, creative new ways to fulfill the historic vision. This vision is worth considering both by the experienced and the novice.

Professor David V. Loertscher
School of Library and Information Science,
San Jose State University

Acknowledgments

The editors express their appreciation to the contributors to this volume. Without their enthusiasm and dedication to the project, it would not have happened. We also thank Jacqueline C. Mancall at Drexel University and Sharon Coatney at Libraries Unlimited for the editorial support they provided to the project. By posing the tough questions, they helped us move toward new understandings that shaped our vision for the book.

Introduction

Violet H. Harada and Sandra Hughes-Hassell

They keep moving the cheese.

—Spencer Johnson

In his national bestseller *Who Moved My Cheese,* Spencer Johnson (1998) tells the story of two mice (Sniff and Scurry) and two little people (Hem and Haw). The four characters live together in a maze and share the same food supply—a big pile of cheese. One morning the four arrive at their cheese station to find it empty. Sniff and Scurry are not surprised—they had noticed that the pile of cheese was getting smaller and had begun to make plans to look for new cheese. They simply put on their running shoes and proceed to explore the maze in search of new cheese. Hem and Haw, on the other hand, are totally unprepared for what they find. They had taken for granted that the cheese would always be there. They feel betrayed, angry, and afraid. Rather than taking action, they are immobilized, spending precious time waiting for the status quo to return and blaming one another for their situation. Finally, Haw begins to examine and alter his beliefs about change and is able to venture into the maze in search of new cheese. What about Hem? We're not sure. The last time we see Hem, he is waiting for his old cheese to return and adamantly declaring that he is not going to change until he gets what he wants.

Johnson's message is clear. Change happens. To be successful, and happy, we need to not only anticipate and adapt to change, but we need to be ready to quickly change again and again.

Nowhere is Johnson's message more applicable than in the world of education, where change is often described as "ubiquitous and relentless" (Fullan 1993, vii). Since the publication of *A Nation at Risk: The Imperative for Educational Reform* in 1983, the number of reform efforts has grown exponentially (National Commission on Excellence in Education 1983). Politicians, educators, parents, and the community have struggled with questions such as: What should American students know and be able to do to compete in a global marketplace? What is the best way to meet the needs of an increasingly diverse student population? What impact will technology have on teaching and learning? How should schools be structured, governed, and financed? What role should the federal government play in dictating educational policy at the state and local level?

In this new millennium, we find ourselves at the "epicenter of a continuing tempest" calling for change (Kinsler and Gamble 2001, 3). Reform initiatives have focused on topics like standards, choice, and school-based management. They have targeted specific disciplines and specific populations of students including special education students, English language learners, preschoolers, adolescents, and at-risk students. The federal government has mandated changes through legislative actions such as the passage of the No Child Left Behind (NCLB) Act and the Individuals with Disabilities Act (IDEA).

While reform efforts have taken many forms, the emerging international body of research about the characteristics of effective schools reveals striking similarities across countries (Reynolds and Cuttance 1992). According to Levine and Lezotte (1990), distinguishing features of effective schools include: focus on student acquisition of central learning skills, appropriate monitoring of student progress, practice-oriented staff development at the school site, outstanding leadership, and salient parent involvement. Academic excellence, accountability, diversity, digital literacy, and professional leadership have been persistent themes in the reform initiatives (Marsh 1999; Newmann and King 1997). We elaborate on each of these themes in the following sections.

ACADEMIC EXCELLENCE

The call for academic excellence has prompted reformers at the federal and state levels to revisit the core curriculum, promote national standards for the major disciplines, and emphasize new basics that go beyond the traditional three Rs. Earl (2002) says these basics involve accessing, interpreting, and applying information, making informed judgments, and working effectively in groups. More rigorous learning has also prompted a pedagogical shift from mechanistic and behavioral approaches to progressive, constructivist approaches to teaching and learning. Central to a constructivist approach is the notion of active engagement in the process of construction whereby learners build upon their previous or preexisting knowledge and seek meaningfulness in these constructions (Darling-Hammond 1997).

ACCOUNTABILITY

The challenges of improvement become more complex and demanding as performance increases, and the demands on existing instructional practices and existing organizational norms more direct and difficult (Elmore 2004). Accountability at the school level must reflect an appreciation for the fact that schools are not alike and that each school must assess its instructional practices and determine best ways to communicate demonstrable gains in student performance.

Student achievement has traditionally been assessed through standardized quantitative measures. Current reformers, however, argue that more realistic assessment of student performance is possible through a range of qualitative and quantitative approaches that include strategies to carefully observe student performance and analyze student work (Hartzell 2001). To build this type of authentic assessment, school professionals must identify clear standards for student performance, collect information to inform themselves about their levels of success, and exert peer pressure within their staffs to meet the goals (Meier 1997). As an organic part of the school experiences, these assessments inform self-improvement and modifications in teaching. In short, they provide a solid foundation for evidence-based practice.

DIVERSITY

National statistics reveal that students in our schools come from an increasingly diverse range of cultural and socioeconomic backgrounds. There are over five million school-age children that have limited English proficiency (McElroy 2005). Over nine percent of our student population currently receives special education instruction (U.S. Department of Education 2005). If all students are to be judged against the same standards, the underserved minority populations and our children in special education must have access to the full scope of what is measured (Stevens 1993). Yet these are the very students who often receive a "watered-down and slower-paced curriculum" (Kinsler and Gamble 2003, 109). Current reform initiatives recognize the need to address these critical issues if all students are to succeed.

DIGITAL LITERACY

While technological advances in past decades failed to deliver the revolutionary changes in education that they promised, the present digital explosion and the ubiquity of technology tools hold unprecedented promise in designing technology-rich, customizable learning environments. Today's students live in a "wireless mediasphere where video, iPods, cell phones, instant messaging, and blogging are reshaping fundamental definitions of what it means to be literate" (Gordon 2006, 9). Advances in information and communications technology demand that we look seriously at digital literacy as central and not supplemental to learning in our schools.

PROFESSIONAL RENEWAL AND LEADERSHIP

When advocates push for the adoption of new instructional methodologies, they frequently assume that teachers can implement these practices with little or moderate preparation and training. For example, teachers are expected to foster abstract and critical thinking skills in children and yet they are frequently unskilled in questioning techniques to develop higher-order thinking. There is increasing recognition that the one-day workshops with no follow-up support are ineffective ways to help teachers internalize these skills and significantly modify their immediate practices.

Newer paradigms for professional renewal focus on analysis and reflection in small groups or teams (York-Barr, Sommers, Ghere, and Montie 2006). The professional development is not formulaic but is inquiry-based and focused on an examination of actual practice. Collaboration, risk taking, and feedback are crucial conditions in building the trust that is essential in developing such learning communities.

THE SCHOOL LIBRARY MEDIA
SPECIALIST AND SCHOOL REFORM

In the midst of all of these reform efforts sit school library media programs. The editors of this volume believe that the capacity of library media specialists to deal with educational change proactively and productively is critical to the overarching goal of school reform, as well as to the mission of school library media programs. We also believe that when library media specialists act as skilled change agents, they make a difference in the lives of students regardless of background. This is the theme of this book.

OVERVIEW OF THE BOOK

The purpose of this book is twofold: to provide insight into the elements of change agentry and to demonstrate strategies for effective change agentry using a subset of current reform initiatives. The book is not intended to provide comprehensive coverage of all aspects of school reform. Rather, the editors have identified reform-related topics and targets that we deem most relevant for the school library media specialist. Therefore, we have focused on issues that deal with (1) what library media specialists teach and how we might effectively teach and assess for learning, (2) the literacies that are central to the services provided by the library media center, (3) student populations that reflect the diverse range of learners with whom we work, and (4) professional development that might help us achieve our goals.

The authors are educators, library media specialists, and researchers who share a common belief in classroom teachers, administrators, library media specialists, parents, and community members working together to create schools that make a difference in the lives of students, and helping to produce citizens who have a capacity to cope with future change. The book is organized around the following strands.

Librarian as Change Agent

In Chapter 1, "Change Agentry: An Essential Role for Library Media Specialists," Sandra Hughes-Hassell and Violet Harada define the major characteristics of an effective change agent, the potential of the library media specialist to assume this role, and possible strategies to develop skills in becoming agents of change.

Partners in Student Achievement

In Chapter 2, "The Impact of Standards-Based Education on School Library Media Programs," Marjorie Pappas provides an overview of the standards movement, with an emphasis on No Child Left Behind (NCLB). She describes both the positive and negative impact of NCLB on school library media programs and challenges school library media professionals to participate in the ongoing conversation about standards and their role in improved student learning.

In Chapter 3, "Teaching for Understanding," Barbara Stripling explains how understanding goes beyond fact gathering and comprehension. She describes how understanding is developed and how library media specialists and other educators might foster the disciplinary knowledge, dispositions, and cognitive and metacognitive processes that are essential for deep understanding.

In Chapter 4, "Evidence-Based Practice and School Libraries: From Advocacy to Action," Ross Todd challenges library media specialists to go beyond input measures of program effectiveness (e.g., circulation statistics and collection counts) to output strategies that measure direct learning impacts. He provides historical background on the evidence-based practice (EPB) movement and articulates the principles underlying EPB. He stresses that empirical evidence and familiarity with existing research must be combined with professional wisdom and suggests strategies to demonstrate how libraries make a real difference in student learning.

Developing Literacy in the Twenty-First Century

In Chapter 5, "Family Literacy: The Dynamic Roles School Librarians Can Play," Bonnie Mackey and Sharon Pitcher explore the differences between family involvement and family literacy. They emphasize the value of engaging families in reading and learning together and present specific strategies that might be an exciting extension of the library media center's program.

In Chapter 6, "Reading the Web: The Merging of Literacy and Technology," Elizabeth Dobler focuses on what the act of reading "looks like" in a digital environment. She culls from the research as she tackles the following questions: How is reading online similar to or different from reading in a text-based environment? What strategies do readers use to decode and comprehend online text? She thoughtfully discusses the implications of reading and writing in a web-based environment for the library media specialist.

In Chapter 7, "Literacy and Learning in a Digital World," Pam Berger challenges the reader to consider what it means to be literate in a digital age. She argues that digital literacy requires a variety of cognitive, social, and emotional, as well as technical skills. Berger highlights key initiatives underway that provide educators with guidelines and strategies to integrate information and communications technology across the curriculum. She also proposes critical action steps for the library media specialist in building these twenty-first century skills into today's schools.

Serving Diverse Student Populations

In Chapter 8, "Special Education and Inclusion: Opportunities for Collaboration," Mary Jo Noonan and Violet Harada center on the inclusion reform in the U.S. They maintain that working with students with disabilities poses both a challenge and an opportunity for library media specialists, and they provide ideas for resources, services, and instruction that are appropriate and effective for this student population.

In Chapter 9, "Language, Culture, and the School Library," Denise Agosto and Sandra Hughes-Hassell focus on an underserved and burgeoning segment of our school population, students with limited English proficiency. They examine how language and culture shape student learning and how students' linguistic and cultural backgrounds affect educators' assessments of student skills and student socialization. The writers present ways in which the library media specialist can create a learning environment that supports and nurtures students' academic and personal growth.

Building Professionalism

In Chapter 10, "The Real Thing: Authentic Teaching through Action Research," Carol Gordon presents a compelling case for conducting action research to develop best practices that are based on rigorous and systematic data collection and analysis. She urges library media specialists to become practitioner-researchers and provides examples of action research in actual school settings.

In Chapter 11, "Professional Development in Communities of Practice," Joyce Yukawa, Violet Harada, and Daniel Suthers introduce the concept of communities of practice and describe how they implemented this concept in a course involving inquiry partnerships between teachers and library media specialists. They conclude with guidelines for staff development that center on developing professional learning communities.

THE JOURNEY BEGINS

Everyone wants schools to get better. All members of a school community must take part in choosing how to catalyze changes that help students succeed. The editors and contributors to this book strongly believe that school library media specialists can be key participants in school reform.

Questions that we must ask ourselves as school library professionals: Are we willing to open the doors to reform in our schools? Are we willing to convince others to participate in the improvement of our students' lives in the new millennium? In short, are we willing to take the lead in searching for the new cheese?

EDITORS' NOTE

Throughout this book, the terms "school librarian," "teacher librarian," and "library media specialist," and the terms "library media center" and "library" are used interchangeably.

REFERENCES

Darling-Hammond, Linda. 1997. *The Right to Learn: A Blueprint for Creating Schools that Work.* San Francisco, CA: Jossey-Bass.

Earl, Lorna. 2002. "Assessment As Learning." In *Keys to Effective Schools: Educational Reform as Continuous Improvement,* ed. Willis D. Hawley and Donald I. Rollie, 85–98. Thousand Oaks, CA: Corwin Press.

Elmore, Richard F. 2004. *School Reform from the Inside Out.* Cambridge, MA: Harvard Education Press.

Fullan, Michael. 1993. *Change Forces: Probing the Depths of Educational Reform.* Bristol, PA: Falmer Press.

Gordon, David T. 2006. "A Short History of School Reform." http://www.fcd-us.org/pdfs/AShort HistoryGordon.pdf [accessed January 19, 2007).

Hartzell, Gary N. 2001. "The Implications of Selected School Reform Approaches for School Library Media Services." *School Library Media Research* 4. http://www.ala.org/ala/aasl/ aaslpubsandjournals/slmrb/slmrcontents/volume42001/hartzell.htm (accessed October 6, 2006).

Johnson, Spencer. 1998. *Who Moved My Cheese?* New York: Putnam.

Kinsler, Kimberly, and Mae Gamble. 2001. *Reforming Schools.* New York: Continuum.

Levine, Daniel. U., and Lawrence W. Lezotte. 1990. *Unusually Effective Schools: A Review and Analysis of Research and Practice.* Madison, WI: National Center for Effective Schools Research and Development.

Marsh, David D. 1999. *Preparing Our Schools for the 21st Century. Yearbook 1999.* Alexandria, VA: Association for Supervision and Curriculum Development.

McElroy, Edward J. 2005. "Supporting English Language Learners." *Teaching PreK-8,* 36, no. 3: 8.

Meier, Deborah. 1997. "Habits of Mind: Democratic Values and the Creation of Effective Learning Communities." In *Common Schools, Uncommon Futures: A Working Consensus for School Renewal,* ed. Barry S. Kogan, 60–73. New York: Teachers College Press.

National Commission on Excellence in Education. 1983. *A Nation at Risk: The Imperative for Educational Reform.* Washington, DC: Government Printing Office.

Newmann, Fred M., and M. Bruce King. 1997. "Accountability and School Performance: Implications from Restructuring Schools." *Harvard Educational Review,* 67, no. 1: 41–74.

Reynolds, David, and Peter Cuttance. 1992. *School Effectiveness: Research, Policy and Practice.* London: Cassell.

Stevens, Floraline I. 1993. *Opportunity to Learn: Issues of Equity for Poor and Minority Students.* Washington, DC: National Center for Educational Statistics.

U.S. Department of Education, Office of Special Education and Rehabilitative Services, Office of Special Education Programs. 2005. *25th Annual (2003) Report to Congress on the Implementation of the Individuals with Disabilities Education Act.* Washington, DC: U.S. Government Printing Office.

York-Barr, Jennifer, William A. Sommers, Gail S. Ghere, and Jo Montie. 2006. *Reflective Practice to Improve Schools: An Action Guide for Educators.* 2nd ed. Thousand Oaks, CA: Corwin.

Part I

Librarian as Change Agent

1

Change Agentry: An Essential Role for Library Media Specialists

Sandra Hughes-Hassell and Violet H. Harada

One of the greatest pains to human nature is the pain of a new idea. It . . . makes you think that after all, your favorite notions may be wrong, your firmest beliefs ill-founded . . . Naturally, therefore, common men hate a new idea, and are disposed more or less to ill-treat the original man who brings it.

—Walter Bagehot

Is change agentry really an essential role for library media specialists? Absolutely. Why? Because change is the norm in education today. Not only are schools affected by planned educational changes in the form of systemic reform and legislative mandates, they are also affected by changes in the information and cultural landscape of society. The change process is exceedingly complex—too complex for any one person to understand or navigate alone. Successful change requires every person working in a school to be committed to change and to strive for individual and collective improvement. As Fullan (1993) emphasizes, educators who want to make a difference in the lives of students need to act as "skilled change agents pushing for changes around them, intersecting with other like minded individuals and groups to form the critical mass necessary to bring about continuous improvement" (40).

WHAT IS CHANGE AGENTRY AND WHAT DO CHANGE AGENTS DO?

Fullan (1993) defines change agentry as "being self-conscious about the nature of change and the change process" (12). Change agents bring about, or help to bring about, change. They may support, assist, nurture, encourage, persuade, and/or push people to change, to adopt an innovation, and to use it in their daily work (Hord, Rutherford, Hulling, and Hall 2006). They do not necessarily *lead* the change process. Instead, they may act as caregivers, facilitators, coaches, enablers, negotiators, or catalysts. Regardless of the role they assume, the goal of the change agent is "to fill the gaps of expertise and to assist in charting and implementing courses of action" (Fullan and Stiegelbauer 1991, 215). Change agents provide support and technical help. They contribute to greater mastery, confidence, and ownership. Key to the success of change agents is their ability to appreciate the unpredictable and volatile nature of change and to openly pursue ideas and competencies that positively influence the change process (Fullan 1993).

WHAT CORE CAPACITIES ARE REQUIRED TO BE AN EFFECTIVE CHANGE AGENT?

Many authors have delineated the characteristics or core capacities required for individuals to be effective change agents. Among these are: moral purpose and personal vision-building (Fullan 1993), a high level of commitment (Glickman 2002), inquiry and abstract thinking skills (Fullan 1993; Glickman 2002), knowledge and mastery (Fullan 1993; Fullan and Stiegelbauer 1991), collaboration (Fullan 1993), resiliency (Conner 1998), and interpersonal skills (Grossman 1974; Lippitt and Lippitt 1978). Table 1.1 provides key questions to ask yourself as you consider each characteristic.

Table 1.1.
Core Characteristics of Effective Change Agents—Questions to Ask Yourself

Characteristic	Key Questions to Consider
Moral purpose	How do you make a difference in the lives of your students? The school community? The broader society? Can you think of specific examples?
	How do you nourish your sense of moral imperative? What do you do to stay optimistic about your potential to positively impact the lives of your students? To contribute to an improved society?
Personal vision-building	Why did you become a school library media specialist in the first place?
	What do you stand for as a school library media specialist?
	What do you want your legacy to be?
Commitment	How do you demonstrate your commitment to the profession? To your school community? To students?
	What methods do you use to continually improve yourself? As a school library media specialist? As a collaborative colleague? As a mentor for students? As a learner?
	How do you help your colleagues continually grow and improve themselves?
Capacity of inquiry	What strategies do you use to examine and improve your practice?
	What do you know about action research? Evidence-based practice? Critical friends? Peer mentoring?
	Have you ever kept a personal journal in which you reflected on your practice?

(continued)

Table 1.1. *(continued)*

Characteristic	Key Questions to Consider
High abstract thinking skills	How well are you able to view innovations from multiple perspectives (your own, students', parents', aides' and administrators')?
	How do you use what you observe to generate action plans? To predict problems? To provide interventions and support?
Knowledge and mastery	What strategies do you use to keep up with the latest in educational and technological innovations?
	What strategies do you use to know what is happening in your school community and to understand how it might be affecting morale, relationships, decision-making, etc.?
	How do you negotiate the politics of your school community? Can you name the opinion leaders in your school?
	Do the other members of your school community view you as knowledgeable and competent?
Collaboration	How committed are you to the idea of collaboration?
	How comfortable are you sharing decisions regarding teaching and learning, the selection of resources, the development of policies and procedures, etc. with your colleagues and with students?
	What methods of communication do you use to openly discuss issues and convey information?
	How flexible and open to new ideas are you?
Resiliency	What strategies do you use to manage ambiguity and to effectively implement change?
	How well do you use all available resources to leverage support for change? To develop strategies for responding to change?
	How adept are you at identifying the opportunities associated with change, rather than focusing on the negative, or the downside?
	On a scale of 1–10, where would you place yourself in terms of your comfort with risk-taking? Are you comfortable taking risks or do you avoid them, seeking comfort instead?
Interpersonal skills	How do the members of your school community view you? Do they view you as caring? Friendly? Trustworthy? Empathetic?
	Do you project a positive and competent attitude?

Fullan (1999) defines moral purpose as "making a difference in the life-chances of all students" at the individual level and "education's societal development and democracy" at the societal level (1). He argues that moral purpose is "a critical motivator for addressing the sustained task of complex reform because the effort is gargantuan and must be morally worth doing" (Fullan, 2003, 18).

Related to moral purpose is the idea of personal vision-building. Fullan (1993) emphasizes that to be effective, change agents must have a personal vision of what is important to them as educators. They need to ask themselves why they came into teaching and what difference they are trying to make personally. A clearly articulated personal vision not only gives meaning to the work, but it "forces [educators] to take a stand for a preferred future" (Block 1987, 102). It gives them a goal to continually strive to meet and sets a high standard for their practice.

Commitment emanates from moral purpose and personal vision-building. Successful change agents are committed to "continually improving themselves, their students, and their fellow faculty members" (Glickman 2002, 89). They expend both extra energy and extra time to do more for students and to help their colleagues, often going far beyond the "official" job description or the contracted hours of the job.

A capacity for inquiry is another essential characteristic. Change agents must exhibit the habit of continuous learning. As Fullan (1993) points out, "lifelong inquiry is the generative characteristic needed because post-modern environments themselves are constantly changing" (15). Using strategies such as reflective practice, action research, personal journals, critical friends groups, and peer coaching, successful change agents continually examine their practice and actively seek improvement (Fullan 1993; Fullan and Hargreaves 1991).

Tied to inquiry are high abstract thinking skills. High abstract thinking skills enable change agents to view innovations from many perspectives (their own, students', parents', aides', administrators') and to generate multiple plans for implementation. High abstraction makes it possible for change agents to think through the advantages and disadvantages of an innovation, to see problems that might arise, and to systematically provide interventions and support (Glickman 2002).

Knowledge and mastery, too, are crucial. Change agents must have a command of the content of the new practice, and its purpose, as well as the benefits that will result from its use (Fullan and Stiegelbauer 1991). They must understand how the innovation interfaces with programs and practices currently in place. Additionally, they must have a working knowledge of the environment (Rogers 1962). They must be cognizant of the culture, or core values, of the school as well as the power structure, and of different factions that exist within that school (House 1979; Sarason 1996). Gaining knowledge and mastery requires strong initial education, continuous staff development, and political astuteness.

Collaboration is also essential for effective change agentry (Fullan and Hargreaves 1991). As Fullan emphasizes, "there is a ceiling effect to how much we can learn if we keep to ourselves" (1993, 17). Learning is a social activity—people need one another to learn and to accomplish things. Without collaborative skills and relationships it is not possible to learn and to continue to learn, nor is it possible to create meaningful change.

Resiliency is another necessary capacity for change agents. According to Conner (1998), the single, most important factor that affects one's ability and speed to change is resilience. He identifies five characteristics that constitute resiliency: positiveness, focus, flexibility, organization, and proactivity (1998, 189). Change agents and leaders are more likely to have higher levels of resilience, and those with high resilience are more likely to be change agents and leaders.

Finally, change agents must possess the interpersonal skills needed to work effectively with people. Successful change agents are usually described as sincere, honest, patient, perceptive, realistic, enthusiastic, empathetic, and trustworthy (Feehan 1991). Recognizing the feelings of concern, anxiety, and uncertainty teachers may experience during the change process, they use imaginative ways to encourage participation and demonstrate the value of change (Grossman 1974; Hord et al. 2006).

WHAT ARE SOME KEY POINTS ABOUT THE CHANGE PROCESS?

There is an extensive body of literature about the change process in the literature of both the education and business community. We have included five key points below.

"Change is a journey, not a blueprint" (Fullan 1993, 21). One of the key lessons learned over the past four decades of research is that change is a process, not an event (Hord et al. 2004). Significant change takes time. There are too many unknowns and unknowables for change to occur quickly and easily. As McGregor (2003) points out, that's good news for change agents—it means "there is no right or wrong way to make things happen in his or her particular situation" (204). Successful change efforts require flexibility, ongoing monitoring, attention to the specific needs of the staff and students, and continual assessment.

"Conflict and diversity are our friends" (Fullan 1993, 18). Conflict and problems are inherent in the change process. Successful school change is more likely when problems are treated as a natural and expected part of the process. It is through solving problems that we learn. Acknowledging problems and working to solve them can broaden attitudes, knowledge, and skills (Kaser et al. 2006).

"Change is accomplished by individuals" (Hord et al., 2006, 6). It is only when each individual in a school has changed that an innovation can be deemed a success. Individuals must thus be the focus of attention in implementing any new educational program or practice.

The Concerns-Based Adoption Model, developed by Hord, Rutherford, Huling, and Hall (2006), identifies five roles that individuals involved in change assume: innovator, leader, early majority adopter, late majority adopter, or resister.[1]

Innovators are individuals who try new ideas, are open to change, and are willing to take risks. They are frequently the ones who conceive, develop, and introduce new ideas to their colleagues. Unfortunately, innovators are often not trusted by their peers. Approximately eight percent of any group can be considered innovators.

Leaders are also open to change; however, they are more thoughtful about getting involved. These individuals are often described as opinion-leaders. They tend to be respected by their colleagues and to be viewed as trustworthy. Seventeen percent of any group can be considered leaders.

Early majority adopters are cautious and deliberate about deciding to adopt an innovation. They watch innovators and leaders to see what ideas seem useful or acceptable. Approximately 29 percent of any group can be considered early majority adopters.

Those in the *late majority* are often described as "set in their ways." They are skeptical of adopting new ideas and tend to do so only after an idea has proven its value based upon experience and empirical evidence. Approximately 29 percent of any group can be considered late majority adopters.

Finally, there are the *resisters*. These individuals are suspicious and generally opposed to new ideas. They are usually unwilling to change unless it seems like the only alternative. Approximately 17 percent of a group can be considered resisters.

As Hord and her colleagues point out, these labels, or identifiers, should not be viewed as negative or positive. Instead, they provide change agents with valuable information that can be used to develop support and intervention strategies.

Figure 1.1
Stages of Concern: Typical Expressions of Concern about the Innovation

	Stages of Concern	Expressions of Concern
IMPACT	6 Refocusing	I have some ideas about something that would work even better.
	5 Collaboration	How can I relate what I am doing to what others are doing?
	4 Consequence	How is my use affecting learners? How can I refine it to have more impact?
TAKS	3 Management	I seem to be spending all my time getting materials ready.
SELF	2 Personal	How will using it affect me?
	1 Informational	I would like to know more about it.
	0 Awareness	I am not concerned about it.

Source: Hord, Shirley, William Rutherford, Leslie Huling, and Gene E. Hall. 2006. *Taking Charge of Change.* Rev. ed. Austin, TX: Southwest Educational Development Laboratory. Reprinted with permission of Southwest Educational Development Laboratory.

Change entails developmental growth in feelings and skills (Hord et al. 2006). Everyone involved in change has different concerns that evolve over time. The Concerns-Based Adoption Model (Hord et al. 2006) identifies seven stages of concern that individuals experience when adopting and implementing an innovation (see Figure 1.1). The seven stages are defined by the expressions of concern that individuals make at the various stages. The stages are not mutually exclusive and the intensity of specific stages varies as adoption and implementation progress. Assessing people's concerns about change and diagnosing their needs, allows change agents to develop appropriate support and intervention strategies.

When an innovation or change is first introduced, individuals are very likely to have self-concerns (Stage 1 and Stage 2). They will want to know more about the innovation, how it is similar to and different from what they are already doing, when the change will begin, what kind of preparation they will receive, how and why it is supposed to work, and how it will affect them personally (Hord et al. 2006).

During Stage 3 teachers are concerned with the nuts and bolts of implementation. They ask questions such as: How do I do it? How can I use these materials efficiently? How can I organize myself? and Why is it taking so much time? These concerns are usually most intense right before teachers actually begin to implement the innovation and in the early stages of use (Hord et al. 2006).

When teachers reach the final three stages of the model, they are concerned with how the change is affecting students and how they can improve its effectiveness. Some of them may even begin to think about how they can work better with others to implement and improve the innovation (Hord et al. 2006).

Change alters and is altered by the culture of the school (Rossman, Corbett, and Firestone 1988; Sarason 1996). The process of change is embedded in the complex culture of the school. The culture describes the way things are, interprets acts, behaviors, events, words, and gives them meaning. The introduction of an educational innovation challenges the prevailing culture, causing teachers to compare their current norms and beliefs to those embedded in the proposed change. Staff members respond to the innovation according to how well they believe the innovation fits the existing cultural context. Successful change must either accommodate core beliefs and values or engage in the difficult job of reinterpreting, redefining, or reshaping them.

WHAT ASSETS DO LIBRARY MEDIA SPECIALISTS BRING TO THE CHANGE PROCESS?

Library media specialists have a number of assets that make them particularly well-positioned to act as change agents. First, library media specialists are often one of the few members of the school community that has a "big picture view" (McGregor 2003, 210). Library media specialists work with every teacher and student in the building. They have a broad view of the curriculum, student learning needs, teaching styles, resources, and technology use. They are in a prime position to implement changes in a comprehensive and continuous manner, to identify concerns and problems, and to assist teachers and administrators.

Second, library media specialists are experienced collaborators. Collaboration is the cornerstone of a successful library media program. Library media specialists possess knowledge and experience with collaborative planning, teaching, and assessment that can be shared with the school community.

Third, most library media specialists have the flexibility and time to model effective teaching practices and to act as coaches and mentors. Flexible scheduling allows library media specialists to spend time in classrooms co-teaching with teachers, modeling new practices, identifying and discussing issues, and working collaboratively with teachers to develop solutions to problems and to improve practice.

Fourth, the nature of their job requires that school library media specialists engage in continuous learning. To be effective, library media specialists must stay current with educational trends, emerging technologies, new resources in all formats, and community connections.

Finally, library media specialists do not supervise or evaluate teachers like principals and other administrators. They are viewed as their peers and colleagues. Teachers may, therefore, be more willing to express their concerns to and seek assistance from them.

STRATEGIES FOR BECOMING A CHANGE AGENT

Just as the process of change is a journey, likewise the process of becoming a change agent is a journey—a journey filled with periods of ambition and excitement, but also self doubt, uncertainty, and disappointment. Before you can effectively facilitate the change process, you have to view yourself as a change agent—you have to believe you can make a difference and that you can provide support for your colleagues. You also have to recognize your own strengths and limitations and reconcile your own subconscious feelings about change. Below are 11 strategies for becoming a change agent.

Strategy 1: Follow the advice of Livsey and Palmer (1999) and revisit your moral purpose. Ask yourself the following questions:

1. Why did I become a library media specialist in the first place?
2. What do I stand for as a library media specialist?
3. What are the gifts I bring to my work?
4. What do I want my legacy to be?
5. What can I do to "keep track of myself"—to remember my own heart? (16).

Figure 1.2
Glickman's Four "Types" of Teachers

Quadrant III Analytical Observers	Quadrant IV Professionals
Have a low commitment but high level of abstraction. Intelligent, highly verbal, and full of great ideas. Know what needs to be done but are unwilling to commit the time, energy, and care necessary to carry out plans.	Have both a high level of commitment and a high level of abstraction. Can think about a task, consider alternatives, make a rational choice, and develop and carry out an appropriate plan of action. Provide activities, ideas, and resources. Others regard them as informal leaders, people to whom they go willingly for help.
Quadrant I Teacher Dropouts	Quadrant II Unfocused Workers
Have both a low level of commitment and a low level of abstraction. Simply go through the minimal motions in order to keep the job. See no reasons for change. Come to work exactly on time and leave school as soon as officially permissible.	Have a high level of commitment but low level of abstraction. Enthusiastic, energetic, and full of good intentions. Unfortunately, lack the ability to think change through and act fully and realistically. Usually get involved in multiple projects and activities but become discouraged and swamped by self-imposed and unrealistic tasks.

Adapted from: Glickman, Carol D. 2002. *Leadership for Learning: How to Help Teachers Succeed.* Arlington, VA: Association for Supervision and Curriculum Development, 87–89.

Strategy 2: Use Conner's (1998) five factors (positiveness, focus, flexibility, organization, and proactivity) to rate your level of resiliency. How confident are you in your ability to implement changes and to assist others in their efforts? How focused are you on your personal vision? How well do you manage ambiguity? Are you flexible and willing to take risks?

Strategy 3: Determine what "type" of teacher you are. Glickman (2002) has developed an instrument to assess the status of teachers (see Figure 1.2). Use the instrument to evaluate yourself honestly. If you recognize yourself in Quadrant I or Quadrant II, think about what you need to become re-energized and more focused—to move to Quadrant IV. If you position yourself in Quadrant IV, work to make sure your colleagues and the administration recognize you as a *Professional* by demonstrating a high level of commitment to teaching and a high level of abstraction.

Strategy 4: Surround yourself with likeminded individuals who complement your strengths and compensate for your limitations. As Lieberman (2001) points out, change agents often find themselves at odds with others in the school community. In order not to become overwhelmed and discouraged, you need to belong to a community of your own—one that understands the difficulties and stress involved in facilitating the change process.

Strategy 5: Educate yourself about the change process and the role of change agents. The more familiar you are with how change happens and the role change agents can play, the less formidable it becomes. A good way to do this is to make a habit of reading the literature on change, both inside and outside the field of education. We have provided a bibliography to get you started in Table 1.2.

Strategy 6: Understand how you generally react when faced with change. Would you identify yourself as an innovator? A leader? An early majority adopter? A late majority adopter? A resister? Do you react quickly and positively like Sniff and Scurry, or do you dig in your heels and wait for the status quo to return like Hem (Johnson 1998)? Are you comfortable letting go of established ways of doing things in order to embrace new practices?

Table 1.2.
Understanding the Change Process: A Bibliography to Get You Started

Change Agent's Guide. Ronold G. Havelock and Steve Zlotolow. 2nd ed. Englewood Cliffs, NJ: Educational Technology Publications, 1995.

Change Forces: Probing the Depths of Educational Change. Michael Fullan. Bristol, PA: Falmer Press, 1993.

Change Forces: The Sequel. Michael Fullan. London: Falmer Press, 1999.

Change Forces: With A Vengeance. Michael Fullan. London: Routledge Falmer, 2003.

Guiding School Change. Frances O'Connell Rust and Helen Freidus, eds. New York: Teachers College Press.

New Meaning of Educational Change. Michael Fullan. 3rd ed. New York: Teachers College Press, 2001.

Revisiting the Culture of the School and the Problem of Change. Seymour B. Sarason. New York: Teachers College Press, 1996.

Strategies for Planned Change. Gerald Zaltman and Robert Duncan. New York: Wiley, 1997.

Surviving Change: A Survey of Educational Change Models. James B. Ellsworth, Syracuse, NY: ERIC Clearinghouse on Information & Technology, 2000.

Taking Charge of Change. Shirley M. Hord, William L. Rutherford, Leslie Huling, and Gene E. Hall. Rev. ed. Austin, TX: Southwest Educational Development Laboratory, 2006.

Who Moved My Cheese? Spencer Johnson. New York, Putnam, 1998.

Strategy 7: In relation to the particular innovation being considered, determine which stage of the Concerns-Based Adoption Model (Hord et al. 2006) best describes your stage of concern. Make sure you have a support network in place to help you address your concerns. You cannot help others until you consider and address your own concerns.

Strategy 8: Make sure you understand the content of the innovation. As Lieberman (2001) points out, many reform efforts falter because the leadership does not have a deep understanding of the content.

Strategy 9: Determine how to balance your feelings about the innovation with your "responsibility to help students [and teachers] succeed at whatever has been set before them" (Eisenberg 2004, 22). As Eisenberg points out, while you may not be a proponent of the particular innovation (in this case he is referring to No Child Left Behind), you do need to provide students and teachers with the resources, skills, and tools needed to meet the demands of that particular innovation. Use other avenues, such as meetings of the site-based management team, school board, and professional associations, to articulate your concerns and to advocate for education reform that more closely aligns with your philosophy or beliefs.

Strategy 10: Cultivate your relationship with the administrator and teacher-leaders in your school. Become recognized as a critical member of the school's leadership team—as someone who adds value to the educational conversation.

Strategy 11: Dedicate yourself to being a continual learner and to seeing problems as opportunities for learning and change—not as "show stoppers." Join professional education associations, such as ASCD (Association for Supervision and Curriculum Development), NCTE (National Council of Teachers of English), IRA (International Reading Association), NCTM (National Council of Teachers of Mathematics) and AERA (American Educational Research Association) so that you are on the cutting edge of educational change. Subscribe to and read publications such as *Education Week.* Monitor listservs such as ASCD's *Smart-Brief* and the Public Education Fund's *NewsBlast.*

STRATEGIES FOR ACTING AS A CHANGE AGENT

Now that you have examined your feelings about change and positioned yourself to act as an agent of change, how do you proceed? We've included four strategies to get you started.

Strategy 1: Focus on the people affected by the change, as well as the change itself. Be empathetic. Show genuine concern. Recognize the problems and dilemmas teachers are facing. Provide support. As McGregor (2003) points out, "the encouraging word provided at the right moment might make the difference between a teacher giving up on the idea and trying one more time" (211).

Strategy 2: Become a member of the school's leadership team. Volunteer for other leadership positions within the school and to represent the school on system-wide committees, especially those that deal directly with the innovation being adopted and implemented.

Strategy 3: Clearly articulate and demonstrate how the school library media program overlaps, complements, and supports the reform effort being implemented. Gather and analyze data from your program. Talk to other library media specialists to gather evidence. Search the literature for research-based evidence. Be proactive—don't wait until you are asked how the library supports the innovation; prepare and present the evidence in advance.

Strategy 4: Use the Concerns-Based Adoption Model: Level of Use Index (Hord et al. 2006) to assess the concerns other people have and provide appropriate support and interventions (see Figure 1.3).

WHY ACT AS A CHANGE AGENT?

So what's in it for you? Why should library media specialists act as change agents? After all, as Brown (1998) reminds us, "being a change agent or an instructional leader . . . goes far beyond the requirements of the job" (70). Studies have shown that taking on a leadership role can yield significant personal benefits, including intellectual and professional growth, decreased isolation, and increased feelings of efficacy.

Teachers report that their knowledge and skills increased dramatically as a result of their involvement in leadership positions (Lieberman, Saxl, and Miles 1988; Porter 1986). Growth occurred as teacher leaders worked with administrators, observed and assisted other teachers, and were exposed to new concepts and ideas (Boyd-Dimock and McGree 1995).

Teacher leaders also report a significant decrease in isolation as a result of opportunities to work with others (Boyd-Dimock and McGee 1995). Isolation is a potential problem for school library media specialists since they are often the only librarian in the building. Working with teachers and administrators to facilitate the adoption and implementation of an innovation may provide an avenue for cultivating collaborative relationships and reducing feelings of isolation.

Figure 1.3
Intervention Strategies for Each Stage of the Concerned-Based Model

Stage 0—Awareness Concerns

Begin to talk informally with teachers about the change. Initiate the conversation. Take note of their questions and concerns.

Begin to gather resources for teachers about the innovation. Consider developing a Web page, wiki, blog, and/or pathfinder that includes journal articles, books, Web resources, and conferences or workshops. Be careful not to overwhelm people with too much information.

Locate videos or other materials that show the innovation being implemented in other locations. Focus on videos that highlight the complete change journey, including "the detours, dead ends, and cloverleafs" (Kaser et al. 2006, 88). Order these materials for the library's professional collection.

Stage 1—Informational Concerns

Make clear and accurate information about the innovation available to teachers. Set up displays of materials in the library. Publicize the Web page, wiki, or blog you developed. Post the pathfinder electronically, but also distribute it in print. Remind teachers of the dates of various professional development opportunities.

Make a list of schools in the area where the innovation is in use. Share these with the principal and staff. Encourage the principal to provide opportunities for the faculty and staff to visit these places. Contact the school library media specialists at the schools to discuss the innovation and its impact on teachers, students, and the library program.

Encourage teachers to use the wiki or blog you have created to share resources and discuss their concerns with each other.

Work with teachers and administrators to determine the types of library resources needed to successfully implement the innovation. Develop a collection development plan that includes budgetary requirements. Share this plan with the leadership team, or person responsible for finances in your school. Order the resources.

Be enthusiastic about the innovation's potential impact on the learning community.

Stage 2—Personal Concerns

Use personal notes and conversations to provide encouragement.

Help teachers connect with others whose concerns have diminished and who will be supportive.

Share your personal concerns with teachers.

(continued)

13

Figure 1.3
Intervention Strategies for Each Stage of the Concerned-Based Model *(continued)*

Stage 3—Management Concerns

Discuss implementation issues during collaborative planning meetings with individual teachers, grade levels, or departments.

Encourage teachers to use the "innovation" wiki or blog to discuss "how-to" issues with each other.

Gather advice and suggestions from the teachers in your building. Develop a frequently asked questions (FAQ) section for the Web page, blog, or wiki you have developed about the innovation.

Implement the innovation in the library and offer to demonstrate aspects of the innovation for teachers.

Acknowledge your failures and what you have learned. Be willing to share with your colleagues.

Stage 4—Consequence Concerns

Collect evidence of successes in your building and draw attention to them.

Engage in action research.

Display student work in the library. Highlight successful units on the library Web site or library blog. Interview teachers and students for the school news program.

Provide support by identifying what has worked well, presenting new teaching resources, and proposing possible changes.

Stage 5—Collaboration Concerns

Highlight successful collaborative efforts in your building. Focus on the benefits to students and to you as professionals.

Provide professional development for individuals interested in learning how to collaborate more effectively.

Stage 6—Refocusing Concerns

Connect teachers with the resources they may need to refine their ideas and put them into practice.

Suggest avenues for sharing their ideas, such as conferences and professional journals. Offer to assist teachers in preparing a presentation, writing an article, or developing a blog or wiki.

14

Finally, teacher leaders report increased confidence and a stronger commitment to teaching (Boyd-Dimock and McGee 1995). This benefit ties directly to Fullan's ideas of moral purpose and personal vision building. Teachers who have participated as change agents often have felt empowered, especially when the school culture supports collegiality and the sharing of ideas. They have felt like they made a difference in the lives of their students, which, "is what drives the best of [us]" (Fullan 1993, 40).

FINAL THOUGHTS

As Donald Schön (1983) reminded us, professionals often learn what they are doing in the process of doing. As you read the following chapters, we invite you to relate our authors' thoughts and experiences with educational change to your own. Which of these reform efforts are currently being implemented in your school? How did teachers, administrators, and students react when the innovation was first introduced? Who is leading the change? What role have you played in the change process? How can you implement the change in the library media center? What strategies can you employ to help teachers, students, and the administration succeed?

We are now facing unprecedented challenges and opportunities in education (Rust and Freidus 2001). By taking on the role of change agents, we believe school library media specialists have the opportunity to help rethink, reshape, and re-vision what teaching and learning looks like, to work with teachers within true communities of practice, and to transform library media programs to ensure that all children succeed.

Make no mistake. Taking on the role of change agent will not be easy. Brown (1998) offers this advice: Be a lifelong learner. Work with your fellow teachers in true partnership. Never lose sight of the value of what you have to offer. And most importantly, keep faith in what you are doing.

NOTE

1. Hord, Rutherford, Huling-Austin, and Hall drew on the work of Everett Rogers (1962) in the development of their model.

REFERENCES

Bagehot, Walter. 1999. *Physics and Politics, or, Thoughts on the Application of Principles of "Natural Selection" and "Inheritance" to Political Society.* http://bagehot.classicauthors.net/PhysicsPolitics/PhysicsPolitics5.html (accessed January 8 2007).

Block, Peter. 1987. *The Empowered Manager.* San Francisco, CA: Jossey-Bass.

Boyd-Dimock, Victoria, and Kathleen M. McGee. 1995. "Leading Change from the Classroom: Teachers as Leaders." *Issues About Change* 4, no 4. Southwest Educational Development Laboratory. http://www.sedl.org/change/issues/issues44.html (accessed September 6, 2006).

Brown, Jean. 1998. "Navigating the 90s—The Teacher Librarian as Change Agent." In *Foundations of Effective School Library Media Programs,* ed. Ken Haycock, 65–72. Englewood, CO: Libraries Unlimited.

Conner, Daryl R. 1998. *Leading at the Edge of Chaos.* New York: Wiley.

Eisenberg, Michael B. 2004. "It's All about Learning: Ensuring That Student Are Effective Users of Information on Standardized Tests." *Library Media Connection* 22, no. 6: 22–30.

Feehan, Pat E. 1991. "State Library Agency Youth Services Consultants: Their Potential As Agents of Change." Doctoral dissertation, University of North Carolina at Chapel Hill. Dissertation Abstracts International, 52/10, 3466.

Fullan, Michael. 1993. *Change Forces: Probing the Depths of Educational Change.* Bristol, PA: Falmer Press.

Fullan, Michael. 1999. *Change Forces: The Sequel.* London: Falmer Press.

Fullan, Michael. 2003. *Change Forces: With a Vengeance.* London: Routledge Falmer.

Fullan, Michael, and Andrew Hargreaves. 1991. *What Is Worth Fighting For in Your School?* Toronto, Ontario: Ontario Public School Teachers' Federation.

Fullan, Michael, and Suzanne Stiegelbauer. 1991. *The New Meaning of Educational Change.* 2nd ed. New York: Teachers College Press.

Glickman, Carol D. 2002. *Leadership for Learning: How to Help Teachers Succeed.* Arlington, VA: Association for Supervision and Curriculum Development.

Grossman, Lee. 1974. *The Change Agent.* New York: AMACOM.

Hord, Shirley M., William L. Rutherford, Leslie Hulling, and Gene Hall. 2006. *Taking Charge of Change.* Rev. ed. Austin, TX: Southwest Educational Development Laboratory.

House, Ernest R. 1979. "Technology Versus Craft: A Ten Year Perspective on Change." In *New Directions in Curriculum Studies,* ed Phillip H. Taylor, 137–151. Sussex, England: The Falmer Press.

Johnson, Spencer. 1998. *Who Moved My Cheese?* New York: Putnam.

Kaser, Joyce, Susan Mundry, Katherine E. Stiles, and Susan Loucks-Horsley. 2006. *Leading Every Day: 124 Actions for Effective Leadership.* 2nd ed. Thousand Oaks, CA: Corwin Press.

Lieberman, Ann. 2001. "The Professional Lives of Change Agents: What Do They Do?" In *Guiding School Change: The Role and Work of Change Agents,* eds. Frances O'Connell Rust and Helen Freidus, 155–162. New York: Teachers College Press.

Lieberman, Ann, Ellen R. Saxl, and Matthew B. Miles. 1988. "Teacher Leadership: Ideology and Practice." In *Building a Professional Culture in Schools,* ed. Ann Lieberman, 148–166. New York: Teachers College Press.

Lippitt, Gordon, and Robert Lippitt. 1978. *The Consulting Process in Action.* San Diego, CA: University Associates.

Livsey, Rachel, and Parker Palmer. 1999. *The Courage to Teach: A Guide to Reflection and Renewal.* San Francisco, CA: Jossey-Bass.

McGregor, Joy. 2003. "Collaboration and Leadership." In *Curriculum Connections through the Library: Principles and Practices,* eds. Barbara K. Stripling and Sandra Hughes-Hassell, 199–219. Chicago: American Library Association.

Porter, Andrew C. 1986. "Teacher Collaboration: Partnership to Attract Old Problems." *Kappan* 69 (2): 147–152.

Rogers, Everett M. 1962. *The Diffusion of Innovations.* New York: The Free Press.

Rossman, Gretchen B., H. Dickson Corbett, and William A. Firestone. 1988. *Change and Effectiveness in Schools: A Cultural Perspective.* Albany: State University of New York Press.

Rust, Frances O'Connell, and Helen Freidus. 2001. "Introduction." In *Guiding School Change: The Role and Work of Change Agents,* eds. Frances O'Connell Rust and Helen Freidus, 1–15. New York: Teachers College Press.

Sarason, Seymour B. 1996. *Revisiting the Culture of the School and the Problem of Change.* New York: Teachers College Press.

Schön, Donald A. 1983. *The Reflective Practitioner: How Professionals Think in Action.* New York: Basic Books.

Part II

Partners in Student Achievement

2

The Impact of Standards-Based Education on School Library Media Programs

Marjorie Pappas

All, regardless of race or class or economic status, are entitled to a fair chance and to the tools for developing their individual powers of mind and spirit to the utmost. This promise means that all children by virtue of their own efforts, competently guided, can hope to attain the mature and informed judgment needed to secure gainful employment, and to manage their own lives, thereby serving not only their own interests but also the progress of society itself. (National Commission on Excellence in Education 1983, 8)

Educators today negotiate their teaching and their students' learning around standards. How did standards-based education become the norm in American educational policy and practice? How has the movement changed since its inception in 1983? What impact has the movement had on student performance? How can school library media specialists support standards-based teaching and learning? What is the role of school library media specialists in discussing the pros and cons of standards-based education? These are the questions this chapter examines.

THE BEGINNING OF THE STANDARDS MOVEMENT

A Nation at Risk, released in 1983 by the National Commission on Excellence in Education, recommended that schools adopt standards to measure academic performance. Standards establish what students need to know and be able to do to be proficient at various levels in their education. They "help educators and their communities to explicitly identify educational goals and expectations, allow teachers to focus and organize their curriculum and instruction, and can help school administrators and teachers to decide on required resources" (Buttram 1997, 1). In short, standards-based education "establishes criteria for holding students, teachers, and school systems accountable" (Buttram 1997, 1).

A Nation at Risk included the following recommendations:

- Standardized tests should be administered at major transition points, for example, junior high to high school and high school to college.
- States and schools should administer these tests nationwide, but the tests are not meant to be federal tests.
- In addition to standardized tests, other diagnostic procedures should be administered to help educators evaluate student progress.
- The school day and/or year should be extended to allow more time to be devoted to basics.
- Teacher education programs should require candidates to meet educational standards that measure their knowledge in a specific academic discipline (National Commission on Excellence in Education 1983).

The report had a significant impact on education. Prior to its release, the perspective of policy-makers and educators in the United States had been on inputs as a means of ensuring that more students achieved a basic education. The report changed the focus to one of *accountability*. Legislators and policy-makers wanted *evidence* that students were meeting proscribed levels of proficiency.

Why this shift in educational policy and direction? Technology was fueling major changes in the business community and the economy. The United States was shifting from an industrialized economy with a workforce that required only basic skills for assembly line jobs, to a knowledge-based economy that required workers who could engage in critical thinking, effectively problem solve, and demonstrate leadership skills. There was a growing understanding that all young people needed an education that would enable them to meet the challenges of the information age. Educators, legislators, and policy-makers realized that the U.S. educational system must be revamped in order to meet these new challenges (Buttram 1997).

The National Council of Teachers of Mathematics (NCTM) was the first content association to develop national standards. The document, *Curriculum and Evaluation Standards for School Mathematics,* was adopted in 1989. Other content area associations quickly followed their example. In 1996, the National Science Education Standards, National Standards for English Language Arts, as well as the National Standards for History were all released.

Individual states also began their own standards development process and by 1993, 45 states were either in the process of developing standards or were in the midst of implementation. Some characteristics across the state standards included "a strong push for higher-order thinking and active models of learning; more interdisciplinary learning and understanding; more in-depth coverage of a core set of topics rather than wide, but superficial coverage of many topics; and more challenging content for all students" (Developing Content Standards 1993). The process for developing these standards often initiated controversy. For example, the concepts of outcomes-based education and affective outcomes fueled debates in many states.

Once the standards were developed, the next step for states was to design and implement standardized tests. Again, concerns were raised among different groups. For example, some educators believed the tests would cause a teach-to-the-test approach by classroom teachers. Other educators were concerned that the efforts of teachers to help average and below-average students reach proficiency would mean a less rigorous curriculum and learning experience for above-average students. Initial writing efforts often resulted in standards that focused on low-level thinking skills.

In 1997, *Education Week* began an annual survey, Quality Counts, to monitor the standards-based reform movement. The study was initiated at the request of Governor Robert Miller (D-Nevada) who believed there should be an "'external, independent, nongovernmental effort' to measure and report on each state's annual progress in raising student achievement and improving the public schools" (Daily Report Card 1996). The survey was developed to gather data in response to two major questions: (1) Have states adopted policies that support standards-based education? and (2) Have states made progress in improving the academic achievement of their students (Swanson 2006)?

In 2001, the results of the Quality Counts survey provided a snapshot of teachers' perspectives on standards-based education and academic achievement of students. Those results showed that many, but not all, teachers believed that:

- The curriculum was more demanding for students.
- Teachers' expectations of students had increased.
- Most states had developed standards aligned with the English/LA and mathematics standards developed by the content associations.
- Teachers in schools were collaborating more.
- Students were writing more; nearly half reported students were reading more.
- Classroom instruction placed too much emphasis on state tests.
- State tests used multiple-choice and short-answer questions and needed greater emphasis on writing essays and performance tasks.
- The state standards were so comprehensive that there was insufficient time to teach the content.
- States needed to offer a better balance between rewards and punishments for levels of performance.
- Teachers needed more support to effectively teach the standards, especially in schools with greater numbers of minority and poor students (Quality Counts 2001).

It is important to note that the Quality Counts 2001 study results reflected the perspective of many educators at the time President George W. Bush took office in January 2001 and presented his educational reform legislation to Congress.

THE NO CHILD LEFT BEHIND ACT

President Bush proposed the No Child Left Behind (NCLB) legislation three days after taking office, declaring that the initiative would be "the cornerstone of my Administration" (NCLB 2001). The primary goals of NCLB were accountability, choice, and flexibility. President Bush stated, "these reforms express my deep belief in our public schools and their mission to build the mind and character of every child, from every background, in every part of America" (NCLB 2001). Congress overwhelmingly supported this legislation with 90 percent of the legislators approving (Reed 2005).

Accountability

The NCLB Act reauthorizes the Elementary and Secondary Education Act (ESEA) and requires states to establish accountability systems that document achievement for students in grades 3–8. Accountability requires states to:

- Develop challenging standards in reading and math.
- Administer annual standardized tests to determine student proficiency based on state standards.
- Ensure that all students reach proficiency in reading and math within 12 years.
- Disaggregate testing results by poverty, race, ethnicity, disability, and limited English proficiency. The goal is to ensure that "no group is left behind."

Accountability requirements for school districts and individual schools are equally rigorous. Schools and school districts must:

- Meet adequate yearly progress (AYP) goals as indicated in the state standards.
- Distribute annual report cards to parents communicating information about those schools that successfully met the AYP and those schools that failed (NCLB 2001).

Rewards apply when the AYP goals are met. Punitive action is taken when the AYP goals are not met.

Choice

NCLB authorizes choice options for parents under two conditions:

1. Schools fail to meet the AYP.
2. Schools are defined as "persistently dangerous"; or students "are victims of violent crime at school." (NCLB 2001)

When either of these conditions occurs, parents may choose to do the following: (1) Send their children to other schools within the same district, including charter schools; or (2) Request supplemental educational services for their children.

School districts are responsible for providing transportation to students who move to other schools, using up to five percent of their Title I funds to cover the expense of that transportation. School districts must provide up to 20 percent of the district funding for Title I when supplemental educational services are required for students (NCLB 2001).

Flexibility

Flexibility is achieved in the use of federal monies earmarked for education by granting districts and schools who successfully meet the annual yearly progress (AYP) goals financial flexibility with grant programs. School districts may transfer up to 50 percent of the monies earmarked in the following grants to Title I programs or transfer monies between these grant programs:

- Teacher Quality State Grants.
- Educational Technology.
- Innovative Programs.
- Safe and Drug-Free Schools.

The law also permits up to seven states to consolidate monies from many federal and state grant programs to local educational agencies. Those states that are allowed to participate are required to enter into five-year performance agreements. The Local Flexibility Demonstration Program permits an additional 70 local education agencies (LEAs) to consolidate monies for any ESEA-authorized purpose from those same grant programs listed above. The participating LEAs must establish performance agreements with the Department of Education (NCLB 2001).

Improving Teacher Quality State Grant Program

The NCLB Act also includes funding to states for programs to improve the quality of teachers, principals, and paraprofessionals. State Departments of Education can apply for funding through a grant application process. This program replaces the Eisenhower and Class Size Reduction Programs although the purpose of the Eisenhower program (focus on math and science instruction) and the Class Size Reduction Program continue to be one part of the more expanded Improving Teacher Quality Program. State Education Agencies (SEA), local school districts (LEA), and state agencies of higher education are encouraged to develop proposals that include partnerships. Proposals should be based on scientifically proven programs and resources. Professional development proposals should focus on strategies to align state standards, assessments, and the improvement of student achievement. Funds can be used for professional development, implementing mentoring programs, teacher retention, and recruitment programs; supporting the training of teachers to better integrate technology; and providing assistance to teachers to meet certification, licensure, or other requirements—including the National Board for Professional Teaching standards (NCLB 2001).

Regrettably, school library media specialists are not included in the Teacher Quality State Grant Program.

NCLB, Reading, and Literacy Programs

Included in the NCLB Act is the authorization for three reading literacy programs: Reading First, Early Reading First, and Improving Literacy Through School Libraries. The Reading First program establishes that all students will be proficient in reading by the third grade. A major focus of the program is an emphasis on scientifically based reading research as the primary criterion for selection of reading instructional programs. The NCLB Act authorizes a grant program with "funds [to be] allocated to states according to the proportion of children ages 5 to 17 who reside within the state and who are from families with incomes below the poverty line" (NCLB 2001). Other Reading First requirements include:

- Screening and diagnostic assessments must be administered to identify students in kindergarten through grade 3 who need remedial reading programs.
- Professional development for K-3 teachers in effective instructional reading practices must be provided.

The goal of the Early Reading First program is to provide instructional resources and professional development for teachers to ensure that children who enter kindergarten have the "necessary language, cognitive, and early reading skills for reading success." The Early Reading First program provides six-year grants for early language, literacy, and pre-reading development of preschool-age children, especially those who are in low-income communities. Programs are required to adopt instructional materials that have been scientifically proven to be effective. This is a competitive grant application process and in 2006 the estimated funding level is over one-hundred million dollars (NCLB 2001).

The Improving Literacy Through School Libraries program is designed to "improve student literacy skills and academic achievement by providing schools with up-to-date library materials and to ensure that school library media centers are staffed by well-trained and professionally certified school media specialists" (NCLB 2001). This is a competitive grant application process administered by the Department of Education with the application and instructions for submission located on the Ed.gov Web site. In 2006, the grant program was funded at $19 million and 100 grants were awarded to schools. The primary criterion for eligibility is the poverty level of school districts. Applications are limited to those school districts with 20 percent of the students from families whose incomes fall below the poverty line. Districts may apply for funding to:

1. Purchase up-to-date school library media resources, including books.

2. Acquire and use advanced technology that is integrated into the curricula to develop and enhance the information literacy, information retrieval, and critical-thinking skills of students.

3. Facilitate Internet links and other resource-sharing networks.

4. Provide professional development for school library media specialists and provide activities that foster increased collaboration among library specialists, teachers, and administrators.

5. Provide students with access to school libraries during nonschool hours, weekends, and summer vacations. (NCLB 2001)

The Improving Literacy through School Libraries program is the first effort by the federal government to provide funding for school libraries since the initial ESEA was funded in 1965. Additional information about this grant program is available on the School Library Funding Web site developed by the American Library Association.

Science Testing Begins in 2007

While NCLB has focused primarily on mathematics, reading, and language arts as content areas for testing, starting in 2007, states will be expected to test student achievement in science in grades 3–5, 6–9, and 10–12. Science teachers are debating a possible change in the science curriculum and instructional practices. The National Science Standards include a focus on inquiry-based learning, and many science teachers and curriculum experts regard the science standards as "a premier guideline on how to teach [science]" (Cavanaugh 2004). Other voices within the science discipline, however, have begun to promote direct instruction as an alternative approach, citing a number of research studies to support the effectiveness of this approach (Cavanaugh 2004). Those science teachers who support inquiry learning fear the direct approach will lead to another example of teaching-to-the-test. There is also concern that direct instruction will regress the discipline back to lectures with an emphasis on regurgitation of facts. "The NSTA [National Science Teachers Association] . . . encourages a blend of both direct teaching and laboratory experimentation" (Cavanaugh 2004). Many believe this combined approach will benefit students by providing them with a higher level of understanding, yet at the same time preparing them for the state tests that are looming (Cavanagh 2004).

A REPORT CARD ON NO CHILD LEFT BEHIND

The No Child Left Behind Act (NCLB) raised the bar on standards-based education, mandating that states should develop standardized tests based on challenging state standards. With that mandate, high stakes testing became the norm in this country. It is important to note that these are not standardized tests administered by the federal government. Instead the NCLB Act establishes policies that mandate accountability outcomes from *state* tests. However, using the funding that the vast majority of school districts receive from Title I as leverage, the federal government now plays a significant role in decisions that impact curriculum, instruction, professional development, textbook selection, and teacher certification

(NCLB 2001; Swanson 2006). What changes has this influence brought to schools over the past five years?

Two important goals of NCLB are to raise the proficiency levels of students in reading and math and to focus greater attention on poverty, race, disabilities, and students with limited English proficiency. The results of these goals receive mixed reviews depending on the perspectives of various stakeholder groups.

Critics of the legislation argue that the law is flawed. They disagree with the use of standardized tests as a fundamental measure of progress (Trotter and Davis 2006), question the viability of severe consequences to raise student achievement (Guilfoyle 2006), and believe the law has led to a narrowing of the curriculum and teach-to-the-test mentality—a practice that has dire consequences, especially for poor, minority children (Whelan 2006). In January 2006, a coalition of school, civil rights, and child advocacy groups provided congressional staff members with a list of 14 recommendations for changing the law (Trotter and Davis 2006).

President Bush, however, declared recently that "the No Child Left Behind . . . has been successful because the annual testing in reading and math hold schools accountable for how they teach and what students learn" (Labbe 2006). The Secretary of Education, Margaret Spellings, responding to criticism about the Reading First program, reiterated her belief that, "the only way to be sure a child is a successful reader is through regular assessments" (Straight Answers 2005, 28). The Achievement Alliance, a coalition formed by two civil rights groups and a prominent business association, continues to support the legislation, despite criticisms from other civil rights and business leaders. According to Achievement Alliance, "The fact that students in larger, more diverse districts are being paid attention to and given extra help is a welcome change in an education system that routinely shortchanges such students . . . This additional support should not be characterized as punishment" (Reid 2005).

The next section explores in more detail some of the positive and negative outcomes of the legislation to date.

Quality Counts Data

The most recent Quality Counts report, released in January, 2006, included the following conclusions:

- Student achievement in mathematics, as measured by National Assessment of Education Programs (NAEP) scores, increased by 18.5 points on a 500-point scale at the 4th grade level—nearly 2 grade levels.
- The mathematics scores of black and Hispanic 4th grade students increased 27.7 points and 24.2 points, respectively.
- The national average in reading barely budged from 1992–2005, inching up only 2 points in both grades 4 and 8.
- Reading scores for black, Hispanic, and low-income 4th grade students increased at nearly triple the national average, or about two-thirds of a grade level. (Olson 2006)

Although overall reading scores show little improvement, math scores from the Quality Counts data suggest that high-stakes testing aligned with the state standards is working. There is, however, disagreement within the education community about how to best interpret this data.

Accountability and Annual Yearly Progress (AYP) Goals

Another goal of NCLB is accountability. School districts and schools that fail to meet their annual yearly progress (AYP) goals are the recipients of sanctions. Schools that do not make their AYP goals in the first year are required to offer parents the option of changing their student(s) to another school in the district, including charter schools, or providing supplemental educational opportunities for the students who do attain the AYP goal. Schools that do not make the AYP in the second year are required to hire different teachers. By the third year schools can be restructured, which means changing the entire faculty and the administration. Schools also essentially lose part of their Title I funding because they are required to use a percentage of that money to pay for the busing and supplemental education options (NCLB 2001). Many educators believe the accountability requirements of NCLB are punitive and actually hurt the low-income students the law was intended to help (Reid 2005).

Anecdotal examples illustrate the potentially negative impact of AYP on schools and teachers. Fletcher (2005) describes the successes of the Cherry Hill Elementary Middle School in Baltimore prior to implementation of NCLB. Located in a low-income area, students had made significant advances on the Maryland standardized tests in both math and reading for several years. Students were so successful that the school had been the recipient of an award, including money to purchase new instructional resources for classrooms and books for the library media center. Student successes continued until 2003, when the school failed to achieve the AYP. The situation deteriorated rapidly with the school still unable to meet the AYP goal in the third year, 2005. This failure resulted in the restructuring of the school and the replacement of staff and administration. Students who had been so proud of their significant advances on state tests now found they could not meet the standards set for the AYP. The failure also brought reduced funding to a school that was already struggling with insufficient funding. Ironically, the new principal and many of the replacement faculty came from other schools in the school district that had also failed to meet the AYP goal (Fletcher 2005).

Some teachers also report feeling pressured to apply instructional strategies that penalize low-achieving students. Booher-Jennings (2006) describes an elementary teacher, "Mrs. Dewey," who was faced with a new strategy, "data-driven decision making." Teachers were advised to gather data on students using regular benchmark assessments and to use that data to make decisions about students that grouped them by their potential to be successful on the state standardized tests, by a professional development consultant. The "triage approach" required Mrs. Dewey and other teachers to divide students into three categories according to their benchmark scores on the tests. Those categories were:

- "Safe cases"
- "Suitable cases for treatment"
- "Hopeless cases"

Mrs. Dewey was told the "safe cases" needed little attention because they would definitely pass. She was to concentrate on the "suitable cases for treatment" because these were the "bubble kids," those students who, with sufficient help, would also pass the test. The others were the "hopeless cases," those students who had no chance of ever passing the test. This scenario put Mrs. Dewey in an untenable position. If she tried to help those students who were in the "hopeless case" category, she would have less time to spend with the middle group or the "bubble group." Her ethics told her she should be helping those students in the "hopeless case" category, but if she did and some students in the "bubble group" failed to pass the test the school would not make their AYP and all teachers, and students, would suffer. Booher-Jennings (2006) suggests this moral dilemma is taking place in schools all over the country. She concludes that the stakes are so high today for schools to meet their AYP that many teachers and administrators feel forced to focus on successfully reaching the AYP regardless of the consequences to those very students that the NCLB Act was meant to help (Booher-Jennings 2006).

Proponents of NCLB counter the above arguments with their own NCLB stories—success stories. Falkener Elementary School in Greensboro, North Carolina, for example, was recently recognized by the White House as an example of an excellent school. Approximately 86 percent of the students attending Falkener receive federally subsidized meals. Since 2001 when No Child Left Behind was passed, Falkener has made significant academic improvement, setting and achieving high standards for all students. As Fernandez (2006) points out, "these are the students Bush wanted to help through the No Child Left Behind Act." Principal Amy Holcombe and PTA president Adeline Blacknall attribute the school's success to NCLB: "No Child Left Behind is working . . . It gives us the motivation to continue what we're doing" (Fernandez 2006).

Narrowing the Curriculum

Lewis (2006) focuses on another potential problem with the AYP requirement. Many schools are now placing so much emphasis on meeting the AYP that teachers are not only teaching to the test with double periods of reading and math, but also reducing the time spent on social studies and science to minimal levels. If it is not on the test, it is not being taught. Lewis argues that this perspective results in a reduced focus on creativity and critical thinking. She poses the question, "What are teachers and schools learning from tests focused on limited subjects and limited skills?" Lewis suggests the solution to this problem is to drop the AYP requirement.

The bottom line to narrowing the curriculum in this manner is that the very students the NCLB Act wanted to help—low-income students and minorities—tend to be the students hurt the most by the narrow focus of teaching primarily math and reading. Jack Jennings, president of the Center of Education Policy, says, "although 78 percent of districts report improved standardized test scores, by narrowing the curriculum the main concern is that low-proficiency students will only master rote learning and fail to obtain a well-rounded education" (Whelan 2006, 17).

One Size Does Not Fit All

Mayers (2006) suggests that the AYP requirement puts school districts and schools in a position where not all test scores are equal. "Annual measurable achievement objectives (AMAO) must be identified for each subgroup [gender, race, ethnicity, migrant status, disabilities, LEP (limited in English proficiency)] and it is by meeting or exceeding these objectives that a state may demonstrate that they are moving forward" (449). The fallacy in the NCLB policy is that not all states set their policies for subgroups using the same guidelines. Many states have negotiated with the federal government for exceptions in their policy guidelines for subgroups (Mayers 2006). NCLB requires all states and schools to meet the AYP and to report the AMAO to parents and community members through their annual report card, but all states are not required to follow the same rules that produce those results.

The Department of Education is attempting to address some of the concerns about the way NCLB uses test scores to determine AYP by altering requirements and introducing new flexibility. They are also exploring a growth model pilot program that would enable states to track individual student progress, thus ensuring that the schools get credit for helping their lowest-performing students (Guilfoyle 2006). It is hoped that these changes will stop some of the "cheating" that has been reported that "raise test scores, but do nothing to help students" (Laitsch, Lewallen, and McCloskey 2005).

Reading Educators and NCLB

The Reading First program has received mixed reviews by those who teach reading. The International Reading Association (IRA) surveyed the membership in March, 2005, using a random sample of 4,000 members with a survey return of 1,557. When asked to agree or disagree on the statement, "Children's reading achievement will improve when research-backed curriculum and instruction are fully implemented," 77.9 percent agreed. The sample responded negatively, however, to the statement: "NCLB implementation in your school or district has been sufficiently funded to achieve reading proficiency"; 74.3 percent disagreed. Other questions received mixed responses. The survey results suggest that members of IRA have strong opinions on NCLB, some positive and others negative (Micklos 2005). The IRA has expressed support for professional development, believing that highly qualified teachers will benefit students. They also firmly believe that multiple methods of reading instruction will be the most beneficial for students taught by qualified reading teachers and reading specialists (Farstrup 2005).

The Reading First initiative has generated some controversy related to the methodology, assessment strategies, and selection of instructional reading programs. One requirement of NCLB states that selection of instructional reading programs must be based on "scientifically based research" (Grunwald 2006). The emphasis on phonics to the exclusion of the whole language approach has caused school districts to abandon reading programs that were working in favor of programs strongly recommended by the Department of Education. The Center on Education Policy (CEP) released a report in June, 2005, reflecting survey evidence that 40 out of 49 states responding perceived the ED (Department of Education) as "strictly or very strictly enforcing the Reading First program" (McCallion 2006). The Inspector General's Final Inspection Report of the Reading First program confirmed the CEP report, finding that the U.S. Department of Education inappropriately influenced the selection of reading programs by state and local education agencies, included requirements within the application process that were not part of the NCLB Act, and established a review panel that lacked objectivity with regard to specific reading programs (United States Department of Education 2006). Despite the flawed selection process, Richard Long, who lobbies for the International Reading Association, believes that the influx of one billion dollars a year has helped "kids [learn] to read" but he also adds, "it's been very frustrating for those of us who really believe in evidence-based programs" (Grunwald 2006).

Proponents of the Reading First approach believe that children need to start with phonetic awareness, progress to phonics, and eventually achieve comprehension. According to Manzo (2006), some states, particularly those that have been taking part in the program for several years, credit Reading First with "driving dramatic changes" (24). Florida, for example, has trained over 16,000 of its 35,000 k-3 teachers and has seen some gains in 3rd grade reading scores and teachers in Colorado have been learning to use assessment results to design more immediate intervention plans for struggling students (Manzo 2006).

NCLB AND THE SCHOOL LIBRARY MEDIA PROGRAM

NCLB has the potential to both positively and negatively impact school library media programs. How school library media specialists respond to the challenges posed by the legislation is critical. Reed (2005) suggests "NCLB is a wake-up call for library media specialists," and she provides the following recommendations:

- Research NCLB and develop an understanding of the law.
- Develop an understanding of the state standards and local curricula.
- Collaborate with teachers to map all content areas of the curriculum and use that information to provide library media center resources that correlate.
- Actively promote reading and literary appreciation.
- Become a resource for national research relevant to the curriculum and instructional programs and issues of the school. (56)

Toni Buzzeo offers similar advice to library media specialists: "[i]f you have not yet begun true collaboration, team-designed, team-taught, and team-assessed units of study that integrate information literacy skills into content area teaching, now is the time to begin collaborating from the center of your school universe" (Buzzeo 2006, 20).

Potentially Positive Impacts

NCLB includes significant funding opportunities for school library media centers in low-income areas. The Improving Literacy through School Libraries Grant is obviously aimed at school library media center programs. However, while school librarians cannot directly apply for other NCLB grants such as Reading First or Enhancing Education through Technology, these funds can be earmarked for libraries if school library media specialists make a convincing case that the library program contributes to student learning (Whelan 2004). In North Carolina, for example, the Department of Public Instruction used its NCLB technology grant to provide a five-day training camp for teams of principals, school library media specialists, technology directors, and teachers from 11 schools with high poverty rates and little technology. Through this training, it became clear that school media programs are central to helping schools meet the law's requirements in relation to technology (Whelan 2004).

St. Lifer challenges school library media specialists to become adept grant writers or work with someone or a group who is successful. As he points out, "the money will not follow you; you have to follow the money" (St. Lifer 2003, 13). The 2004 Improving Literacy through the School Library awardees, for example, successfully secured funds that "focused on library books, materials development, online database subscriptions, acquisition of computer hardware and software, expanding library hours to allow students to easily access resources after school, facilitating family literacy programs, and curriculum writing that integrates information literacy standards and technology use across content areas" (Georges 2004, 28). Numerous grant writing resources can be found on the Web. Grant writing assistance is even available by emailing the Department of Education at lsl@ed.gov.

NCLB underscores the importance of teaching students to read. This provides school library media specialists with the opportunity to advocate for the connection between the library media program, literary appreciation, and reading proficiency. Della Curtis, coordinator of the Office of Library Information Services for Baltimore County, believes that NCLB offers school library media specialists a golden opportunity to really get engaged with literacy (Whelan 2004, 41). Curtis's office, for example, along with principals, teachers, school library media specialists, and parents developed a master plan, outlining strategies and goals for complying with NCLB regulations. The plan includes "a literacy campaign aimed at increasing visits to local public libraries, a K-12 read-a-thon that encourages kids to read books to raise money for a literacy fund for underprivileged peers, an independent reading program called Strive for 25, and a Get Carded campaign to distribute library cards . . . to all the district's 7,000 kindergartners" (Whelan 2004, 41).

Scott Knickelbine suggests that supporting literacy development can start simply, with the school library media specialists approaching reading specialists, department heads, and teachers to inquire about their needs and to offer books and other helpful resources, especially staff development books geared towards literacy development (Whelan 2004). In a recent issue of *Knowledge Quest* focused on teen reading, editor Debbie Abilock provided yet another connection between the school library media program and reading—vocabulary development. Abilock suggests that library media specialists can have a dynamic influence on developing and broadening students' vocabulary. School library media specialists cannot "afford to relegate the intentional teaching of vocabulary to the classroom, unless we are willing to forfeit our credibility and respect among the very teachers we want to work with" (Abilock 2006, 8).

The emphasis of NCLB on accountability can also be viewed as an opportunity for school library media specialists. As the American Association of School Librarians (AASL) brochure "Your School library Media Program and No Child Left Behind" points out, many state tests do ask students to apply skills as well as to recall facts (2004). Testing of this nature opens the door for school library media specialists to work collaboratively with teachers to design information literacy units tied to classroom curriculum. In this way, school library media specialists can help students learn to not only memorize information, but to also use it in meaningful and memorable ways. In order to do this, however, it is imperative that school library media specialists provide evidence of the correlation between information literacy and state standards. Eisenberg (2004) suggests "we need to address the specific questions of performance on standardized tests." Some specific strategies to gather this information include:

- Analyzing state standards and test items to determine direct connections to information skills instruction.

- Targeting information skills instruction actions to specific standards and test items.

- Evaluating the impact of these interventions on student performance on test items (25–26).

NCLB will soon require that all students be technology-literate by the end of eighth grade (NCLB 2001). Again, this requirement provides school library media specialists with a leadership opportunity (AASL 2004). Technology skills are an integral part of the information literacy curriculum. School library media specialists are knowledgeable and practiced in teaching children how to use information technologies to answer questions and solve problems. They can provide ready access to computers and information technologies, especially for students who do not have home access. They can provide guidance to students using technology to complete school assignments, as well as explore personal interests. Finally, they can provide support for teachers struggling to integrate technology into teaching and learning in meaningful ways.

In 2007, states will begin administering standardized tests in science. As Curtis points out, "school library media specialists have a lot to offer science teachers and their students" (Whelan 2004, 41). At the most basic level, they can provide resources to supplement science textbooks that often fall short of supporting required standards. More importantly, however, they can help create learning environments that support inquiry and encourage students to engage in challenging scientific research in the library, and in the classroom.

Finally, NCLB provides an opportunity for school library media specialists to strengthen their relationships with public libraries. St. Lifer (2003), for example, suggests that school libraries and public libraries proactively work together to provide rich, diverse resources to support student learning, and offer innovative programs that target rich learning experiences for students.

Potentially Negative Impacts

While the NCLB Act has infused new life into library media centers through the Improving Literacy through School Libraries program, the high-stakes testing mandate and significant focus on phonics-based reading programs have resulted in some limitations on library media specialists' ability to collaborate with classroom teachers to integrate information fluency across the curriculum. As Goldberg (2005) points out, the obsession of administrators and teachers with "achiev(ing) NCLB benchmarks (has led to) 'a real narrowing of the curriculum,' as decision makers throw all available resources into prepackaged 'drill-and-kill' programs to boost scores. That can bode ill for school library media specialists, who have found themselves losing technology dollars to the purchase of software that can track achievement-test data" (40). Some school library media specialists have found the primary function of the library media center relegated to students using computers with software that teaches test-taking skills.

While the literacy focus of NCLB should bode well for school library media programs, this has not been the case everywhere. As Loertscher (2006) points out, "many schools are so focused on the skill of reading that they hire reading specialists or literacy coaches rather than teacher-librarians to boost achievement, and they never mention the love of reading or lifelong reading habit" (9). In some cases, funding has been diverted from school library media program budgets to purchase classroom collections of books—books only accessible to a limited number of students.

As stated earlier in this chapter, the development of highly qualified teachers is an emphasis of NCLB. Library media specialists are not specifically mentioned in the legislation, however, and thus have not benefited from the increased focus on professional development. While the mandate to place "highly qualified" teachers in all schools is commendable, the act is silent with regard to "every school library should be staffed by a highly qualified, certified library media specialist" (ALA 2006). The omission of the school library media specialist from NCLB suggests that members of Congress lack an understanding of the school library media center as a learning laboratory and a fundamental requirement of effective learning programs in schools.

Table 2.1.
Positive and Negative Impacts of NCLB on Schools and School Libraries

Positive Impacts

NCLB has forced states to develop content area standards.

The emphasis on reading and math has brought about at least modest increases in student achievement.

Significant increases in federal funding have enabled professional development and updating of instructional resources and school library technology, resources, and services for low income areas.

An improvement has been seen in the qualifications of classroom teachers.

Funds from NCLB grants such as Reading First or Enhancing Education through Technology can be earmarked for school libraries if school library media specialists make a convincing case that the library program contributes to student learning.

The emphasis on literacy provides school library media specialists an opportunity to advocate for the connection between the library media program, literary appreciation, and reading proficiency.

The requirement for students to be technology—and science—literate by the end of eighth grade provides school library media specialists with a leadership opportunity.

Negative Impacts

The AYP requirement is viewed by many as punitive with a greater negative impact on low income areas and the very students the law was meant to help, that is, low-income and ethnic and minority populations, special needs students, and students with limited English proficiency.

NCLB Act has given the federal government control over many aspects of education at the expense of local control.

The legislation is based on a false premise—one size fits all—while in reality, special dispensations, unequal funding, cultural disparities, and punitive consequences result in significant differences among states and school districts.

The high-stakes testing focus has fueled a teach-to-the-test mentality by some teachers and a narrowing of the curriculum.

Many schools have become so focused on reading skills that they no longer emphasize pleasure reading.

Some schools are diverting funding from library media center budgets to use to develop classroom collections.

REAUTHORIZATION OF NCLB AND SCHOOL LIBRARY MEDIA SPECIALISTS

The NCLB legislation is scheduled for reauthorization in 2007. What is the role of school library media specialists as legislators discuss the pros and cons of this landmark legislation? As Table 2.1 shows, NCLB has had both a positive and negative influence on America's schools and school libraries.

Accountability in education is a priority focus today and will continue into the future. The challenge for lawmakers, community leaders, and educators is how to establish accountability that recognizes the diversities that exist across the country and fosters positive changes rather than punitive consequences. Legislators and policy-makers believed they had the magic answer to the problems in education and were unwilling to involve experts within the education profession in their decisions. Change that is successful and ongoing requires buy-in by all parties involved in the outcome. The NCLB Act resulted in change, both positive and negative. Before the legislation is—hopefully—changed and then reauthorized, legislators should require an objective review of the outcome of the law and use that information to make changes.

How can library media specialists influence the change process? St. Lifer (2003) challenges school library media specialists to "accept the new paradigm and take action" (13).

The Recommendations for Action proposed by the School Libraries Task Force represent an aggressive effort by the American Library Association (ALA) and AASL to address the "critical current issues that threaten the existence of school libraries in states throughout the country" (Lowe 2006). The proposed Delphi Study and the final report of the Task Force to the Executive Board are scheduled to be discussed at ALA's annual conference in 2007.

School library professionals at all levels need to become informed about the existing law and the influence it has had on their school and community. School librarians are information specialists, so this is their opportunity to contribute to the local knowledge base. School librarians need to become strong and vocal advocates for school library media programs as vital and significant contributors to the learning experience for students. Ross Todd and Keith Curry Lance have advocated for evidence-based practice, but they need the participation of practitioners and library educators. The lobbying voices of ALA, AASL, and state associations will have greater significance with scientific and evidence-based research.

REFERENCES

Abilock, Debbie. 2006. "'Portkeys' to Vocabulary." *Knowledge Quest* 35, no. 1: 8–11.

American Association of School Librarians. 2004. *Your School Library Media Program and No Child Left Behind.* http://www.ala.org/ala/aasl/aaslpubsandjournals/aaslbooksandprod/aaslbooksproducts. htm#principals (accessed September 24, 2006).

American Library Association. 2006. "A 'Highly Qualified' Librarian in Every School Library." http://www.ala.org/ala/aasl/aaslissues/nclb/nclb.htm (accessed September 29, 2006).

Booher-Jennings, Jennifer. 2006. "Rationing Education in an Era of Accountability." *Phi Delta Kappan* 87, no. 10: 756.

Buttram, Joan L. 1997. "Improving America's Schools through Standards-Based Education." *The National Association of Secondary School Principals. NASSP Bulletin* 8, no. 590: 16.

Buzzeo, Toni. 2006. "Collaborating from the Center of the School Universe." *Library Media Connection* 24, no. 4: 18–20.

Cavanagh, Sean. 2004. "NCLB Could Alter Science Teaching." *Edweek.org* (November 10). http://www.aeoe.org/news/online/nclb-science-edweek111004.html. (accessed September 15, 2006)

"The Daily Report Card." 1996. *The National Update on America's Education Reform Efforts: A Service of the National Education Goals Panel* 6, no. 31. http://ofcn.org/cyber.serv/academy/rptcard/1996/drc631.html (accessed November 16, 2006).

"Developing Content Standards: Creating a Process for Change." 1993. *Policy Briefs* (October). New Brunswick, NJ: The Consortium for Policy Research Education. http://www.ed.gov/pubs/CPRE/rb10stan.html (accessed September 29, 2006).

Eisenberg, Michael B. 2004. "It's All About Learning: Ensuring That Students Are Effective Users of Information on Standardized Tests." *Library Media Connection* 22, no. 6: 22–30.

Farstrup, Alan E. 2005. "A Classic Case of Mixed Feelings." *Reading Today* 22, no. 6: 7. http://www.reading.org/publications/reading_today/samples/RTY-0506-classic.html. (accessed September 19, 2006).

Fernandez, Jennifer. 2006. "Getting Ready for Bush Visit." *News-Record.com.* http://news-record.com/apps/pbcs.dll/article?AID=/20061017/NEWSREC0101/61016018/-1/NEWSREC0201 (accessed November 18, 2006).

Fletcher, Michael A. 2005. "Issues & Views." *The Crisis* (September/October): 16–19.

Georges, Fitzgerald. 2004. "What Are the Implications for School Libraries?" *Library Media Connection* 23, no. 1: 28–29.

Goldberg, Beverly. 2005. "Why School Libraries Won't Be Left Behind." *American Libraries* 36, no. 8: 38–41.

Grunwald, Michael. 2006. "Billions for an Inside Game on Reading." *Washington Post* (October 1). http://www.washingtonpost.com/wp-yn/content/article/2006/09/29/AR2006092901333.html (accessed on October 3, 2006).

Guilfoyle, Christy. 2006. "NCLB: Is There Life Beyond Testing?" *Educational Leadership* 64, no. 3: 8–13.

Labbe, Theola. 2006. "Bush: No Child Left Behind Closing Achievement Gap." *Washington Post* (October 5). http://www.washingtonpost.com/?nav=globetop (accessed on October 9, 2006).

Laitsch, Dan, Theresa Lewallen, and Molly McCloskey. 2005. "The Whole Child: A Framework for Education in the 21st Century." *Infobrief,* no. 40 (February). Alexandria, VA: Association for Supervision and Curriculum Development.

Lewis, Anne C. 2006. "Clean Up the Test Mess." *Phi Delta Kappan* 87, no. 9: 643.

Loertscher, David. 2006. "What Flavor Is Your School Library? The Teacher-Librarian as Learning Leader." *Teacher Librarian* 34, no 2: 8–12.

Lowe, Katherine. 2006. *Interim Report to ALA Executive Board School Libraries Task.* Chicago, IL: American Library Association. http://www.mslma.org/whoweare/ALAtask/ALAinterim0106.html. (accessed September 15, 2006).

Manzo, Kathleen K. 2006. "Scathing Report Casts Cloud over 'Reading First.'" *Education Week* 26, no. 6 (October 4): 1, 24–25.

Mayers, Camille M. 2006. "Public Law 107–110 No Child Left Behind Act of 2001: Support or Threat to Education As a Fundamental Right?" *Education* 126, no. 3: 449.

McCallion, Gail. 2006. *Reading First: Implementation Issues and Controversies.* Congressional Research Service. The Library of Congress. http://www.opencrs.com/rpts/RL33246_20060120.pdf#search=%22CRS%20Report%20%20January%20OR%202006%20%22Reading%20First%3A%20Implementation%20Issues%20and%20Controversies%22%22 (accessed on September 10, 2006).

Micklos, John. 2005. "IRA Survey Shows Mixed Reactions to NCLB." *Reading Teacher.* http://blog.reading.org/archives/000574.html (accessed on October 4, 2006).

National Commission on Excellence in Education. 1983. *A Nation at Risk: The Imperative for Education Reform.* Washington, DC: Government Printing Office.

No Child Left Behind Act of 2001: Executive Summary. 2001. Washington, DC: U.S. Department of Education. http://www.ed.gov/nclb/landing.jhtml (accessed on September 15, 2006).

Olson, Lynn. 2006. "A Decade of Effort: Quality Counts at 10." *Edweek.org* (January 5). http://counts.edweek.org/sreports/qc01/articles/qc01story.cfm?slug=17exec_sum.h20 (accessed on September 25, 2006).

"Quality Counts 2001 Executive Summary: Seeking Stability for Standards-Based Education." 2001. *Education Week* (January 5). http://www.edweek.org/ew/articles/2006/01/05/17overview.h25.html (accessed September 25, 2006).

Reed, Donna. 2005. "Marian the Librarian Meets NCLB." *Library Media Connection* 23 (7): 56–58.

Reid, Karla Scoon. 2005. "Civil Rights Groups Split Over NCLB: Accountability Provisions Stirring Heated Debate." *Education Week* (August 31). http://www.edweek.org/ew/articles/2005/08/31/01 (accessed November 16, 2006).

St. Lifer, Evan. 2003. "Is NCLB Really 'The Da Vinci Code'?" *School Library Journal* 49, no. 12: 13.

"Straight Answers from Margaret Spellings." 2005. *American Libraries* 36, no. 8: 28.

Swanson, Christopher B. 2006. *Making the Connection: A Decade of Standards-Based Reform and Achievement.* Editorial Projects in Education Research Center. http://www.epe.org/rc (accessed December 5, 2006).

Trotter, Andrew, and Michelle Davis. 2006. "At 4, NCLB Gets Praise and Fresh Call to Amend It." *Education Week* 25, no. 19 (January 18): 26, 30.

United States Department of Education. Office of Inspector General. 2006. "The Reading First Program's Grant Application Process: Final Inspection Report." http://64.233.161.104/search?q=cache:eRyPYfCjbOkJ:www.ed.gov/about/offices/list/oig/aireports/i13f0017.pdf+Inspector+General+Report+%22Reading+First%22&hl=en&gl=us&ct=clnk&cd=1 (accessed on November 10, 2006).

Whelan, Debra Lau. 2004. "A Golden Opportunity." *School Library Journal* 50, no. 1: 40–42.

Whelan, Debra Lau. 2006. "Schools Narrowing Their Curriculums." *School Library Journal* 52 no. 5: 17.

3

Teaching for Understanding

Barbara K. Stripling

The tenth-grade English class had been studying short stories, the unit culminating in the reading of "A Worn Path" by Eudora Welty. The young teacher and her students carefully dissected the story about an "old Negro woman with her head tied red rag" named Phoenix Jackson who was walking into town from her home in the country to get medicine for her grandson. Satisfied that her students understood the story, Miss Moser gave an essay exam with questions to probe the deep, underlying significance of the path and of Grandma's journey into the white world. With few exceptions, the students reacted to the essay questions with perplexity—wasn't the story simply about an old woman walking to town?

I still remember my dismay that my students did not understand the deeper meanings of Welty's powerful story. I realized that I had failed as a teacher; I had taught for comprehension, but not understanding. As a first-year teacher, I learned a powerful lesson about the necessity of teaching for understanding. As a lifelong educator, I am still defining what teaching for understanding means in terms of student learning, teaching practices, and school librarianship.

WHAT IS UNDERSTANDING?

Lewis Carroll provides some sound advice about how to learn to teach for understanding: "Begin at the beginning . . . and go on till you come to the end: then stop" (Guiliano

1982, 76). The first step is defining what "understanding" means. The definition used by the Teaching for Understanding Project at the Harvard Graduate School of Education is, "Understanding is the ability to think and act flexibly with what one knows" (ALPS 2006). Understanding is the end stage of a continuum of learning: facts to information to knowledge to understanding.

Facts have been glorified as the underpinning of problem solving since Joe Friday became a cultural icon with his "Just the facts, Ma'am" approach in the 1950s television police drama, "Dragnet." Facts are supposed to stand on their own, without bias or interpretation. Inevitably, however, facts are collected and organized in some way to provide *information* about a subject. The selection process of what facts to include and the connections made among facts automatically build in interpretation by the author or publisher. Both facts and information exist outside of the learner.

When the learner interacts with information to organize and attach meaning to it, the learner is building *knowledge;* knowledge exists within the mind of that learner. Knowledge is more easily organized within the mind if information can be attached to larger ideas, so that all information on biomes is interconnected and mentally filed under that idea, for example. Grant Wiggins and Jay McTighe call this level of ideas "Important To Know and Do" (Wiggins and McTighe 2005, 71).

The next level of learning is *understanding,* which is the conceptual framework and power of learning that a learner develops when he or she interprets, evaluates, and applies or transfers knowledge to a new context. Understandings (what Wiggins and McTighe call Big Ideas and Core Tasks) are built on knowledge, but knowledge alone is not understanding. Grant Wiggins and Jay McTighe, in *Understanding by Design,* refer to Benjamin Bloom's explanation of understanding: "As Bloom (1956) put it, understanding is the ability to marshal skills and facts wisely and appropriately, through effective application, analysis, synthesis, and evaluation" (Wiggins and McTighe 2005, 39).

The process of gaining understanding is metacognitive transfer: the meaning is used by the learner beyond the particular context in which it is first learned and the learner is thinking about his active application. The learner might go through the following mental process:

- Organize facts and information gained in one context to create meaning (knowledge);
- Challenge, interpret, question, and extend the knowledge to see how it applies to a new context;
- Select knowledge that is relevant and appropriate to a new context; and
- Apply the knowledge to make sense of the new situation or context (understanding).

Understanding goes beyond comprehension. For years, educators have congratulated themselves on moving children beyond decoding to comprehension of text, to being able to state the meaning in their own words. But comprehension stops at that text. To push children to understanding, educators must ask them to use what they learned from the text to make inferences about what is not in the text, understand a different text, or create meaning from new contexts.

Understanding is not inert; understanding is actively developed through the mental process of using knowledge and thinking skills in new applications. Understanding cannot, therefore, be taught, because it must be created by the learner. Educators can only teach *for* understanding by creating learning experiences that require the development of essential knowledge, the use of cognitive and metacognitive skills, and the application and transfer of knowledge.

WHAT NEEDS TO BE UNDERSTOOD? WHO GETS TO SAY?

Defining the curriculum and priorities of our educational system is a political battle that has gone on for decades. The publication in 1983 of *A Nation at Risk* with its dire predictions of a "rising tide of mediocrity that threatens our very future as a nation and a people" precipitated a movement toward national standards (National Commission on Excellence in Education 1983, 5). The National Council of Teachers of Mathematics (NCTM) was the first national professional association to start writing standards. National mathematics standards were published in 1989, followed immediately by national science standards. The federal government became involved in the standards movement with the appointment of a National Education Goals Panel (NEGP) by Congress in 1990, a Secretary's Commission on Achieving Necessary Skills (SCANS) by the Secretary of Labor in 1990, and a National Council on Education Standards and Testing (NCEST) by Congress in 1991.

Standards were written and published in every major content area over the next few years, but they became increasingly politicized, as exemplified by the January 1995 rejection of the national history standards by Congress in a 99–1 vote as well as increasing political pressure for a national curriculum and national testing. The passage of No Child Left Behind Act of 2001 accelerated the testing momentum by mandating that states test all students in grades 3–8 annually in reading or language arts and mathematics, as well as continue previously mandated testing in reading and mathematics at least once for students in grades 10–12. NCLB also mandated that states develop and administer science assessments at least once in grades 3–5, 6–9, and 10–12 by 2007–2008. Adequate Yearly Progress (AYP) of schools is determined by their results on the reading and mathematics assessments (McREL 2004).

Teachers are under so much pressure that they may resort to "teaching to the test" rather than take a chance that their students will under-perform on the mandated testing. Their diverse responses to the accountability frenzy depend on their experience level, depth of knowledge of the curriculum area being taught, the requirements of the state tests, and local pressures and mandates. Teaching goals are so correlated with testing that one teacher participant in a workshop was overheard saying, "Should I be teaching for understanding or for achievement?" (Nelson 2001, 13).

The question of "Who gets to say what students are learning" seems to have been answered by the political system; however, the picture is not as bleak as it appears on the surface. The state assessments are constructed around national and state standards; therefore, if the standards allow students to target understandings rather than accumulations of facts, then the testing should measure understanding and students will perform well if the educators teach for understanding.

A look at the national standards in the four major content areas provides hope that teaching in our schools can focus on the essential ideas, critical thinking processes, and intellectual frameworks that lead to understanding. The mathematics standards state, for example: "Students must learn mathematics with understanding, actively building new knowledge from experience and previous knowledge" (National Council of Teachers of Mathematics 2000, 2). These math standards define both the content and the thinking processes necessary for achieving understanding of mathematical concepts. The process standards include problem solving, reasoning and proof, communication, connections, and representations.

The conceptual framework of the science standards leads directly to teaching scientific concepts that transfer from one science content area to the next, especially in the Unifying Concepts and Processes Standard (including concepts like systems, order, organization, evidence, change, evolution, and equilibrium) and the Science as Inquiry Standard (which includes understanding of scientific concepts, understanding of the nature of science, and the skills necessary to become independent inquirers about the natural world) (National Research Council 1996, chap. 6).

The history standards developed by the National Center for History in the Schools at UCLA support and promote teaching for understanding because they include five historical thinking standards along with content standards for K–4 and 5–12 (National Center for History in the Schools 1996):

Standard 1: Chronological Thinking

Standard 2: Historical Comprehension

Standard 3: Historical Analysis and Interpretation

Standard 4: Historical Research Capabilities

Standard 5: Historical Issues—Analysis and Decision-Making

The Standards for the English Language Arts, sponsored by the National Council for the Teachers of English and the International Reading Association, highlight the thinking processes that underlie understanding, including reading to "build an understanding of texts, of themselves, and of the cultures of the United States and the world"; applying strategies to "comprehend, interpret, evaluate, and appreciate texts"; communicating effectively for a variety of purposes to a variety of audiences; conducting research on issues and interests, and participating as "knowledgeable, reflective, creative, and critical members of a variety of literacy communities" (NCTE and IRA 1998–2006).

HOW IS UNDERSTANDING DEVELOPED?

Understanding frames the way one interprets and interacts with the world; it is a way of *doing,* not a way of *knowing.* The acquisition of understanding, then, must be an active process that is an amalgam of the "world" to be understood and the mental processes and dispositions that enable understanding. In other words, the process–content debate (Should librarians teach process while content teachers teach content?) is meaningless in the realm of understanding, because process and content cannot be separated. Roland Case forcefully makes the case for the blending of process and content: "The traditional 'content-process' division is based upon a false dichotomy; in fact, thinking without content is vacuous and content acquired without thought is mindless and inert" (Case 2005, 46).

A number of educational theorists and researchers have investigated the attributes of content and process that lead to understanding (Case 2005; Chambers 2000; Gardner 1983; Perkins 1994; Scholes 1985; Sherman and Kurshan 2004/2005; Taylor 2000; Wiggins and McTighe 2005). Although each has his or her own priorities, their ideas may be synthesized to form a framework for the development of understanding (see figure 3.1).

Certain aspects of background knowledge, cognitive skills, dispositions, and metacognition emerge as essential to any process of developing understanding.

Background Knowledge

Students need to start with meaningful knowledge, or information that they have connected to what they already know and organized within their own heads. A collection of memorized facts does not lead easily to understanding. Ferretti, MacArthur, and Okolo

Figure 3.1
Framework for Development of Understanding

Background Knowledge / Curriculum	Cognitive Skills and Strategies	Habits of Mind / Dispositions
Overarching themes, patterns (Throughlines)	Connect / Relate	Engaged
Key concepts	Observe	Empathetic
Depth	Question	Curious
Context	Hypothesize	Active
Critical conflicts	Analyze	Critical
	Contextualize	Open-minded
	Challenge	Fluent
	Interpret	Multi-sensory
	Infer	Collaborative
	Balance perspectives	Creative
	Organize	Reflective
	Find patterns	Tolerant of ambiguity
	Construct	
	Conclude	
	Apply	
	Express	
	Reflect	

have developed four characteristics of a curriculum for understanding (Ferretti, MacArthur, and Okolo 2001, 60).

- *Conceptual Coherence*—Ideas are held together by overarching themes, perspectives, patterns, and trends, sometimes called "throughlines."

- *Depth*—Educators move beyond breadth of coverage to in-depth learning of core ideas.

- *Context*—Educators help students contextualize the core ideas by addressing human motives and decisions, multiple causations, and differing perspectives.

- *Conceptual Scaffolding*—Teachers provide structures and vocabulary to help students think about the content in a meaningful way (e.g., common definitions of important vocabulary, criteria for assessing validity, processes and strategies for thinking in that discipline).

Cognitive Processes

The mental processes and attitudes that enable the development of understanding are similar across all subject areas, although they may be applied differently depending on the subject being learned (e.g., interpretation of historical information may look different from interpretation of scientific evidence).

Understanding is propelled by questioning. Students who question while they learn reveal hidden assertions, missing information, conflicting ideas, and author bias. Through this challenge process, they develop understanding. Robert Scholes said, "If *wisdom*, or some less grandiose notion such as heightened awareness, is to be the end of our endeavors, we shall have to see it not as something transmitted from the text to the student but as something developed in the student by questioning the text" (Scholes 1985, 14).

Not only should students question throughout the process of developing understanding, but they also should think critically. They need to interpret, judge, evaluate, infer (Taylor 2000, 11) and maintain a "critical disposition of setting aside personal biases and seeking multiple points of view" (Facione 1990, in Chambers et al. 2000, 58).

Roland Case asserts that learners' thinking at this stage should be supported by some cognitive scaffolds—criteria for judgment (not only about the information, but also about the product they will use to communicate their understandings); a critical thinking vocabulary (e.g., a solid understanding of the concepts of inference, cause, comparison); and thinking strategies (complex combinations of skills that enable learners to draw conclusions or summarize) (Case 2005, 48).

Students also need to make sense of the ideas by organizing them and connecting them to broader conceptual frameworks. When knowledge is connected with other concepts and well-organized, it can be used by the learner in new ways, new contexts. "Organization facilitates applying knowledge in different situations and on novel problems, a process called transfer" (Sherman and Kurshan 2004/2005, 9).

Habits of Mind

The habits of mind or dispositions that emerge as essential in the literature about understanding revolve around the willingness of learners to engage with the work and with fellow learners and open themselves to new, often conflicting, ideas and multiple perspectives. Just as the cognitive skills are applicable to gaining understanding in any content area, so too are the habits of mind. Learners need to be fluent in both their skills and dispositions to respond flexibly and effectively to each learning situation. Roland Case expects all learners to be "open-minded, fair-minded, tolerant of ambiguity, self-reflective, attentive to detail" (Case 2005, 48). Chambers expects students to be active, collaborative, and reflective (Chambers et al. 2000, 58).

The habits of mind required for developing understanding include empathy. Students need to understand the emotional and personal aspects that have shaped the generation of ideas and information in all subject areas. Wineburg says that when you read historical texts, you should seek to understand the bias of the source by putting the emotional context of the writer back in (Wineburg 2001, 63). All historical text is interpretation—a part of understanding the meaning of the text is understanding the emotions that drove it. Indeed, all information is biased by those human aspects. Students who identify and empathize with those biases develop a richer context for understanding the meaning.

Students also must make a habit of using all their senses to learn and express themselves. Howard Gardner calls these "multiple entry points" in his theory of multiple intelligences (Gardner 1983). Isadora Duncan once said, "If I could explain it, I wouldn't have to dance it" (Brabazon 2002, 58).

Metacognition

Metacognition is essential for developing understanding. Throughout the process, students need to look at their own growth in understanding by comparing what they are learning to what they already knew. They need to see how their new understandings conflict with what they previously thought and be able to correct their misconceptions and false assumptions. They need to reflect on how knowledge can be used in different contexts. Most importantly, they must see themselves as learners and be able to call up the necessary knowledge, skills, strategies, and dispositions to meet any new learning context. Teachers can drive metacognition by confronting students with conflicts, opposing ideas, and counterintuitive demonstrations, so that they have to confront the "disequilibrium created by the differences between current and new information" (Sherman and Kurshan 2004/2005, 10).

HOW IS UNDERSTANDING DEVELOPED IN THE REAL WORLD?

Most educators believe that the reason to teach for understanding is so that students will be able to apply their school-related learning to their lives outside of school, both in the present and in the future. Looking at how people develop understandings in the real world, often termed "informal learning," reveals a fuller picture of how to teach for understanding and transfer. Informal learning depends on information gathered through texts (as in formal learning) to some extent, but it more often depends on information gained through social construction (how others influence our understanding) and through embodied knowledge (the practice of a workplace or culture) (Lloyd 2005, 84).

Annemaree Lloyd studied the information literacy practices of firefighters that enabled new recruits to go beyond their knowledge of what firefighters *do* to *become* firefighters. They had to move beyond textual sources to (1) social sources, the interchange of ideas, beliefs, and attitudes with those who were already part of the culture (firefighters), and (2) physical and sensory sources, the embodied learning and practice inherent in a community of practitioners (Lloyd 2005, 85). Lloyd's important conclusion is that we must understand the "formal, informal, social, and embodied sources of information available to the learner" (Lloyd 2005, 87). For students to understand fully, they must have access to textual sources and formal learning, but they must also develop their understanding through tapping into their informal learning from their own life experiences, communicating with others (including experts and practitioners in the field) and acting on the understanding (or applying and practicing it in multiple contexts).

HOW DO WE TEACH FOR UNDERSTANDING?

Even when educators have a solid mental concept of understanding and its connection to content area standards, recognize the necessity of teaching for understanding, and have a deep understanding of the skills and dispositions required, they still may have difficulty in teaching for understanding. Switching from lecture-driven, fact-based lessons to constructivist, understanding-based lessons requires a repertoire of specific teaching strategies and the courage of one's convictions. Teaching for understanding is moving from the What? and How? to the So What? of teaching.

Maintaining a commitment to understanding is natural for many educators (who seem to have a "save the world" mentality), and even more so for school library media specialists because of their focus on building lifelong learners, on empowering students to learn on their own. Translating this focus into specific and successful strategies to teach for understanding is essential. The father in a fiction book by Jodi Picoult called *My Sister's Keeper* expressed the importance of specificity when he said, "I became a firefighter because I wanted to save people. But I should have been more specific. I should have named names" (Picoult 2004, 147).

The specific frame that an increasing number of educators in every content area are using to teach for understanding is inquiry. Indeed, all of the processes and attitudes of understanding can be captured under the overarching stance of inquiry (the active questioning, investigation, and construction of meaning by the learner). Perhaps, then, the best way to prepare ourselves to teach for understanding is to design instruction and develop teaching methodologies that facilitate inquiry.

HOW DO WE DESIGN INQUIRY-BASED INSTRUCTION THAT LEADS TO UNDERSTANDING?

Inquiry-based instruction that leads to student understanding is designed most powerfully when content and process specialists work together—a collaborative team of library media specialist and classroom teacher. The process of developing instruction outlined in *Understanding by Design,* called backward design, provides guidance in the first steps: (1) target specific understandings; (2) determine how students will demonstrate their learning; (3) design the instructional activities (Wiggins and McTighe 2005).

Target Specific Understandings

The curriculum must be organized coherently in a way that leads students to build conceptual frameworks that enable them to gain understanding through retrieval and transfer of knowledge (Nelson 2001, 15). The number of topics covered is reduced and the pacing is slowed so that students have time for in-depth learning and making connections from one idea to another. Such a curriculum approach allows teachers and students to focus on the most important ideas (Nelson 2001, 15). The Teaching for Understanding Framework from Harvard's Project Zero calls these Generative Topics (topics for exploration that build on previous topics and are central to the discipline and engaging) (ALPS 2006). Educators must then look at these generative topics and determine broader themes and key concepts (overarching throughlines), so that students can connect new understandings to ideas that will carry them into the future (ALPS 2006; Colantonio 2005, 26).

The targeted understandings of an inquiry unit revolve around the important ideas of the discipline and what students should understand about those ideas. Wiggins and McTighe suggest that educators use the stem, "Students will understand *that. . .*" because it will lead to a clear statement of what students should understand about the concept. Using an example provided by Wiggins and McTighe, educators who are teaching a unit on nutrition might state, "Students will understand that a balanced diet contributes to physical and mental health," rather than "Students will understand about balanced diets" (Wiggins and McTighe 2005, 24).

Once the important, targeted understandings have been identified, educators must develop essential questions that intrigue, motivate, and challenge the students with authentic problems (Bransford, Brown, and Cocking 1999) and conflicting issues. Authentic problems are ill-defined—they require the learner to focus the issues and sort through the questions and information to define the problem and develop a solution. Students develop more understanding through this process than if they seek one right answer to a question.

Library media specialists and teachers can embed authentic problems and conflicts into an inquiry unit through the essential questions driving the unit. For the unit on nutrition, they might pose an essential question like, "Why do we like foods that aren't good for us?"

Determine How Students Will Demonstrate Their Learning

The next important piece in designing instruction for understanding is the assessment product—how students will demonstrate their new understandings. Rick Stiggins says there is a difference between assessment *of* learning and assessment *for* learning (Stiggins 2002). We must assess *for* understanding (Colantonio 2005, 25). If the measure of understanding is that students apply and transfer knowledge, then the assessment products built into instructional units *must* call for students to create products and performances that demonstrate their understanding in a new context—authentic tasks in which they must present their solutions to the authentic problems (e.g., they are asked to extend their understanding of the Westward Movement by putting together a wagon train: they must decide what types of people they would select for their wagon train, what they would pack in their wagons, what route they would take, where they would settle, and what challenges they would face along the way and how they would overcome them). The Teaching for Understanding project from Harvard offers both examples and guidance in designing these "Performances of Understanding" (ALPS 2006).

The assessment product and the essential questions combine to offer students opportunities to present their own answers to intriguing questions in formats that have credibility in the real world (e.g., an editorial on "Is our rebellion justified?" written by an American colonist rather than a two-page report on the American Revolution).

Design the Instructional Activities

The processes and attitudes previously identified as critical to understanding (see Figure 3.1) are the same as those that are necessary for inquiry; therefore, teachers and library media specialists can develop the day-by-day instructional plan around the framework of inquiry. The chart in Figure 3.2 shows the application of these processes and attitudes throughout an inquiry learning experience using the Stripling model of inquiry (Stripling 2003). Although all of the listed skills and dispositions may be necessary throughout the inquiry process, they are placed at the phase where they are primarily important. Metacognition must continue through every phase.

In teaching the cognitive processes involved in understanding, teachers and library media specialists must push past superficial, activity-based instruction to deeper, constructivist approaches in which the student is expected to engage actively and thoughtfully in building meaning. A constructivist teaching strategy is suggested for each phase and more detailed descriptions of the strategies follow the chart.

Concept Map: The Connect Phase of Inquiry

A concept map is a visualization of what a student knows about a topic, including the major ideas and the relationships among ideas. This is a useful technique at the Connect Phase, because it is important for students to recognize what they already know and do not know before they start the unit. Concept maps are also very useful for bringing misconceptions to the surface, because students will often draw their understandings in clearer ways than they can express in words. Students can use the following process to create concept maps:

1. Create a visual symbol of the main idea for the center of the map.

2. Brainstorm all that you already know about the topic using visual symbols or words, writing each on a separate card or slip of paper.

3. Prioritize and organize the ideas, placing the major ones in some relationship to the central idea. When you are satisfied that your organization expresses your ideas well, transfer the major ideas to the concept map. Draw appropriate connections among the ideas (arrows, straight lines, question marks).

4. Add the rest of your facts and ideas to the concept map where they are most appropriately placed and show the connections and relationships among the ideas by using lines, graphics, or visual placement.

Figure 3.2
Teaching for Understanding through Inquiry

Inquiry Phase	Cognitive Skills and Strategies	Dispositions	Metacognition	Teaching Strategies
Connect • Connect to self, previous knowledge • Gain background and context • Observe, experience	Connect/Re-late Observe	Engaged Empathetic		Concept map
Wonder • Develop questions • Make predictions, hypotheses	Question Hypothesize	Curious		Six thinking hats questioning
Investigate • Find and evaluate information to answer questions, test hypotheses • Think about the information to illuminate new questions and hy-potheses	Analyze Contextualize Challenge Interpret Infer Balance mul-tiple perspec-tives	Active Empathetic Critical Open-minded Fluent Multi-sensory Tolerant of ambiguity	Reflection and self-knowledge	Construction of context Corroborating information
Construct • Construct new understandings connected to previous knowledge • Draw conclusions about questions and hypotheses	Connect/Re-late Organize Find patterns Construct Conclude	Collaborative Fluent		Narrative frame-work Constructive con-versation
Express • Apply understand-ings to a new context, new situation • Express new ideas to share learning with others	Apply Express	Creative Active Collaborative Fluent Multi-sensory		Gallery walk
Reflect • Reflect on own learning • Ask new questions	Reflect	Reflective		Reflection logs

Six Thinking Hats Questioning: The Wonder Phase of Inquiry

Although students are innately curious, they may have a hard time thinking of interesting questions to drive their research. Different scaffolds can help them with this phase, including question stems, sample questions, and question wheels or dice. The Six Thinking Hats Questioning technique offers another possibility to help students brainstorm and think creatively about their questions. It was developed by Carol Koechlin and Sandy Zwaan (2006) based on Edward de Bono's Six Thinking Hats. Each colored hat represents a different way of thinking, or, in this case, questioning. If students are trying to develop questions on Ancient Rome, for example, they could be asked to develop questions for each hat (see Figure 3.3).

Construction of Context: The Investigate Phase of Inquiry

Students often do not understand a situation because they rely on limited information and do not try to understand the larger context in which that situation occurred. Context is difficult to teach because the learner must construct context him- or herself by weaving together the evidence. Students may have to be provoked to search for evidence that extends beyond the easily obtainable information. The following template in Figure 3.4 may be used to push students' thinking about context while they are investigating.

Corroborating Information, Verifying Sources: The Investigate Phase of Inquiry

Verifying the validity and accuracy of a source is an essential piece of any investigation, especially in this age of self-published Web sites. Although the following questions were

Figure 3.3
Six Thinking Hats Questioning Technique

Hat	Characteristic	Example
White	Neutral	What were the characteristics of daily life in ancient Rome?
Black	Judgmental	What were the good and bad features of Roman government if you were a soldier? A slave? A woman? A statesman?
Yellow	Optimistic	What did ancient Rome contribute to the world that has had a lasting effect?
Red	Intuitive	How would you have felt if you had lived during the time of Nero?
Green	New Ideas	If ancient Romans were alive today, what would be their favorite television show and why?
Blue	Metacognition	How did ancient Rome affect the world at that time and the world in times thereafter?

Figure 3.4
Developing Context to Gain Understanding

What if?

The student poses some What if? questions: What if something hadn't happened? What if one of the contributing factors had not been present? What will happen if something occurs? The student then seeks alternative views that might answer his questions.

Why?

The student seeks answers to intriguing Why? Questions like why something happened, why it was important, why people reacted the way they did. Here the student summarizes or visualizes the main idea of his investigation.

Here the student summarizes or visualizes the main idea of his investigation.
Examples:
- *Excerpted text from the Emancipation Proclamation*
- *The removal of Pluto as a planet*
- *Buying an MP3 player*

What else?

The student asks What else? What other information sheds a light on this subject? What additional information should be found? What other sides to a controversial issue should be represented?

Who says?
What do others say?

The student looks at whose point of view is represented? Are there other points of view that should be considered? Is it possible to find stronger evidence for one point of view over another?

So what?
The student asks So what? What was the impact of this topic? What kind of continuing impact can be seen? Why should we care?

adapted from Seixas who created them for historical investigations, they could be used to corroborate information in any subject areas (Seixas 1996):

- Where did the source come from?
- Who created the source and for what purpose?
- What other sources could be checked to verify the accuracy of this source?
- How reputable does this source seem to be?

Narrative Framework: The Construct Phase of Inquiry

The Construct Phase of inquiry is perhaps the least taught and the most difficult to teach. Educators struggle to teach students how to construct their own understandings. One strategy that offers promise is the Narrative Framework, because it enables students to use the narrative structure, which they generally understand, to get a picture of a historical event. Since history is basically a story, students can develop and maintain knowledge of history better by constructing a narrative framework: they will gather information about the people, the problems they faced, the reasons for their actions and decisions, the challenges they faced when they acted, and the outcomes that occurred (Ferretti, MacArthur, and Okolo 2001, 63).

Constructive Conversation: The Construct Phase of Inquiry

A second strategy to help students construct understanding is the *"constructive conversation"* (Ferretti, MacArthur, and Okolo 2001, 63), which leads students through a process of analyzing, interpreting, and communicating the information they have gathered. Students read their evidence out loud; other students question, offer additional evidence, and help them interpret the evidence to draw conclusions in group discussion. Teachers monitor these conversations to clarify misunderstandings, offer additional evidence, and ask critical questions.

Gallery Walk: The Express Phase of Inquiry

A Gallery Walk is a display of students' final assessment products with an opportunity for the students to go from exhibit to exhibit and learn from their classmates. The walk can be organized as a group tour with a docent at each exhibit (the student who completed that project) who highlights the main points, tantalizes the group with controversial or intriguing ideas, and asks provocative questions to generate group discussion. Alternatively, students can tour the gallery on their own, as critics or reporters, with the task of discovering the main ideas, challenging superficial or careless thinking, and illuminating connections among the different exhibits.

Reflection Logs: The Reflect Phase of Inquiry

Students should have reflected and thought metacognitively throughout their inquiry experiences, but the reflection log at the conclusion of their project should ask them to think about the whole content/process learning experience. Students must identify their new understandings at this point—they should express how their ideas have changed. Two simple reflection techniques that capture their change in understanding are:

Reflecting on a two-column sheet, with the left column labeled "I used to think . . . " and the right column labeled " . . . but now I understand. . .. " A box at the bottom of the sheet labeled "I still wonder . . . " reinforces the idea that inquiry at its best leads to more questions.

Adding to the concept maps that they created at the first phase of inquiry. In a different color, students add the ideas and evidence that they learned during the project. They also identify and cross out misconceptions that they had previously included on their concept maps. Then as a class, the students reflect on the new understandings gained by the group.

In addition to thinking about their new content understandings, students need to reflect about the process that they just experienced. Question prompts will help guide their thinking: What was the most important new skill you learned during your inquiry project? What was your most frustrating time during your research? What did you need to know how to do to keep from being frustrated? What phases of inquiry still seem confusing or challenging and why?

HOW DO WE INVITE STUDENTS TO THINK METACOGNITIVELY ABOUT THE PROCESS OF DEVELOPING UNDERSTANDING IN ALL CONTENT AREAS?

By giving students numerous occasions to practice developing new understandings, teachers develop an inquiry stance in students and enable them to translate the attributes of good learning to any situation. Teachers should push the class to construct understandings around the following questions (adapted from questions about historical inquiry by Ferretti, MacArthur, and Okolo 2001, 64):

- What is history/science/mathematics? How do experts in the field know and learn about their field?
- What is evidence? What kinds of evidence are most important for the subject being studied?
- What is an opinion vs. a fact? How can both facts and opinions be used?
- How do you know a piece of evidence is biased? What should you do?
- Is it all right for a person doing inquiry to have his or her own opinion? What happens when evidence conflicts with the researcher's opinion?
- When would you feel pretty sure that a source's opinion is right?

WHAT ARE THE CHALLENGES THAT STUDENTS ENCOUNTER WHEN THEY ARE TRYING TO DEVELOP UNDERSTANDING?

Students may encounter multiple challenges to developing understanding.

Challenge 1: New understandings are limited by preconceptions and overshadowed by misconceptions. If a student thinks that the only reason for the Civil War was the conflict over slavery, then he or she is likely to interpret everything within that frame. Evidence that does not fit with the preconception is often discarded. Misconceptions are especially prevalent in science, because people form naive theories about the natural world from their life experiences. Misconceptions also emerge in the social sciences, according to Howard Gardner, in the form of stereotypes or "scripts" that are learned when we are young and carry over through the years unless they are challenged. Gardner offers the example of the Stars Wars script: ". . . the good guys look like you, the bad guys look different, the two gangs struggle, and, in the end, the good guys win" (Brandt 1993).

These misconceptions are not easily changed; it takes an active process of confronting the misconception and replacing it with more accurate information. "Misconceptions cannot be ignored, because new and accurate information inconsistent with these misconceptions is likely to be learned superficially, recalled only for tests, and then forgotten" (Sherman and Kurshan 2004/2005, 7).

Challenge 2. One of the greatest challenges to developing historical understanding is the bias of presentism (Ferretti, MacArthur, and Okolo 2001, 68). Students cannot get beyond their own grounding in the present to understand historical times in their own context. That is a good reason for starting a unit with a historical novel or a video—the connect phase becomes particularly important not only for background information, but for an understanding of the historical context. Without that context, students will tend to fit the past into boxes they have created in the present (Wineburg 2001)—for example, deciding to find out what teenagers were like in American colonial times, when the concept of "teenager" did not even exist until the 1940s.

Challenge 3. The essence of understanding is the ability to resolve two conflicting pieces of information, and yet that is one of the biggest challenges that students face in all subject areas (Ferretti, MacArthur, and Okolo 2001, 68). Students have a difficult time deciding what to believe when they find credible evidence that conflicts with other credible evidence. Certainly, teaching them strategies to evaluate the validity of information is important, but students may simply not have enough experience to judge the credibility of certain information. The author of a piece on the Web may not even be cited or his authority may not be given. Students may not be familiar with experts in the area or with the reputations of certain organizations. Textbooks rarely list the author of a piece and they are written in the omniscient third person point of view, which seems very authoritative to students.

Challenge 4. Students have difficulty interpreting primary sources (Ferretti, MacArthur, and Okolo 2001, 68). They are often not familiar with the context within which the source was created and they may not be able to determine the purpose of the primary source or the bias inherent in it. Photographs and artifacts may be particularly troubling because students do not know how to collect evidence from the source without overgeneralizing (the child's face is dirty; therefore, all children at that time were poor and neglected by their parents).

Challenge 5. Students are often not given enough time to learn in depth. A look at a typical school schedule shows that, when all the nonacademic time (assemblies, testing, vacations) is subtracted, students may be left with only 120 hours of instruction in each subject area each year (Nelson 2001, 14). "Translate that into a typical adult context—three 40-hour work weeks dedicated to each subject each year" (Nelson 2001, 14).

HOW DO LIBRARIANS AND CLASSROOM TEACHERS CREATE A COMMUNITY THAT HELPS STUDENTS BUILD UNDERSTANDING?

Teaching for understanding is certainly a desirable goal, but the complexities of building understanding cannot be overcome by individual teachers acting alone. Librarians and classroom teachers must create a community in the school that frames the learning; engages, challenges, and supports the learners; provides opportunities for interactivity; fosters questioning and metacognition, and incorporates the informal learning attributes of embodied knowledge and social construction.

The learning frame that supports student understanding is a seamless blend of content learning with the process/thinking skills necessary for students to create meaning for themselves. The librarian must provide leadership in extending the frame throughout the school by helping students learn to apply the underlying skills in multiple situations and by developing inquiry-based instructional units with teachers in every content area that target the development of understanding. Together, librarians and classroom teachers can ensure that students who learn to interpret conflicting texts about the Great Depression can adapt those strategies to interpret controversial issues in science.

A community that builds understanding is one in which learners are actively engaged. Teachers cannot deliver understanding to their students; instead, teaching must be constructivist, or designed so that each learner is constructing his own understanding and applying it to new contexts. Students are both motivated and engaged when the community supports active questioning (Harpaz and Lefstein 2000), the curriculum includes authentic problems, and students are asked to demonstrate their understandings through authentic assessment products. To help students develop understandings as embodied knowledge, library media specialists and teachers should provide enough opportunities for guided and independent practice that the thinking processes and understandings become part of the culture of the community.

Students must not only be engaged, but they must also be challenged and supported in their learning if they are to go beyond acquiring knowledge to developing understanding. Students will not reach their full potential unless teachers challenge them to extend beyond their comfort zone. All learners need opportunities to grapple with conflicting evidence, complex issues, and ill-defined problems. Teachers have a responsibility to balance the challenges with supports by providing scaffolds before students get lost in the struggle. Because inquiry units require so many skills for successful completion, librarians often choose to teach certain skills and scaffold the others (such as providing pathfinders instead of teaching search strategy or guiding note taking through templates instead of offering a detailed lesson on taking notes). The balance of provocation and support enables all students to succeed in developing new understandings.

Students today desire interactivity and sharing during learning; they seek out opportunities for "collective knowledge building" (Clifford 2005, 16) in school, just as they engage in social construction of ideas in their informal learning. The digital world allows us to respond to this hunger for interacting with others so that students do not have to "power down" when they enter the school. Interaction by itself, however, does not mean that students are building understanding, even when they are personalizing the interactions through blogs, chats, and personal space entries. Each individual must still act on the knowledge and transform it to solidify the understanding.

Technology is not the panacea we might wish it to be. It has to be managed carefully because the digital environment can both facilitate and thwart the development of understanding. For example, although access to multiple perspectives is improved through the digital environment, students may be less likely to encounter those perspectives as they follow the same point of view from link to link unless they are provoked by a teacher's question or evidence of a conflict. Increased access to primary sources should drive active construction of meaning by students, but teachers have to structure the learning to overcome presentism and the difficulty students have in drawing evidence from those sources (especially visual sources). The digital environment makes it much easier for students to revise and improve their writing but also to cut and paste someone else's work. Teachers must craft assignments that provoke students into their own thinking and cannot be copied.

As long as librarians and classroom teachers plan carefully, technology can be very helpful in teaching for understanding. It can be interactive and can present students with robust and complex simulations that confront students with all sides to an issue, with scientific experiments that challenge common misconceptions, and with multiple situations in which they can try out different answers and solutions and keep trying until they have formulated an understanding that resolves the conflicting ideas (Sherman and Kurshan 2004/2005, 10).

The most important aspect to building a community of understanding is the type of thinking engendered and supported by the environment. Educators can use questioning strategies to motivate students, provoke deeper thought, facilitate self-reflection, and nurture an inquiry stance. Students who master the skills of inquiry to develop deep understandings in their academic content areas will be able to apply their insights to new situations, both in and out of school. Students who learn to think metacognitively develop as independent thinkers and learners.

WHAT IS THE ROLE OF LIBRARIANS AS LEADERS IN CREATING COMMUNITIES THAT FOSTER UNDERSTANDING?

Changing the culture of a school to one that fosters understanding is a complex process that requires an advocate and leader. School librarians must step up to that leadership role by acting as a coach, caregiver, connector, and catalyst (Stripling 2003, 33–36). For a number of years, school reformers have advocated facilitative teaching, the "teacher-as-coach" method, in order to provoke and support active learning by the students. Librarians must transfer this same approach to their leadership role to become a "leader-as-coach," because school reform is a learning process that involves challenging old ideas and scaffolding the development of new methods and attitudes. Librarians know through experience in collaboration that critical questioning can provoke new thinking, but it must be handled delicately so that the focus is on exploration of new ideas, not on challenging the expertise of fellow educators. Librarians may want to both provoke and support change to a community of understanding through a transparent process of posing the tough questions about their own practice and enlisting teachers in the exploration of answers (e.g., How will I know that students have really developed new understandings? What should I do if students construct their own understanding, but it's wrong?).

Librarians as leaders of reform also serve as caregivers to the community of teachers. Teachers invest emotional as well as cognitive energy in their practice. To support the teachers emotionally through the process of changing to a pedagogy that fosters understanding, the librarian can forge relationships with the teachers that are framed by the same habits of mind and dispositions necessary for developing understanding. Librarians must develop, and help teachers develop, fluency in teaching for understanding by trying new strategies and approaches, reflecting on the experience, revising, and trying again. This cycle of action and reflection is bolstered by an attitude of empathy and collaboration and a cognitive stance that is both critical and open-minded.

For a school-wide change to a culture of understanding, the librarian must lead from the middle by relinquishing "control" and connecting teachers to the ideas and each other. Many effective librarians create change by empowering teachers to integrate information fluency instruction into their classrooms, fostering collaborations among teachers, and putting the latest professional research and best practice articles directly into the hands of teachers.

Finally, the librarian who is a leader in reform serves as a catalyst for change. The process of school change is much like the process of developing understanding—the educators construct the culture of teaching for understanding by gathering information, finding patterns and connections to create knowledge, and then actively applying that knowledge to their teaching practice. At every phase, the librarian-as-leader provokes thinking by asking contextual questions like What if, Why, What else, Who says, and So what. As educators wrestle with their answers, they move toward new understanding and changed practice.

Librarians can lead a school to develop a culture of understanding by building strong relationships with teachers and administrators and assuming the roles of coach, caregiver, connector, and catalyst. In all of those roles, the librarian must be positive, active, strategic, and focused on the empowerment of teachers and students. Our most important goal is to create a community in which teachers and students challenge and support each other in acquiring new ideas and applying them to understand the world.

REFERENCES

ALPS. *Teaching For Understanding: Putting Understanding Up Front.* 2006. http://learnweb. harvard.edu/alps/tfu/index.cfm (accessed August 26, 2006).

Bloom, Benjamin S., ed. 1956. *Taxonomy Of Educational Objectives: Classification Of Educational Goals.* New York: Longman, Green.

Brabazon, Tara. 2002. *Digital Hemlock.* Sydney, Australia: University of South Wales Press.

Brandt, Ron. 1993. *On Teaching for Understanding: A Conversation with Howard Gardner.* http://www.nea.org/teachexperience/undk030908.html (accessed August 26, 2006).

Bransford, John D., Ann L. Brown, and Rodney R. Cocking. 1999. *How People Learn: Brain, Mind, Experience, and School.* Washington, DC: National Academy Press.

Case, Roland. 2005. "Bringing Critical Thinking to The Main Stage." *Education Canada* 45, no. 2: 45–49.

Chambers, Antonia, Kathryn Bartle Angus, JoAnn Carter-Wells, Jan Bagwell, JoAnne Greenbaum, Donna Padget, and Carla Thomson. 2000. "Creative and Active Strategies To Promote Critical Thinking." *Yearbook: Claremont Reading Conference 2000* 63: 58–69.

Clifford, Pat. 2005. "CYBERkids." *Education Canada* 45, no. 2: 14–16.

Colantonio, John N. 2005. "Assessment for a Learning Society." *Principal Leadership* 6, no. 2: 22–26.

Facione, Peter A. 1990. *Critical Thinking: A Statement of Expert Consensus for Purposes of Educational Assessment and Instruction.* Report prepared for the Committee on Pre-College Philosophy of the American Philosophical Association (ERIC Document Reproductive Service No. TM 014 423).

Ferretti, Ralph P., Charles D. MacArthur, and Cynthia M. Okolo. 2001. "Teaching for Historical Understanding in Inclusive Classrooms." *Learning Disability Quarterly* 24, no. 1: 59–71.

Gardner, Howard. 1983. *Frames of Mind.* New York: Basic Books.

Guiliano, Edward, ed. 1982. *The Complete Illustrated Works of Lewis Carroll.* New York: Avenel Books.

Harpaz, Yoram, and Adam Lefstein. 2000. "Communities of Thinking." *Educational Leadership* 58, no. 3: 54–57.

Koechlin, Carol, and Sandy Zwaan. 2006. *Q Tasks.* Markham, Ontario, Canada: Pembroke Publishers.

Lloyd, Annemaree. 2005. "Information Literacy: Different Contexts, Different Concepts, Different Truths?" *Journal of Librarianship and Information Science* 37, no. 2: 82–88.

Mid-continent Research for Education and Learning (McREL). 2004. *Content Knowledge,* 4th ed. http://www.mcrel.org/standards-benchmarks/docs/purpose.asp (accessed August 20, 2006).

National Center for History in the Schools. 1996. *National Standards for History Basic Edition.* http://nchs.ucla.edu/standards (accessed August 12, 2006).

National Commission on Excellence in Education. 1983. *A Nation at Risk: The Imperative for Educational Reform.* http://www.ed.gov/pubs/NatAtRisk/index.html (accessed August 25, 2006).

National Council of Teachers of English (NCTE) and International Reading Association (IRA). 1998–2006. *Standards for the English Language Arts.* http://www.ncte.org/about/over/standards (accessed August 12, 2006).

National Council of Teachers of Mathematics. 2000. *Principles and Standards for School Mathematics.* http://www.nctm.org/standards/12752_exec_pssm.pdf (accessed August 12, 2006).

National Research Council. 1996. *National Science Education Standards.* http://newton.nap.edu/htm1/nses/6a.html (accessed August 12, 2006).

Nelson, George D. 2001. "Choosing Content That's Worth Knowing." *Educational Leadership* 59, no. 2: 12–16.

Perkins, David. 1994. "Putting Understanding Up Front" *Educational Leadership* 51 (February): 4–7.

Picoult, Jodi. 2004. *My Sister's Keeper.* New York: Washington Square Press.

Scholes, Robert. 1985. *Textual Power: Literary Theory and the Teaching of English.* New Haven, CT: Yale University Press.

Seixas, Peter. 1996. "Conceptualizing the Growth of Historical Thinking." In *The Handbook of Education and Human Development,* eds. David R. Olson and Nancy Torrance. Oxford, UK: Blackwell Publishers, 765–783.

Sherman, Tom, and Barbara Kurshan. 2004/2005. "Teaching for Understanding." *Learning and Teaching with Technology* 38, no. 4: 7–8.

Stiggins, Rick. 2002. "Assessment Crisis: The Absence of Assessment for Learning." *Phi Delta Kappan* 83, no. 10: 758–765.

Stripling, Barbara K. 2003. "Inquiry-Based Learning." In *Curriculum Connections through the Library,* eds. Barbara K. Stripling and Sandra Hughes-Hassell. Westport, CT: Libraries Unlimited, 3–39.

Taylor, Rhonda Harris, and Lotsee Patterson. 2000. "Using Information Literacy to Promote Critical Thinking." *Teacher Librarian* 28, no. 2: 9–14.

Wiggins, Grant, and Jay McTighe. 2005. *Understanding by Design,* expanded 2nd edition. Alexandria, VA: Association for Supervision and Curriculum Development.

Wineburg, Sam. 2001. *Historical Thinking and Other Unnatural Acts.* Philadelphia: Temple University Press.

4

Evidence-Based Practice and School Libraries: From Advocacy to Action

Ross J. Todd

THE BEGINNINGS

Historically library services worldwide have been based on the assumption that they contribute to the social good, the growth of democracy, and the development of a knowledgeable and creative society. An examination of any random number of library mission statements affirms the centrality of this societal value. The International Federation of Library Associations and Institutions (IFLA), representing some 1,700 member library and information associations in 150 countries, has identified as one of its core values "the belief that people, communities and organizations need universal and equitable access to information, ideas and works of imagination for their social, educational, cultural, democratic and economic well-being" (The International Federation of Library Associations and Institutions n.d.). In a similar vein, the Library of Congress, the world's largest library of some 130 million books, positions its mission "to make its resources available and useful to the Congress and the American people and to sustain and preserve a universal collection of knowledge and creativity for future generations" (Billington n.d.). In articulating the integral relationship of the school library to the educational process, the United Nations Educational, Scientific and Cultural Organization (UNESCO) School Library Manifesto asserts that the provision of information is "fundamental to functioning successfully in today's information and knowledge-based society" (UNESCO n.d.). Such value statements make the assumption that the provision of information can make a difference to the lives and well being of people; that there is a widely accepted relationship between the provision of information and personal and social benefits. An integral aspect of this provision is the recognition that this does not happen by chance, and that professional intervention is to

57

equip people "with life-long learning skills and [to]develop the imagination, enabling them to live as responsible citizens" (UNESCO n.d.).

Against this backdrop, it might seem perplexing, perhaps confronting, that a focus on evidence-based librarianship has emerged, and that the acceptance of libraries as integral to the life-stream of a nation and its educational process is seemingly in question. Evidence-based practice is not questioning libraries as a basis of a knowledgeable society; rather, it is an approach to articulating the basis of our beliefs and the claims we can make about the value and role of libraries. Its basis is a move from a tradition of public belief statements that invoke variously named rhetorical ultimates, such as "development of a democratic society," or the development of "independent lifelong learners" or "information literate students," to articulating user-centered outcomes and the basis on which those outcomes have been derived. It is a move from a rhetorical warrant to an evidential warrant: from a "tell me" framework to a "show me" framework, from a persuasive framework to a declarative framework.

The evidence-based practice movement has its origins in the health care area, emerging strongly in the early 1990s in the United Kingdom in the fields of medicine and health care services. It emerged initially to teach medical students how to independently find, appraise, and apply the best evidence from a plethora of clinical trials, research studies and other documentary evidence and to apply it to solving clinical problems (O'Rourke 1996; Sackett et al. 1996). Sackett et al. defined evidence-based medicine as the "conscientious, explicit and judicious use of current best evidence in making decisions about the care of individual patients. This practice means integrating individual clinical experience with the best available external clinical evidence from systematic research" (Sackett et al. 1996, 71).

In its earliest iterations, three central dimensions of evidence-based practice were established: the ability to collect, read, interpret, and integrate valid and applicable user-observed and research-derived evidence; the combining of this evidence with professional expertise, insight, experience, and leadership; and the application of this evidence and wisdom to ensure significant and optimal outcomes (Coe 1999). At a fundamental level, the early evidence-based practice movement in medicine had as its goal the tangible capacity to make a difference to the lives of people, through carefully informed decision-making and interventions based on available research to achieve optimal outcomes. Expressed simply, the fundamental tenets of evidence-based practice—access to and utilization of research-based evidence, the melding of research-based knowledge with personal knowledge derived through experience, and its application to day-to-day practice for optimal outcomes, and monitoring the outcomes—were founded at this time.

This chapter provides a reflective overview of evidence-based practice as an emerging mindset and framework for decision-making, professional action, continuous improvement, and building active support for school librarians and school libraries. It describes the emergence of this concept and its practice in librarianship and education and its rationale and central dimensions. It elucidates a set of organizational principles to shape and implement evidence-based practices in a school community.

EVIDENCE-BASED LIBRARIANSHIP

Interest in evidence-based practice grew considerably from the early 1990s, and its application quickly extended from medicine to allied disciplines such as nursing, pathology, and cardiology. While the call for a more scientifically based approach to library science education extends back several decades (e.g., Houser and Schrader 1978), medical and health care librarians in particular responded to the initiative to propose the core characteristics of evidence-based librarianship (EBL). As Ritchie (1999) explained: "Evidence-based decision-making is a methodology which can be extended from its beginnings in the medical world to all other professions which have a body of research-based knowledge. As a profession which has the ability to manage the literature of research, librarianship is uniquely placed to model the principles of evidence-based practice, not only as they apply to other disciplines which we serve, but also as they apply to our own professional practice" (33).

Booth (2000) defines evidence-based librarianship as "an approach to information science that promotes the collection, interpretation, and integration of valid, important and applicable user-reported, librarian-observed, and research-derived evidence. The best-available evidence moderated by user needs and preferences, is applied to improve the quality of professional judgments." Both Booth and Eldredge, two key proponents of evidence-based librarianship, highlight its focus to employ the best available evidence based on library science research to arrive at sound decisions about solving practical problems in librarianship (Booth 2000; Eldredge 2000). Positioning evidence-based librarianship as a dynamic and evolving approach to integrating research into practice, Eldredge (2000) acknowledges that this does not take place in a "remote, ivory tower" microcosm; rather, it acknowledges that librarians "operate their libraries in the real world context of providing services and collections through managing budgets and other resources" (289). Thus, EBL constitutes an *applied* rather than theoretical science. EBL merges scientific research with the pressing need to solve practical problems (Eldredge 2000). Subsequently, Eldredge has proposed a seven-part conceptual framework for evidence-based librarianship:

1. EBL seeks to improve library practice by utilizing the best-available evidence combined with a pragmatic perspective developed from working experiences in librarianship;

2. EBL applies the best-available evidence, whether based upon either quantitative or qualitative research methods;

3. EBL encourages the pursuit of increasingly rigorous research strategies to support decisions affecting library practice;

4. EBL values research in all its diverse forms and encourages its communication, preferably through peer-reviewed or other forms of authoritative dissemination;

5. EBL represents a global approach to information seeking and knowledge development, involving research but not restricted to research alone;

6. EBL supports the adoption of practice guidelines and standards developed by expert committees based upon the best available evidence, but not as an endorsement of adhering to rigid protocols; and

7. In the absence of compelling reasons to pursue another course, EBL adheres to the hierarchy (or levels) of best available evidence, lending priority to higher levels of evidence from rigorous research that includes:

    • Systematic reviews of multiple rigorous research studies;

    • Systematic reviews of multiple but less rigorous research studies, such as case studies and qualitative methods;

    • Randomized controlled trials;

    • Controlled-comparison studies;

- Cohort studies;
- Descriptive surveys;
- Case studies;
- Decision analysis; and
- Qualitative research (e.g., focus groups, ethnographic observations, historic).

This seven-part conceptual framework suggests the following reflective, responsive, and integrative approach to evidence-based practice:

1. Access evidence;
2. Know evidence;
3. Question evidence;
4. Integrate evidence and wisdom;
5. Apply evidence;
6. Communicate evidence; and
7. Reinvest evidence.

These dimensions are action-based dimensions, explicitly placing the locus of control and responsibility on the deliberate engagement and intervention by the practitioner. These dimensions parallel the conception of evidence-based practice in the field of education.

EVIDENCE-BASED EDUCATION

Today evidence-based practice is acknowledged as an important approach to professional practice in many disciplines in addition to librarianship, such as education, social work, and law. Comings (2003) argues that while practitioners in various education systems sometimes base professional decisions and actions on learning theories and research, most base their decisions on tradition, the opinion of experienced practitioners, and personal experience gained through trial and error. He argues that these theory-based and experienced-based approaches "can lead to decisions that support effective learning, but the program models that have grown out of these approaches do not have strong evidence of their effectiveness" (Comings 2003, 5).

The Institute of Education Science, in the U.S. Department of Education, defines evidence-based education as the "integration of professional wisdom with the best available empirical evidence in making decisions about how to deliver instruction" (Whitehurst 2001a). In defining empirical evidence, Whitehurst refers to scientifically based research not just undertaken in educational settings, but from a range of allied disciplines, such as psychology, sociology, and neuroscience so that a cumulative and integrative knowledge base can be the foundation of practice. The primary characteristic of scientifically based research is its use of objective measures to compare, evaluate, and monitor progress, and to identify causal and associative relationships and interactions, particularly in situations where decisions about competing approaches to educational interventions need to be made (e.g., the use of classroom libraries, reading incentive schemes, and computer-aided instruction). Also underpinning the argument for scientifically based research as a framework for professional decision-making and action is the need to avoid fad, fancy, and personal bias, and the advocating of stances and positions without the supporting evidence derived from empirical research.

Figure 4.1
Evidence-Based Education

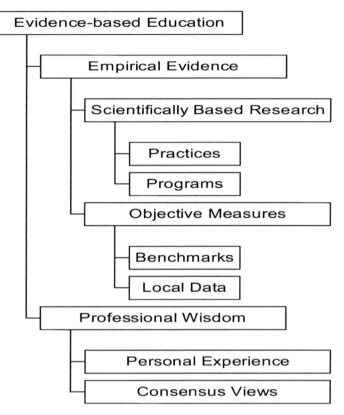

Source: Whitehurst, Grover J. 2001b. *Evidence-Based Education (EBE)*.
URL: http://www.ed.gov/offices/OERI/presentations/evidencebase.ppt#3
(accessed November 7, 2006).

Central to evidence-based education is the acknowledgement that empirical evidence does not stand alone, outside of the context of practice. Rather, it is melded with professional wisdom, defined by Whitehurst (2001b) as the judgment that individuals acquire through experience and through views derived from professional consensus. Evidence-based education does not ignore professional wisdom; rather, as shown in Figure 4.1 (Whitehurst 2001b), it acknowledges that this wisdom plays a key role in the interpretation and integration of local circumstances, conditions, and constraints in the planning, design, delivery, and evaluation of instructional interventions. The meshing of local evidence is also an aspect of this approach.

Embedded in this evidence-based focus is using empirical evidence to support claims of impact and effectiveness. This is based on the argument that policy and practice "should be capable of being justified in terms of sound evidence about the likely effects" (Coe 1999). Underpinning education is the belief that student learning and student learning outcomes are "too important to allow [them] to be determined by unfounded opinion, whether of politicians, teachers, researchers or anyone else" (Coe 1999). In other words, evidence-based education is not just using empirical research to inform and enable professional action through teaching and learning processes, but also being able to develop processes and strategies to measure learning impacts, and to articulate claims of learning outcomes based on evidence-based practices.

SCHOOL LIBRARIES AND EVIDENCE-BASED PRACTICE

The professional practice of school libraries sits at the confluence of education and librarianship. The focus on evidence-based practice of school libraries has emerged strongly within the last five years. One of the earliest elaborations of this concept was in my keynote address at the International Association of School Librarianship conference in Auckland, New Zealand, in 2001, titled: "Transitions for Preferred Futures of School Libraries: Knowledge Space, Not Information Place; Connections, Not Collections; Actions, Not Positions; Evidence, Not Advocacy" (Todd 2001). As a prelude to my focus on evidence-based practice at that time, I stated that in order for school libraries to play a key role in the information age school and be perceived to add value to the learning agenda and learning outcome of a school, there needs to be a fundamental shift from thinking about the movement and management of information resources through school library structures and networks, and from information skills and information literacy, to a key focus on knowledge construction and human understanding, implemented through constructivist, inquiry-based frameworks. I viewed a part of this shifting mindset to be also a shift away from the rhetorical, advocacy basis for ongoing development and maintenance of professional practice, to an evidence-based framework that focused on learning outcomes rather than information inputs and processes. I argued that while information is the heartbeat of meaningful learning in schools, it is not the hallmark of the twenty-first-century school library; rather, the hallmark of a twenty-first-century school library will be actions that show that it makes a real difference to student learning, that it contributes in tangible and significant ways to the development of human understanding, meaning making, and knowledge construction. In essence, the focus of the professional practice of school librarianship revolves around learning outcomes of students—the knowledge, attitudes, values, and skills that students develop because of school libraries, and the demonstration of these dispositions—rather than around the information infrastructure, that is, resources, technology, and organizational processes.

MERGING RESEARCH AND PRACTICE

From a student outcomes orientation, I posited that evidence-based practice focuses on two things. First, it is the conscientious, explicit, and judicious use of current best research evidence in making decisions about the instructional role of the school librarian. It is about using research evidence, coupled with professional expertise and reasoning to implement learning interventions that are effective. Why instructional? All the research evidence points clearly to this dimension of the school librarian's role as a primary enabler of learning outcomes. Second, evidence-based practice is about ensuring that professional efforts focus on gathering "meaningful and systematic evidence on dimensions of teaching and learning that matter to the school and its support community, evidences that clearly convey that learning outcomes are continuing to improve" (Todd 2001). Since that time, there has been a burgeoning interest in the arena of evidence-based practice, particularly in the context of the school library's relationship to student learning outcomes, and how this is achieved through partnerships and instruction. It has become the theme of school library conferences and publications across the world (Loertscher and Todd 2003; Todd 2002a; Todd 2002b; Todd 2003; Scholastic Library Publishing 2006).

Evidence-based practice is more than getting research into practice to guide day-to-day decision-making and actions. It is also about focusing on the delivery of services based on stated goals and objectives, systematically demonstrating outcomes and endpoints in tangible ways, and critically reflecting on inputs and processes to build an evidence-based cycle of continuous improvement. It plays an important role in learner-centered services to show that the rhetoric about those services is real, that expectations are met, and that promised outcomes are actually delivered. In the context of school libraries and school goals and objectives, evidence-based practice means that the day-by-day work of school librarians is directed towards demonstrating the tangible impact and outcomes of services and initiatives in relation to student learning outcomes. It involves critically analyzing the accumulated data and on the basis of indicators, deriving statements about student learning outcomes. What is important is that such evidence is cumulated, analyzed, and synthesized so that a learning outcomes profile of students engaging in library learning initiatives can be constructed. As a particular approach to practice, evidence-based practice moves beyond intelligent guesswork and clever hunches to establishing a sound basis for making claims about the impact of that practice. In doing so, it moves from a persuasive framework to a declarative framework in building active support for school libraries.

Identifying Learning Outcomes

For school libraries, the emergence of an evidence-based practice approach comes at a time of opportunity, challenge, perhaps even turbulence in the profession—factors that have driven and continue to drive the focus. In a dramatically changing educational landscape, the increasing emphasis on evidence-based education, measurable student attainment and learning outcomes, continuous improvement, equity of educational opportunity, and accountability have shifted the basis on which value statements can be made about school libraries if they are to be perceived as playing a strong role in the school. Whether we like it or not, terms such as *data-driven, measurable, accountable, gaps,* and *demonstrate* are shaping the politics, processes, and policies of the educational agenda, and they provide an interrogative framework for school librarians to be positioned in the educational reform agenda, rather than be marginalized from it. This can feel confrontive, particularly when practices historically have not been based on data-driven accountability measures, and where professional skills may not have been strongly developed in terms of empirical evidence, objective evidence, benchmarking, and assessment beyond information literacy competencies.

In addition, the changing information landscape itself continues to create dynamic, if not formidable challenges for school librarians, as well as for classroom teachers, administrators, and information technology specialists. For school librarians, the fusion of appropriate and productive pedagogies centering on information literacy, the use of information technology as both a tool for information access and a tool for knowledge construction, and student attainment are perceived to be highly important in the learning process. However, in a standards-based, competency driven environment where test scores are the major measures of achievement, these dimensions are often overlooked, and school librarians struggle for the recognition and contribution that they feel they deserve. At the nexus of education and librarianship, it is clear that value claims about school libraries can no longer be made solely on the basis of deep-seated beliefs about the social, educational, cultural, democratic, and economic value of school libraries. Rather, the basis for these claims, and the school-based processes that lead to these claims, centers on evidence that they make a difference to student achievement as defined by curriculum standards and the learning goals of the school.

PRINCIPLES OF EVIDENCE-BASED PRACTICE

Against this background, evidence-based practice can be conceptualized as a framework of three interrelated and integrated phases: evidence *for* practice, evidence *in* practice, and evidence *of* practice. These phases are not linear and static; rather, they are a dynamic, iterative, and integrative process of welding evidence from multiple sources in a cycle of continuous transformation of data, information, knowledge, and wisdom to inform practice, to generate practice, and to demonstrate outcomes of practice. They are built on accessing appropriate evidence, reflecting on it, meshing it with knowledge and experience, taking action on it, and interrogating the outcomes as part of a cycle of reinvestment, reuse, and regeneration. Based on this F-I-O framework, six guiding principles for building an evidence-based practice framework in the school library can be elucidated. These are:

1. Know the research, and know the research intimately;
2. Make visible the research foundations of your practice in your school;
3. Make student learning outcomes the center of your evidence;
4. Integrate evidence-generating strategies in your practice that focus on learning outcomes;
5. Mesh results of local evidence of learning outcomes with other evidence in the school, as well as with existing research to establish evidence-based claims, and to build a continuous improvement plan;
6. Disseminate, celebrate and build together on the evidence-based outcomes.

Know the Research, and Know the Research Intimately

Research informing practice, and practice informing research, is a fundamental cycle in any sustainable profession. Simplistic as it might seem, evidence-based practice asks school librarians to engage with the body of research knowledge of their profession in a deep and precise way. Knowing the research does not simply mean knowing the existence of available research, such as individual reports of the range of statewide studies undertaken in our profession, nor does it simply mean knowing the existence of compilations and syntheses of this research, for example, Scholastic's important compilations, "School Libraries Work" (2006) and "Compendium of Read 180 Research 1999–2004" (2004), or various analytical and summative reports (e.g., Haycock 2003, Lonsdale 2003), or monograph compilations (e.g., Loertscher and Woolls 2002). Knowing the research goes beyond telling stakeholders that it exists; it means having a deep and explicit knowledge of the complex array of findings, and being able to speak with confidence about how these findings shape your professional practice, how you utilize these findings, as well as being able to show how these findings, when meshed with evidence at your school or district level, can be powerful platforms for local school library interventions and initiatives. This is evidence-based education in action through school libraries.

One of the fundamental requirements with knowing the research in such an explicit way is that the research needs to be read deeply and meaningfully. There is some evidence to suggest that librarians across the different information sectors do not read research a great deal, and that their use of research is low (McClure and Bishop 1989, Turner 2002).

This also raises the question: What sources do school librarians consider important to read, and what do they actually read? Here is a simple reflective task to undertake. You might want to pose this to a group of school librarians in your district, as well. Take a look at the list of information sources in Figure 4.2 that are typically available to school librarians to inform them of their work, and how their practice might be developed. Rate

Figure 4.2
Professional Resources: What Role Do They Play in Your Decision Making?

Source	Importance Rating	Reading Frequency Rating
Scholarly journal articles		
Scholarly research reports		
Professional books about practice		
Conference proceedings Atendance at conferences		
Informal and formal conversations and discussions		
Publishers' blurbs and advertisements		
Professional and trade magazines		
Professional Web sites		
Listservs		
Others?		

Importance Rating:

How important is each source to you for finding information about and making decisions for your daily activities?
1 = No importance
2 = A little importance
3 = Some importance
4 = A good deal of importance
5 = Greatest importance

Reading Frequency Rating:

How often do you read the information resources to inform your decision-making in practice?
1 = Never, I don't read these
2 = Rarely (e.g. once every few months)
3 = Sometimes (e.g. once a month)
4 = Often (e.g. weekly)
5 = A great deal (e.g. several times weekly)

how important each source is to you for finding information about and making decisions for your daily activities. Having done that, indicate how often you read the information resources to inform your decision-making in practice.

Having worked in a number of school library forums recently where I posed these questions, I have seen one predominant pattern. While the research-based literature published in scholarly journals (e.g., *School Library Media Research* and *School Libraries Worldwide*) together with research reports and professional books are regarded as highly important sources of research for informing practice, they are read far less than informal sources such as listserv conversations, and professional and trade magazines. Often the argument is raised that busy school librarians do not have time to read the research literature, or librarians claim that the research is not used because it is removed from practical reality. Such a stance devalues the profession as a thinking and informed profession, and cuts off the profession from advances in knowledge, which shape sound practice. A profession without reflective practitioners willing to learn about the advances in research in the field is a blinkered profession, one that is disconnected from best practice and best thinking, and one that by default often resorts to advocacy and position as a bid for survival. As part of their own ongoing professional development, it is important that school librarians continue to engage with this research, as it provides a rich understanding of the dynamics of the learning process when students engage with information sources, as well as practical insights into how local evidence might be gathered, analyzed, and utilized to position the school library as central to the learning process.

A deep knowledge of the specific findings of research provides the empirical basis for making and justifying decisions, and for identifying gaps on which continuous improvement programs can be built. These research findings also enable school librarians to pose questions in their school communities. For example, statistics about California school libraries (California Department of Education n.d.) show that while 99 percent of their public schools have a place designated as a library, only 20 percent of California schools have a credentialed school librarian in the building. In Delaware, as a point of contrast in 2005 (Todd 2005a), 71 percent of school library employees were state-certified school librarians. Although the average national ratio of school librarians to students is 1:870, California ranks 51st in the nation with a ratio of 1:4,541. In Delaware, with 124 certified school librarians in a total school population of 108,500 students, the ratio is 1:875. In terms of library books, the average number of school library books per kindergarten through grade twelve (K–12) students in California is 16.4. In Delaware, the average number of books per student is 12.65. Nationally, school libraries average 22 books per student. Where is your state positioned in relation to these numbers? How about your school district? How about your school? Can you clearly and precisely paint a picture of your school and how it benchmarks with available data at your state level, or national level? When meshed with the data from the statewide studies, and their relationship to student achievement as measured through test scores, what does this say? What actions might your school take on this comparison? Knowing the research creates an evidential basis to open dialogue, and a central key to this is the effective communication of research findings.

Make Visible the Research Foundations of Your Practice in Your School

Communicating research findings effectively in a school and developing effective practice on the basis of these findings is not an easy task. Lau (2002) presents the findings from a study of 242 school principals, 50 percent of whom were in elementary schools, with the remainder split between middle and high schools. The study found that 37 percent of those surveyed said their school librarians familiarized them with current research on library media programs and student achievement, and only 35 percent said librarians informed them about current research on reading development. These figures raise some important concerns. To what extent do we demonstrate at the local level that research forms not just the foundation of our practice, but that we engage in the research in an active and meaningful way to build highly effective practice? To whom do we actively talk in our schools about our research, and how do we communicate it? It is not a matter of thrusting various documents, such as research articles, reports, and professionally generated compilations, into the hands of key decision-makers; rather, we have to judiciously and carefully shape that communication to show how it is situated in and responsive to school goals, initiatives, and improvement agendas, and to provide ideas as to how the whole school community might begin to take action on the findings. Here is a starting checklist:

- Does your school library Web site present key research findings at the national, state, and local levels in a compelling way that is succinct, clear, and easily understood by various stakeholders?
- Are student learning outcomes the focus of your communications?
- Do your mission and goal statements for student learning in the school library link to key research claims?
- Do you have a collection of research resources available for teachers in each of the curriculum standards?

- When you communicate to the school board, or to the school community, do you showcase the latest research and elaborate how you are continuing to improve your school library program based on that research?

- When you present the outcomes of collaborative initiatives in school and community forums, do you link your local evidence explicitly to published research?

- Are library-related learning resources part of the professional collection and available to classroom teachers?

- In your quarterly library reports to the school administration and school board, do you highlight findings of significant research that have been the basis for school library initiatives?

Make Student Learning Outcomes the Center of Your Evidence

Spotlight student learning outcomes as defined by school goals and curriculum standards as the central organizing principle and outcome of the school library. Such a principle does not diminish or dismiss the importance of developing students' information literacy competencies. It serves to highlight that learning outcomes as the transforming effects of the school librarians' pedagogical and collaborative interventions and services, and as defined by curriculum and content standards, are the raison d'être for school libraries. This does not mean that school librarians should stop talking about students reaching information literacy standards. My concern is that standards are sometimes presented as separate from the various curriculum standards in a school. For example, a focus on the development of students' information and critical literacies surrounding the use of print and electronic information sources is viewed by school librarians as an essential standard for effective learning in the school library—it is embedded in the code of standards as defined by the American Association of School Librarians (AASL) and the Association for Educational Communications and Technology (AECT). It is important to communicate this. But we also need to communicate what are the outcomes of reaching this standard, in terms of content and skills standards as expressed in various curriculum documents. For example, what has been the impact of reaching this standard on students coming to develop deep knowledge of science concepts and their relationships?

The goal of a school library is not just the development of information literacy standards, but being able to competently show that reaching these standards has an impact beyond the school library. Information literacy is not an end point. This is often perceived by classroom teachers to be a library's doing, an add-on to an already crowded curriculum, and something not necessarily valued outside of the library. The destination is not an information literate student nor even an information literate school community, but rather, the development of knowledgeable and skillful students who demonstrate mastery beyond the library.

Delaware Study

In the Center for International Scholarship in School Libraries (CISSL) study of Delaware's public school libraries in 2005 (Todd 2005a), 154 school librarians were asked to identify the main information literacy focus of their instruction and the significant student learning outcomes enabled by this information literacy focus. Two important findings stand out. First, clearly the school librarians engaged in a range of information literacy instruction initiatives. This instruction primarily centered on knowing about the school library, knowing about different sources and formats, applying effective research strategies in doing effective research, learning how to use the resources, evaluating information for quality, and learning to use information ethically. The question becomes: so what?

In terms of learning outcomes, 39.6 percent of the school librarians indicated that their school library helped students become effective researchers, who improved their skills in locating and selecting sources, organizing and evaluating information, and compiling information; 37.7 percent of the school librarians indicated that their school library helped students improve their reading skills and develop greater interest in reading; 22.1 percent of the school librarians reported that their school library helped students develop a range of technology skills related to using the Internet effectively, and searching online databases and catalogs; 15.6 percent of the school librarians indicated that their work with students helped them develop positive attitudes toward libraries. However, only 4.5 percent of the librarians were able to articulate learning outcomes linked to curriculum standards and goals, that is, how their information literacy initiatives enabled the development of deep knowledge and deep understanding of the content requirements of the curriculum. The challenge of making curriculum outcomes the center of the school library's evidence asks librarians to go beyond *information* outcomes, and to identify *knowledge and skills* outcomes as they relate to curriculum areas. This is elaborated here in two studies.

First New Jersey Study

The first study (Todd 2005b) documented information literacy initiatives in terms of knowledge outcomes of 43 grade 9 students at Gill St. Bernard School in 2004–2005. In a collaboration of seven teachers and the school librarian, 21 girls and 22 boys undertook a semester-long course, "Research Project," which focused on developing research skills, strategic and deep information seeking, and higher-order information analysis and synthesis to represent new understandings as a result of the research. Rather than documenting mastery of information literacy competencies, the study centered on learning outcomes in terms of mastery of content, that is, students' development of deeper knowledge and understanding and their ability to engage in substantive conversation about their content, recognize knowledge as problematic, and use complex terminology in the content area. This project was based on the Productive Pedagogy framework developed by Gore, Griffiths, and Ladwig (2002). The curriculum area under consideration was cultural celebrations. Data collection revolved around a simple knowledge representation protocol at the beginning, midpoint, and end of the instructional process to chart students' development of knowledge of their curriculum topics, as well as a search log to document sources used throughout the process.

The study showed that students' knowledge of their topics developed considerably through the instructional interventions of the librarian. Initially, their knowledge of the topics was simplistic, superficial, and disjointed, and this developed though the process to knowledge that embedded explanations and causal, predictive, and reflective statements about their research areas. The students moved beyond superficial descriptions to demonstrating complex knowledge of their topics. Particularly noticeable was their analysis and organization of ideas into structured conceptual groupings, which conveyed a sense of knowledge, coherence, and depth. Knowledge depth was further represented in the use of specific terminology associated with their topics, and the explanatory details surrounding these subjects. There was substantive evidence that students were using the language specific to the topic domain, not just parroting the terms, but describing them and providing clear explanations.

Given that the students' knowledge representations in this study were constructed from memory, the students progressed in developing deep understanding of their topics, and this matched the cognitive strategies used when searching for information in a range of sources. Overall, their choice of sources showed increasing complexity and depth. The students' search logs revealed that background knowledge was initially built through using encyclopedia references to the particular celebration, or descriptions of the celebration in country-specific books and Web sites. There was also some use of compendiums that briefly described festivals and celebrations around the world. However, as students progressed in their inquiry, there was some change in the nature of the sources used, particularly regarding print and electronic sources that dealt in more depth with the particular celebration as a basis for building deeper knowledge. The analysis of their final written reports showed strong ability to substantially communicate about their topical knowledge in writing. There was also evidence that students could identify and deal with conflicting facts or viewpoints and were able to construct arguments and explanations in relation to conflicting aspects of topics.

Second New Jersey Study

The second CISSL study (Todd 2006) sought to investigate how students built on their existing knowledge of a curriculum topic and how they transformed information into personal knowledge. It developed an approach to identifying and measuring knowledge outcomes of students engaged in inquiry units. The study involved 10 teacher-school librarian teams from 10 public schools in New Jersey working on 17 library-based curriculum projects. Data were collected from 574 students in grades 6 through 12 at the initiation, midpoint, and conclusion of the projects. In order to identify changes in knowledge, five measures were carried out in relation to substance of knowledge, structure of knowledge, amount of knowledge, estimate of extent of knowledge, and label of knowledge. The specific research questions were:

1. *Substance of Knowledge:* What changes in content of relational statements are evident in students' knowledge descriptions as they learn a curriculum topic through the stages of a guided inquiry project?

2. *Amount of Knowledge:* What changes in amount of relational statements are evident in students' knowledge descriptions as they learn a curriculum topic through the stages of a guided inquiry project?

3. *Structure of Knowledge:* What changes in structure of relational statements are evident in students' knowledge descriptions as they learn a curriculum topic through the stages of a guided inquiry project?

4. *Title of Knowledge:* How do the students' titles given to their topics reflect their knowledge descriptions as they learn a curriculum topic through the stages of a guided inquiry project?

5. *Extent of Knowledge:* What changes in perceptions of their knowledge are evident in students' knowledge descriptions as they learn a curriculum topic through the stages of a guided inquiry project?

For the purposes of measuring changes in knowledge, three different writing tasks were used at the initiation, midpoint, and conclusion of the unit.

Writing tasks 1 and 2 consisted of the following questions:

1. Write the title that best describes your research project at this time.

2. Take some time to think about your research topic. Now write down what you know about this topic.

3. What interests you about this topic?

4. How much do you know about this topic? Check (✓) one box that best matches how much you know. Nothing, Not much, Some, Quite a bit, or A great deal.

5. Write down what you think is EASY about researching your topic.

6. Write down what you think is DIFFICULT about researching your topic.

7. Write down how you are FEELING now about your project. Check (✓) only the boxes that apply to you: Confident, Disappointed, Relieved, Frustrated, Confused, Optimistic, Uncertain, Satisfied, Anxious, or Other.

Writing task 3 included additional questions:

1. What did you learn in doing this research project? (This might be about your topic, or new things you can do, or learned about yourself.)

2. How did the SCHOOL LIBRARIAN help you?

3. How did the TEACHER help you?

Students' knowledge was measured through examining the nature of the relational statements about their topics at each of the three stages of data collection. Each statement written by students was coded as Property, Manner, Set Membership, Reason, Outcome, Causality, Implication, or Value Judgment. Overall the students' knowledge of their topics increased, as represented by the number of statements they recorded at each writing task. The data showed that the students represented their topical knowledge predominantly by factual property and manner statements, and that they used increasingly more factual statements to represent their knowledge throughout the three stages. Overall the number of reason and outcome statements was lower than property and manner statements, and did not substantially increase as students progressed, while the cause/consequence and synthesis statements show a decreasing though nonsignificant trend. There was a significant difference between the students' estimates of their knowledge between the stages. The students' perception of their knowledge seemed to particularly increase between the first and second data collection periods when students were building background knowledge and focusing their topics.

The study also identified a group of students who appeared to engage more analytically, conceptually, and reflectively in information use, and who showed an integrative approach to knowledge construction. These students first gathered facts to form an information foundation for manipulating and transforming them in more synthesized and abstract ways, and developing knowledge that showed higher levels of coherence and centrality. Qualitative evidence collected points to the influence of contextual elements shaping the knowledge-building process and its outcome. These elements include the nature of the task; scope of choice within the curriculum area; instructional interventions provided to guide students in information seeking and use; instructional emphasis on information gathering and knowledge-building activities; and attention to affective and motivational aspects of knowledge construction, as well as the cognitive dimensions. Such findings provide an opportunity for school librarians to demonstrate that their information literacy initiatives focusing on knowledge outcomes contribute to students developing deeper and more complex knowledge of their curriculum topics.

Integrate Evidence-Generating Strategies in Your Practice That Focus on Learning Outcomes

The collection of evidence is not something entirely new for school librarians. However, it has traditionally revolved around informational and organizational dimensions, and included such things as: circulation statistics, number of classes in the library, number of students using the library at lunch times, number of items purchased annually, and number of Web searches. Some school librarians have also provided evidence related to library processes and indirect measures of student's experiences of learning, for example, number of coordinations, cooperations, and collaborations with classroom teachers; spreadsheets of information literacy competencies developed across the grades; and records documenting reading enrichment initiatives. These are useful sources of evidence, but it is important to recognize that they are mostly measures of inputs and processes, interventions, and students' experiences, rather than direct measures of learning outcomes.

Direct Measures

In *We Boost Achievement! Evidence-Based Practice for School Library Media Specialists,* Loertscher and Todd (2003) elaborate a useful framework for collecting local evidence from multiple sources. It centers on two types of evidence of learning outcomes: *direct* measures, defined as measures of actual learning, and *indirect* measures, defined as measures of actions and processes that play a key role effecting change. Both direct and indirect measures focus on practice—what school librarians do in relation to instructional collaboration, reading, information literacy, and information technology. The librarians' key goal, however, is to elucidate outcomes and to establish the school library's contribution to these outcomes. They develop direct measures of student learning. Through these measures, school librarians work analytically to develop evidence-based claims about their progress in meeting curriculum outcomes.

Levels of Data Collection

Data can be collected at three levels: the learner level, the teaching level; and the organizational level. At the learner level, a gamut of assessment strategies might be used to measure and inform achievement of curriculum content. It is important to meld this with achievement test scores, which, in the current climate of accountability, have emerged as important sources of evidence. When providing evidence emerging from instructional interventions, it is important that claims revolve around the indicators specified in curriculum standards, such as changes in development of higher-order thinking and depth of content knowledge. Students must be able to provide explanations of end results and causality, substantiate personal positions and viewpoints, demonstrate mastery of conflicting ideas, and develop predictive relations in relation to a topic.

It is critical to work with approaches that enable direct measures of learning outcomes, and where instructional interventions and services can be developed in a cycle of continuous improvement. A useful tool for school librarians might be the following approaches to auditing curriculum standards and auditing standardized tests to integrate evidence-generating strategies into professional practice.

Curriculum Audit

The curriculum audit approach starts with curriculum standards to be developed, not with information literacy standards. It involves carefully examining content standards to identify a critical zone of intervention, a learning point that lends itself to instructional intervention in the curriculum standards through the school library, and working with classroom teachers at that point of intervention. This approach builds solidly on Kuhlthau's

(2004) research in relation to the information search process and zones of intervention. This zone of intervention is where information-to-knowledge processes are embedded in content standards, and where reaching the standards lend themselves to student inquiry in the school library. In other words, the zone of intervention makes explicit an opportunity for developing authentic research through the school library. For example, there is usually a math standard that requires students to do some inquiry related to recognizing and investigating the use of mathematics in real life. Similarly, content standards in science typically require students to analyze a range of science-related ideas, for example, the contributions made by American scientists to the transformation of disciplinary knowledge, or ethical and social issues relating to contentious topics such as stem cell research and genetics modification. For school librarians, these standards are zones of intervention around which library-based inquiry can be developed, and where strategies can be employed to directly measure learning outcomes.

For each of these zones of intervention, the collaborating teacher and school librarian identify the nature of the knowledge and skills to be developed, based on curriculum requirements. This enables the teaching team to select interventions that move from skills in locating sources of information to the development of deeper knowledge.

Embedded in the information-knowledge interventions will be strategies that explicitly target the identification and measurement of student progress. These include pre- and post-knowledge tests, rubrics, concept maps, reflection sheets, self-assessment logs, process documentation tasks, survey responses, and culminating products. It is important to select appropriate measures that can be meaningfully integrated into the instructional process. These measures must provide data that can be analyzed and summarized to substantiate claims about student progress. The goal is not to overwhelm students with multiple evidence-gathering tasks; rather, these should be seen as natural formative and summative processes that provide feedback to learners and instructors alike. The important thing is that these outcomes measures are carefully examined, compared, and summarized so that specific claims can be made about the students' development of content knowledge and skills (Table 4.1).

Over time, this approach provides multiple sources of both direct and indirect evidence (Loertscher and Todd 2003). It not only enables school librarians to make specific claims about the nature of learning outcomes, but it also allows them to chart the scope of curriculum standards they directly address. Librarians can also document the extent and frequency of teacher collaborations across different curriculum domains and track the scope of information literacy competencies covered. When coupled with diverse measures of facility, technology, and resource use, the curriculum audit approach provides multifaceted evidence to support the essential role of the qualified school librarian as an instructional partner.

Standardized Test Audit

A second approach is to undertake a standardized test audit. Many departments of education make available publications that relate to standardized test scores, including examples of practice tests. It is critical that school librarians analyze these tests to identify specific standards that directly relate to school library interventions and to build collaborative opportunities with classroom teachers to facilitate the meeting of these standards. For example, the Louisiana English Language Arts test has multiple-choice and short-answer questions related to using information resources. An analysis of the questions around this

Table 4.1.
Relationship of Outcomes to Standards and Instructional Interventions

Specific Standard	Zone of Intervention	Disciplinary Knowledge to be developed	Instructional Interventions. Students will learn to:	Outcomes Measures (EBP)	Outcomes
As listed in the curriculum document	Specific curriculum standard that lends itself to school library intervention	Identification of nature of knowledge to be developed	Specify the instructional processes targeted to the development of knowledge	Measures to chart the development of knowledge and skills of content, which form a natural part of the instructional process	Specific claims that can be made about the development of content knowledge and content skills

EXAMPLE

Specific Standard	Zone of Intervention	Disciplinary Knowledge to be developed	Instructional Interventions. Students will learn to:	Outcomes Measures (EBP)	Outcomes Claims
Social Science Grade 9	Identify a local issue and plan possible actions to achieve a desired outcome, for example, Increase in homeless; Graffiti in the community	Explore and consider different perspectives; Contest different opinions; Articulate and justify own opinion using supporting evidence; Refine own opinions, values and attitudes; Develop an action plan that demonstrates deep knowledge of topic; Apply knowledge and skills in a range of community-based activities	Map multiple viewpoints: sources, establishing criteria to examine and compare viewpoints; Model the argument: Claim, Data, Warrant, Qualifier, Rebuttal, Backing; Manage conflicting evidence; Utilize strategies to construct personal viewpoint; Create an action plan	For example: pre and post knowledge test of specific issue; Presentation rubric: structure of presentation, quality of argument; depth of content; self-scored rubric of research process; GPA of final product.	Claims about initial level of knowledge and skills; Claims about exit level of knowledge and skills: for example: Level of understanding of concepts; understanding of conceptual relationships—descriptive or explanatory; level of ability in comparing multiple perspectives; extent to which students can explicate links between historical and contemporary issues; and so on

theme shows that the expectation goes beyond students merely finding factual information, to analyzing sets of ideas and constructing responses based on arguments and evidence. This is an information literacy intervention waiting to happen, one that focuses on the development of competencies related to information analysis and synthesis, argument development, and construction of conclusions.

Some state standardized testing procedures also collect survey data in relation to reading habits. Student responses to such questionnaires are factored into test result analyses. School librarians are encouraged to examine carefully the school and subgroup test score data when it is returned to schools, together with careful analyses of test themes. Together, this analysis of both standards and results provide a basis for identifying zones of intervention, targeting particular learning gaps, specifying specific interventions, and evaluating the impacts.

Establishing some baseline data enables progress to be monitored. For example, test score data show that a certain group of grade 10 students in a school are at an unsatisfactory achievement level in relation to some aspects of reading ability. Available data from student questionnaires and library circulation statistics reveal that these students do not read on their own time. In this scenario, ways to gather evidence might include planning and implementing reading interventions, developing sustained and meaningful interventions over time, tracking student progress, charting outcomes, and examining subsequent test scores. At the heart of this action is a commitment to providing the best opportunities for student to learn and to succeed, and to sustain and nourish their learning. It is based on making use of available evidence *for* practice and available evidence *in* practice, to chart evidence *of* practice and its continuous improvement.

Mesh Results of Local Evidence of Learning Outcomes with Other Evidence to Build a Continuous Improvement Plan

Evidence should be cumulative. The evidence from a single instructional intervention or service initiative is not likely to result in dramatic change. Evidence-based practice is an ongoing, constructive, and integrative process, and I would encourage school librarians to develop an evidence-based practice portfolio that brings together the range of data collection instruments, careful summaries of evidences and conclusions drawn, illustrative examples, log book and journal entries, program data about instructional and reading initiatives, and reflective commentaries. The purpose of this is to build up and continually refine and extend a set of claims about how the school library enables students to learn more effectively. As these claims are built, link them with existing research in the field.

For example, when we undertook the "Student Learning through Ohio School Libraries" study (Todd and Kuhlthau 2005), we built the data collection instrument around a set of 48 claims about how the school library helps students with their learning, organized into conceptual groupings such as information literacy, content outcomes, reading, information technology, independent learning, and overall student achievement. These statements were derived from our analysis of research literature available at the time. In testing these claims, we were able to elucidate additional claims:

- The school library saves me time with doing my school work.
- The school library enables me to complete my work on time.
- The school library helps me by providing a study environment for me to work.
- The school library helps me take stress out of learning.
- The school library helps me do my work more efficiently.

- The school library helps me think about the world around me.
- The school library provides me with a safe environment for ideas investigation.
- The school library helps me set my goals and plan for things.

Collectively, this represents one approach to developing and articulating evidence-based claims about how the school library contributes to student learning. The Ohio study also provided an open-ended, critical incident question (Flanagan 1954) to enable students to articulate specific instances of helps and their outcomes, in their own voice. This free writing question asked: *Now, remember one time when the school library really helped you. Write about the help that you got, and what you were able to do because of it.* Given the largely quantitative nature of the survey, the study wanted to provide opportunity for students to give witness in their own way to the help statements provided, and the statements served to prompt the students in identifying concrete examples. The meshing, or triangulation, of both quantitative and qualitative evidence has been an effective tool in conveying the findings of the study, adding a personalization and student perspective. Local evidence of "helps" can be merged with the results of larger studies such as the Ohio study, to demonstrate how you are using research to build your own practice, and to build your local case in light of existing research.

As mentioned earlier, integrating multiple sources of evidence can establish fruitful patterns that form the basis of a stronger claim about the school library's contribution to learning. Bringing together, for example, test score results, evidence of information literacy instruction and curriculum instruction, library scheduling, and reading initiatives can contribute to the strength of your claims.

It is also important to scope out the range of data that a school possesses. For example, test score data may show that there is a need to help grade 9 and 10 students to improve their reading skills. What data exist in and beyond the school library that might provide further insight into this dilemma and provide a basis for building a whole school plan for improvement, one that engages the school library in the process? Look for other sources of data from scheduling; reading remediation, tutoring, and intensive reading programs; curriculum maps; as well as additional classroom and community resources. Continuous improvement plans involve the assessment of the strengths and limitations of a program in the context of a school's goals, and this requires bringing together multiple sources of data to identify specific needs and to justify program and initiative directions. School librarians cannot work alone as they plan and implement improvement plans for student achievement. Such plans are an intersection of school leadership, school culture and climate, curriculum goals, and instructional processes.

Disseminate, Celebrate, and Build Together on the Evidence-Based Outcomes

The message is simple. Let your school library be the center of a knowledge-sharing community, and think strategically about how you will work with the evidence. If you undertake a large data collection initiative in your school, ensure that the presentation of the results in not the first time that the school community hears about it. Show strength in collaboration, by taking a team approach. For example, engage your math teachers in helping you analyze and present the quantitative data; engage the technology team in helping you construct a simple Web-based data collection instrument; get feedback from a group of English teachers as you design a reading motivations survey. Framing the evidence is also very important, because you want your audiences to accept the evidence. Some important guidelines include:

- Is the evidence sufficient to make a strong conclusion?
- Does the evidence speak to school needs, goals, and improvement plans?
- Is the evidence easily understood, and not spoiled by personal opinions?
- Is the evidence verifiable, and can you provide clear details on how you collected the evidence and the scope of the evidence?
- Do you make known the limitations and any biases of your evidence? Also, be prepared to acknowledge negative or problematic evidence, as this can become the basis for a school-wide initiative for improvement.

It is also important to understand the intended audiences, and know how they best like to come to know of such evidence. Understand the beliefs, values, and challenges of your audiences, and structure ideas in ways that do not undermine your evidence. If national and state themes are predominant in your school, such as No Child Left Behind legislation, information technology, and literacy, then build your dissemination accordingly for those audiences. Remember that format of presentation is critical. Capitalize on all opportunities to disseminate evidence, for example, school library Web pages summarizing the process and outcomes of collaborative curriculum units, faculty bulletins, community newsletters, and in-school television. Provide mechanisms for the audience to follow up if additional information or research is needed, for example, an executive summary with accessible links to full documents may be the most appropriate for school administrators.

CONCLUSION

Evidence-based practice is fundamentally about school librarians taking action—action that is informed by systematic research and guided by experience and wisdom. It creates evidence for continuous program development and builds active support for school librarians and school libraries. The principles and processes that underpin evidence-based practice are principles and processes of best practice: working to achieve the highest levels of sustainable performance in order to achieve the highest level of outcomes. At times we might think and feel that evidence-based practice, and best practice for that matter, is about trying to reach some kind of idealistic or elusive standard. I see it as a mindset and action orientation that strives to continuously improve on existing processes as times change, as things evolve, and as research informs. For school librarians to lead learning through school libraries, they must be dedicated to best practice. They must continuously reflect on effective school library practices and translate this thinking into action. Evidence-based practice is a real opportunity for school librarians to move beyond just thinking about improvement, and taking action—implementing research-based local strategies and processes that contribute to a cycle of ongoing improvement. Thinking and believing without action is pointless. Taking action means you are living the solution. Not taking action means that you will be living someone else's dreams and someone else's solutions. And someone else's solutions may not be in the best interest of student learning outcomes through the school library.

REFERENCES

Billington, James H. n.d. *Welcome Message from the Librarian of Congress.* http://www.loc.gov/about/ (accessed October 25, 2006).

Booth, Andrew. 2000. *Evidence-Based Librarianship.* http://www.cilip.org.uk/groups/cofhe/presentations/Andrew%20Booth.ppt#3 (accessed October 25, 2006).

California Department of Education. n.d. *Statistics About California School Libraries.* http://www. cde.ca.gov/ci/cr/lb/libstats.asp (accessed October 25, 2006).

Coe, Robert. 1999. *A Manifesto for Evidence-Based Education.* http://www.cemcentre.org/RenderPage. asp?LinkID = 30317000 (accessed October 25, 2006).

Comings, John P. 2003. *Establishing an Evidence-Based Adult Education System: NCSALL Occasional Paper.* Cambridge, MA: Harvard Graduate School of Education. http://www.ncsall.net/ fileadmin/resources/research/op_comings3.pdf#search='Establishing%20an%20evidencebas ed%20adultpercent20education%20system' (accessed October 25, 2006).

Eldredge, Jonathan D. 2000. "Evidence-Based Librarianship: An Overview." *Bulletin of the Medical Library Association* 88, no. 4: 289–302. http://www.pubmedcentral.nih.gov/articlerender.fcgi ?tool=pubmed&pubmedid=11055296 (accessed October 25, 2006).

Flanagan, John C. 1954. "The Critical Incident Technique." *Psychological Bulletin* 51, no. 4: 327–358.

Gore, Jennifer M., Tom Griffiths, and James G. Ladwig. 2002. *Productive Pedagogy As a Framework for Teacher Education: Towards Better Teaching.* Newcastle, Australia: Faculty of Education, University of Newcastle. http://www.aare.edu.au/01pap/gor01501.htm (accessed October 25, 2006).

Haycock, Ken. 2003. *The Crisis in Canada's School Libraries: The Case for Reform and Re-Investment.* Toronto: Association of Canadian Publishers. http://www.peopleforeducation. com/librarycoalition/Report03.pdf (accessed October 25, 2006).

Houser, Lloyd. J., and Alvin M Schrader. 1978. *The Search for a Scientific Profession: Library Science Education in the U.S. and Canada.* Metuchen, NJ: Scarecrow Press.

International Federation of Library Associations and Institutions. n.d. *About IFLA.* http://www.ifla. org/III/index.htm (accessed October 25, 2006).

Kuhlthau, Carol Collier. 2004. *Seeking Meaning: A Process Approach to Library and Information Services,* 2nd ed. Westport, CT: Libraries Unlimited.

Lau, Debra. 2002. "What Does Your Boss Think about You?" *School Library Journal* 48, no. 9: 52–55.

Loertscher, David V., and Blanche Woolls. 2002. *Information Literacy: A Review of the Research,* 2nd ed. Salt Lake City, UT: Hi Willow Research and Publishing.

Loertscher, David V., with Ross J. Todd. 2003. *We Boost Achievement! Evidence-Based Practice for School Library Media Specialists.* Salt Lake City, UT: Hi Willow Research and Publishing.

Lonsdale, Michele. 2003. *Impact of School Libraries on Student Achievement: A Review of the Research: Report for the Australian School Library Association.* Melbourne: Australian Council for Educational Research. http://www.asla.org.au/research/index.htm (accessed October 25, 2006).

McClure, Charles R., and Ann Bishop. 1989. "The Status of Research in Library and Information Science." *College & Research Libraries* 40 (March): 127–143.

O'Rourke, Alan. 1996. *Seminar 3: An Introduction to Evidence-Based Practice.* http://www.wisdomnet. co.uk/sem3.html (accessed October 25, 2006).

Ritchie, Ann. 1999. "Evidence-Based Decision-Making." *InCite* 20, no. 12: 33.

Sackett, David. L., William M. C. Rosenberg, J. A Muir Gray, R. Brian Haynes, and W. Scott Richardson. 1996. "Evidence Based Medicine: What It Is and What It Isn't." *British Medical Journal* 312, no. 7023: 71–72.

Scholastic Library Publishing. 2004. *Compendium of Read 180 Research 1999–2004.* New York: Scholastic.

Scholastic Library Publishing. 2006. *School Libraries Work! Research Foundation Paper,* 2006 ed. New York: Scholastic.

Todd, Ross J. 2001. "Transitions for Preferred Futures of School Libraries: Knowledge Space, Not Information Place; Connections, Not Collections; Actions, Not Positions; Evidence, Not Advocacy." Paper presented at the International Association of School Librarianship Conference, July 9–12, 2001, Auckland, New Zealand. http://www.iasl-slo.org/virtualpaper2001.html (accessed October 25, 2006).

Todd, Ross J. 2002a. "Evidence-Based Practice I: The Sustainable Future for Teacher-Librarians." *Scan* 21, no. 1: 30–37.

Todd, Ross J. 2002b. "Evidence Based Practice II: Getting into the Action." *Scan* 21, no. 2: 34–41.

Todd, Ross J. 2003. "Evidence-Based Practice III: Difference, Intervention and Transformation." *Scan* 22, no. 4: 30–37.

Todd, Ross J. 2005a. *Report of the Delaware School Library Survey 2004: On Behalf of the Governor's Task Force on School Libraries.* New Brunswick, NJ: Center for International Scholarship in School Libraries.

Todd, Ross J. 2005b. "School Librarians and Educational Leadership: Productive Pedagogy for the Information Age School." In *Information Leadership in a Culture of Change: Selected Papers from the 34th Annual Conference of the International Association of School Librarianship, and Ninth International Forum on Research in School Librarianship,* Hong Kong, China, July 8–12, 2005, eds. Sandra Lee, Peter Warning, Diljit Singh, Eleanor Howe, Lesley Farmer, and Sandra Hughes. Erie, PA: International Association of School Librarianship. [CD-ROM].

Todd, Ross J. 2006. "From Information to Knowledge: Charting and Measuring Changes in Students' Knowledge of a Curriculum Topic." *Information Research* 11, no. 4. http://InformationR.net/ir/11–4/paper264.html (accessed October 25, 2006).

Todd, Ross J., and Carol Collier Kuhlthau. 2005. "Student Learning through Ohio School Libraries, Part 1: How Effective School Libraries Help Students." *School Libraries Worldwide* 11, no. 1: 89–110.

Turner, Kathlyn J. 2002. "Do Information Professionals Use Research Published in LIS Journals?" Paper presented at the 68th IFLA Council and General Conference, August 18–24, 2002. http://www.ifla.org/IV/ifla68/papers/009–118e.pdf (accessed October 25, 2006).

United Nations Educational, Scientific and Cultural Organization (UNESCO). n.d. *UNESCO/IFLA School Library Manifesto.* http://www.unesco.org/webworld/libraries/manifestos/school_manifesto.html (accessed October 25, 2006).

Whitehurst, Grover J. 2001a. *Evidence-Based Education (EBE).* http://www.ed.gov/offices/OERI/presentations/evidencebase.ppt#2 (accessed November 7 2006).

Whitehurst, Grover J. 2001b. *Evidence-Based Education (EBE).* http://www.ed.gov/offices/OERI/presentations/evidencebase.ppt#3 (accessed November 7 2006).

Part III

Developing Literacy in the Twenty-First Century

5

Family Literacy: The Dynamic Roles School Librarians Can Play

Bonnie Mackey and Sharon Pitcher

A child who can read is a child who can learn. And a child who can learn is a child who can succeed in school and in life.

—Secretary of Education Margaret Spellings

Trying to educate children without the involvement of their family is like trying to play a basketball game without all the players on the court.

—Patricia A. Edwards

Since the publication of *A Nation at Risk* in 1983, literacy has been a key component of national education reform efforts (see, e.g., Reading Excellence Act; Goals 2000). The No Child Left Behind Act of 2001 is no exception. Early Reading First and Reading First, two initiatives of this Act, are specifically designed to help states, school districts, and schools ensure that every child can read at grade level or above by the end of third grade. The Early Reading First Program supports preschools and early childhood education providers, especially those serving children from low-income families, so that they can become preschool centers of educational excellence, providing children with the foundational skills necessary to become successful readers (U.S. Department of Education 2005). Reading First targets services to districts that are low-performing and high-poverty by providing funds for the implementation of instructional programs and materials, assessments, and professional development grounded in scientifically based reading research (U.S. Department of Education 2004). A critical element of both initiatives is family involvement. According to the U.S. Department of Education "the quality of family environments and parent-child interactions is central to a child's literacy development and education" (U.S. Department of Education 2005).

81

Recognizing the importance of family involvement to literacy development, many school districts have begun to offer family literacy programs. What are family literacy programs and how can school librarians provide the fire to ignite them in their schools? In this chapter, we define family literacy and highlight current research and related literature about the school librarian's role in family literacy programs. We conclude with a scenario that suggests practical ways for a school librarian to design and implement engaging literacy-related initiatives for families.

WHAT IS FAMILY LITERACY?

According to the National Center for Family Literacy, the U.S. Government defines family literacy as:

> Services that are of sufficient intensity in terms of hours, and of sufficient duration, to make sustainable changes in a family and that integrate all of the following activities: (a) interactive literacy activities between parents and their children, (b) training for parents regarding how to be the primary teacher for their children and full partners in the education of their children, (c) parent literacy training that leads to economic self-sufficiency, and (d) an age-appropriate education to prepare children for success in school and life experiences. (National Center for Family Literacy 2003)

Pitcher and Mackey (2004) differentiate between *family involvement* and *family literacy*. Family involvement centers on what the school asks of parents. This type of participation focuses on what parents can do for the school. Fund-raising and making sure that students get their homework done are two examples (Auerbach 1995). Family literacy, however, focuses on the influence that each unique family has on the child's literacy development.

Research supports the value of family literacy programs and activities. According to Taylor (1983; 1998) family literacy is one of the most significant factors in student achievement. Mulhern, Rodriguez-Brown, and Shanahan (1994) found that children who participated in Project FLAME in Chicago, a family literacy program started in 1989, consistently scored 30 points higher on standardized tests than their peers and required fewer specialized services at school. Other studies have confirmed that parents and children reading together has a positive influence on how children learn to read (Bus, Ijzendoorn, and Pellegrini 1995). Beaty (2004) supports the belief that when families make personal investments in their child's education, they are more likely to support their child's development at home and in later school years. The bottom line is that families offer unique and valuable contributions to the school community; therefore, every opportunity to involve families in literacy opportunities must be considered.

CRITERIA FOR FAMILY LITERACY PROGRAMS

The International Reading Association Commission on Family Literacy identifies five important features of family literacy activities:

- Encompass the way parents, children and extended family members use literacy at home and in their community;
- Occur naturally during the routines of daily living;
- May be initiated purposefully by a parent, or may occur spontaneously;
- Reflect the ethnic, racial, or cultural heritage of families involved; and
- May be initiated by outside institutions or agencies (Asselin 2001, 61).

DeBruin-Perecki and Paris (1997) studied 50 family literacy programs and found that effective programs

- Consider factors that facilitate families participating; such as transportation, food, childcare, and cultural considerations.
- Incorporate activities that are meaningful and useful in the lives of the families.
- Are implemented by staff who understand the needs of the community and work well together.

Pitcher and Mackey (2004) argue that the family literacy programs should provide "models of literacy that can be transferred to homes" (46). Like DeBruin-Perecki and Paris, they underscore the importance of meeting the social and basic needs of families. Having food at the gatherings, for example, transforms the events from purely literacy activities into communal events.

It should be noted that large-scale family literacy programs often require external funding. As we will discuss later, grants to support family literacy programs are available on a competitive basis from many foundations. Even with limited budgets, however, it is possible to implement successful family literacy practices. It requires the visionary leadership of school administrators, school librarians, and teachers; it also requires people bringing together resourceful and creative ideas to engage the school community in these activities.

SCHOOL LIBRARY INVOLVEMENT IN FAMILY LITERACY PROGRAMMING

We have organized our discussion in this section into two parts: critical background knowledge for school librarians and recommended family literacy activities.

Critical Background Knowledge for the School Librarian

If school librarians hope to develop successful family literacy programs, they must first actively seek information about literacies from the students' homes and community. According to Asselin (2001) librarians should carefully analyze the cultures represented in the community and focus on creating open, reciprocal communication between the families and the school library. Griffis (2003) goes further, encouraging school librarians to view families as *resource* models instead of *deficit* models. She suggests that in order to work effectively with parents, librarians should utilize the following elements of successful family literacy programs:

- Build on literacy experiences already present in the home.
- Consider the participants' suggestions;
- Demonstrate the value of the home language by providing translated materials when possible;
- Be flexible so that parents might participate before, during, and after school hours;
- Hold meetings at convenient locations;
- Provide refreshments and child care for young children;
- Develop instruction for children and parents that might include reading, writing and technology skills and activities; and
- Provide access to information and resources (print and electronic) that will help families become self-sufficient.

Griffis also recommends that literacy activities allow for interaction between parents and children and access to information, as well as resources. Additionally, she argues for collaboration with community partners because it expands both the resources available and the range of instruction.

Piazza (2001), a school librarian who managed an extensive literacy project in Georgia, underscores the importance of gathering information about the students and their home life. In the PhOLKS project that he coordinated, Piazza worked closely with teachers, university researchers, administrators, and community members to implement information-gathering strategies that included using cameras and documentation of students' out-of-school lives. By allowing students to reflect on their home lives and heritage, the project not only instilled pride in the uniqueness of each family, but it also enabled teachers and the school librarian to develop culturally relevant literacy experiences.

Librarians must also be aware of the challenges to developing family literacy programs. These include educator's attitudes, retention of participants, implementation of programs in diverse communities, and funding.

While most educators believe that parental involvement in reading instruction is critical, many have a limited view of how parents can and should participate in their child's literacy development. Griffis (2003) argues that "before any family literacy program can succeed, it is important to educate teachers about current family literacy research and help broaden their perspectives about the variety of literacy opportunities families can and do provide for their children" (33).

Although participation in family literacy programs is 24 percent higher than in adult education programs, retention is still a challenge (Griffis 2003, 33). Mulhern and her colleagues (1994), underscore the need to develop programs that meet the specific needs of the participants, to keep attendance records, and to talk to families who leave a program to find out why.

Another challenge involves developing programs in diverse communities, especially linguistically diverse communities. As Griffis stresses (2003), the focus in these situations *must* be on understanding the needs of the participants. Needs assessments can help identify language needs, cultural differences, educational levels, socioeconomic levels, and so forth—all important factors in developing a responsive program.

The final challenge, adequate funding, will be discussed later in the chapter.

Recommended Family Literacy Practices

Numerous case studies and experience-based articles have been written about effective family literacy practices. We highlight several examples in this section.

Reading Nights

Librarian-sponsored family reading nights connect families with the school library, give opportunities to educate parents about early literacy, and help parents to become involved in their child's schooling and in reading with their children. Remsen (2004) describes how his school librarian organized a "Family Adventures in Reading Night." Families read five books together to prepare for the event, attended a school pizza dinner, and discussed viewpoints and shared personal experiences based on the stories they had read. By participating, families were able to practice new skills in reading with their children.

Lending Libraries

Lending libraries can help to even the playing field by putting books directly in more homes and increasing resources for families that might not otherwise be able to offer these experiences and resources to their children. The Family Lending Library Academy (2001) suggests that lending books to families improves the children's academic standing. At the same time, it also strengthens the parent's literacy or English skills, which in turn advances the child's literacy development. This practice might help the adults in their employment and life skills as well. Pitcher and Mackey (2004) also stress the value of books in the home and the importance of the parent's understanding of the relationship between reading activities in the home to reading instruction in school.

Computer Nights

Selwyn, Gorard, and Williams (2001) argue that technology can be used to defeat social exclusion in education and promote lifetime learning practices. They cite institutional barriers to participation and the lack of appropriate local opportunities as obstructions to bridging the digital divide. Pitcher and Mackey (2004) suggest Computer Nights as a family literacy activity. They consider Computer Nights to be one of the best intergenerational activities for encouraging parents and children to learn together. In some school settings, students teach their parents the use of various software applications and Internet navigation. In other cases, the school librarian joins forces with the local public librarian to teach parents and students how online public access catalogs work in both types of libraries (Bayley 2001).

When designing Computer Nights, school librarians need to plan agendas that increase social inclusion of all families in technology opportunities. Providing such experiences can actually increase participation of low social and economic families in education. By reaching families, school librarians help to close the digital gap.

Additional Ideas

Griffis (2003) offers additional family literacy ideas that could be implemented by the school librarian working collaboratively with teachers and parents:

- Lending library programs with reading bags that include a book and extension activity along with a response journal;
- Book sharing, where parents are given easy strategies for sharing books with their children;
- Field trips to the local library;
- Book fairs;
- Parent workshops on selecting quality books, using wordless picture books, devising simple props and costumes to dramatize stories, and so on;
- Bookmaking session;
- Art activities after sharing stories;
- Information sessions on creating home literacy centers;
- Puppet shows and learning how to create these shows at home;
- Book-reading sessions with children authoring books about their families; and
- Parent sessions on basic reading strategies to use with beginning readers, such as using prediction, rhyming words, and picture clues.

PLANNING FOR FAMILY LITERACY PROGRAMS

Eisenberg and Miller (2002) suggest a sensible A-B-C approach to planning that is useful for developing effective family literacy programs.

A: **Articulate a vision and agenda.** Create a library advisory board that includes parents, classroom teachers, and other members of the school community. Start by defining visible and viable goals for the family literacy initiative. Together with members of the board, develop a range of family literacy programs that involve diverse segments of the community.

B: **Be strategic.** Identify priorities and focus your energies in addressing these priorities. Since family literacy is a priority, brainstorm strategies to increase parent participation in literacy and develop ways to involve them in the library. Figure out means to secure support and funding and carefully outline the steps you plan to take.

C: **Communicate continuously.** Publicizing your ideas and programs is a critical feature in effective planning and implementation. Keep your principal informed. Make sure that the library activities are prominently displayed on the school's Web site. Seize opportunities to announce activities and achievements through school bulletins, parent newsletters, and school newspapers.

McGahey (2005) provides a checklist for planning family literacy events. The checklist begins eight weeks prior to the date of the event and ends two weeks afterward and includes the following steps:

- Brainstorm the event including planning and setting goals.
- Determine the level of staff support needed.
- Assemble a team of volunteers.
- Assign tasks.
- Find sponsors and collect door prizes from community businesses in exchange for advertising their company in local community newsletters.
- Create or obtain handouts for parents that inform them about family literacy and the purpose and goals for the event.
- Advertise the event and document it with pictures.
- Evaluate the event.

FUNDING SOURCES

A number of local, state, and national grants are available to support the development of family literacy programs. Table 5.1 provides a partial list of national grants.

The Barbara Bush Foundation awards a total of $650,000 each year to develop and expand family literacy efforts nationwide, and to support the development of literacy programs that build families of readers. No grant exceeds $65,000. Applicants must focus on reading instruction for parents, reading or pre-reading instruction for children, and activities that include parent/child reading time and activities. Grant applicants must provide clear objectives and a concrete plan for measuring how objectives will be achieved. Existing literacy programs can receive funds when they expand their programs to include more than one generation, thus making them family literacy programs.

Grants are also available through the Improving Literacy through School Libraries (ILTSL) grant program that was created in 2001 for the *No Child Left Behind Act* (Rosenfeld and Loertscher 2006). These one-year grants are available for school libraries in districts

Table 5.1.
National Funding Sources for Family Literacy Programs

The Barbara Bush Foundation
www.barbarabushfoundation.com

The Barbara Bush Foundation for Family Literacy, founded in 1989, promotes and supports the development of family literacy programs throughout the nation. Initiatives include an annual "Celebrations in Reading" fundraising event and a national grant award program. A guiding philosophy of the foundation is the belief that home is a child's first school environment, the parent is a child's first teacher, and reading is a child's first subject.

Even Start
www.ed.gov/programs/evenstartformula/index.html

Even Start provides funding to community programs that encourage and integrate early childhood education, adult literacy, parent education, and parent and child interactive literacy initiatives. These programs are intended to provide support to parents and enhance academic achievement of children (birth to seven years old) from families with limited English proficiency, low literacy skills, and/or from lower income neighborhoods.

First Book
http://www.firstbook.org

First Book is a nonprofit national organization that works with community mentoring, tutoring, and family literacy programs to provide new books to children from low-income families.

Books for Kids
www.booksforkidsfoundation.org

Books for Kids promotes literacy through initiatives aimed at underserved and disadvantaged children and youth by creating quality library programs, distributing new books, and providing literacy training opportunities. In addition, Books for Kids has joined forces with the Friends of Libraries USA to dedicate five children's literary landmarks in New York City.

Improving Literacy through School Libraries
http://www.ed.gov/programs/lsl/index.html

Improving Literacy through School Libraries works to increase student reading achievement, information literacy skills, information retrieval skills, and critical thinking skills by providing funds to individual school districts to improve school library media centers. Funding is intended for the purchase of up-to-date technological needs and school library materials. In addition, the organization also works to ensure school libraries are staffed by professionally certified school library media specialists and students have increased access to the facilities and resources during non-school hours.

where at least 20 percent of the students are from families that are living below the poverty level. Schools receiving grants have been able to double expenditures in their libraries and to purchase books and other resources that support literacy development. Some schools have used the funds to staff the library after school hours, thus providing the opportunity for parents to visit the library with their children.

First Book, a national nonprofit organization, has as its mission giving children from low-income families the opportunity to read and own their first new books. The primary goal of First Book is to work with existing literacy programs to distribute new books to children who, for economic reasons, have little or no access to books.

The Books for Kids Foundation promotes literacy among all children, with special emphasis on disadvantaged children and youth. Books for Kids donates books, creates libraries, and participates in reading initiatives within community-based organizations, service agencies, schools, and under-served institutions. In addition to assisting recognized learning programs, such as Head Start, the Books for Kids Foundation seeks to create opportunities for children and parents in under-served or overlooked locations.

In addition, state, regional, and community sources of funding should not be overlooked. For example, the North Carolina School Library Media Association offers Read2Succeed Grants to its members. These grants are available to K–12 school library media specialists, in partnership with classroom teachers. Susan Ward, library coordinator at Burton Geo-World Magnet School in Durham, used the $1,000 grant to develop a program entitled "Fireside Stories—Telling Family Stories Our Way" (NCSLMA 2005). The Barnett Schools Elementary School in Athens, Georgia, garnered $5,000 as a Giant Step Winner for being indispensable to their students and families (Oatman 2005). The funding, provided by Thomson Gale and School Library Journal, allowed the school librarian to sponsor a daylong visit by children's author Susan Stevens Crummel. These are just two examples of the types of grants available to foster family literacy.

FAMILY LITERACY PROGRAMMING: A POSSIBLE SCENARIO

Vashanti Rahaman (1997) in her book, *Read for Me, Mama,* tells the story of Joseph, his mother, and Mrs. Ricardo, the wonderful librarian in Joseph's school, who "knew all of the great big words in the books" and "was the best story reader in the world" (3). Mrs. Ricardo invites the children to take one book to read themselves and a harder book for someone to read to them. Unfortunately, Joseph's mother cannot read. In the story, she joins a literacy program at a local vocational school and discovers the joys of reading with her son.

Rahaman's story takes place in a low-income community. Neuman and Celano (2001) found that low-income families have little opportunity to include print resources in their lives. Through the development of family literacy programs, Mrs. Ricardo could make the school library the hub of literacy in a community where there is limited access to newspapers, books, and magazines. She might consider the following:

Weekly Open Houses where the school library is open for families in the evening. She could develop a special parent resource center within the library that included magazines, newspapers, and paperback books that the parents might borrow. The center might also house videotapes and brochures for parents to borrow. Many times faculty members are willing to donate items.

Family Book Clubs provide an opportunity for families to come together and discuss their personal connections to a book they have read. Kindergarten parents might be taught read-aloud strategies such as chiming, the importance of rhyme, and the use of repetition. Lesson plans and book suggestions to do this are available on Pitcher's Web site at www.towson.edu\~spitcher.

Comprehension book clubs might focus on applying a strategy such as making connections or asking questions when reading. Picture books that offer meaningful text for families to discuss include those by Patricia Pollacco (*The Keeping Quilt, Rotten Richie and the Ultimate Dare, Chicken Sunday,* and *Mrs. Katz and Tush*) and Eve Bunting (*Fly Away Home, The Wall,* and *Smoky Night*).

Family Reading Bingo or Tic Tac Toe (Pitcher and Mackey 2004) are literacy games that families can play at home. The Family Reading Bingo card in Figure 5.1 was created by one of the authors at Cromwell Valley Elementary School in Towson, Maryland, to remind

Figure 5.1
Family Reading Bingo

B	I	N	G	O
Read aloud a book together and parent initial here.	Read a recipe and make dinner together. Take a picture of the result and bring it in to your librarian.	Bake cookies reading a recipe and bring in one for your teacher and librarian.	Go to the public library and bring back a book list of books you may enjoy.	Cut up a comic strip from the newspaper and then put it back together. Bring it in to school pasted back together.
Read together the reviews of movies in the newspaper and choose one to see. Parent initials here when done.	Go to the public library and bring back a book list of books you may enjoy.	Read a poem to five adults and have them initial here.	Read aloud a book together and parent initial here.	Parent and child choose a card for someone special and mail it. Parent initial here when done.
Do an Internet search and find three sites that have information that you would like to read. List the sites here: 1. 2. 3.	Read ads together in the newspaper or Internet before buying something. Parent initial here when done.	*Free Space* ***Read whatever you want for as long as you want!***	Read a recipe and make dinner together. Take a picture of the result and bring it in to your librarian	Go to scholastic.com on the Internet and do one of the parent/child activities together.
Read a poem to five adults and have them initial here.	Bake cookies reading a recipe and bring in one for your teacher and librarian.	Do an Internet search and find three sites that have information that you would like to read. List the sites here: 1. 2. 3.	Go to scholastic.com on the Internet and do one of the parent/child activities together.	Read together the reviews of movies in the newspaper and choose one to see. Parent initials here when done.
Parent and child choose a card for someone special and mail it. Parent initial here when done.	Read aloud a book together and parent initial here.	Bake cookies reading a recipe and bring in one for your teacher and librarian.	Read a poem to five adults and have them initial here.	Go to the public library and bring back a book list of books you may enjoy.

parents that holiday activities can be used to reinforce literacy skills. Every time a family finished a Bingo card, they sent it in to the librarian and it was entered into a drawing for a special prize. The prizes from local businesses included movie tickets, bookstore gift cards, and restaurant gift certificates.

School-Home Links Reading Kit is available through the United States Department of Education's *Compact for Reading Initiative*. The kit consists of easy, one-page literacy activities that parents can do with their K–3 children. Many of the activities involve using any book.

By including one of these activities each week when sending home books, the librarian can support simple family literacy interaction in the home. The activities can also be downloaded and copied from the USDOE Web site at http://www.ed.gov/pubs/Compactfor Reading/index.html.

The Great Poetry Race (Pitcher and Mackey 2004) focuses on fluency as one of the major components of effective reading. The Towson University Reading Clinic and many Baltimore schools have used the Great Poetry Race to promote fluency. Children are given a poem with words that they have learned and are provided with a form that can be signed. They participate in a race to see who can read the poem to the most people in a short amount of time (e.g., a week). The librarian develops a poetry resource area in the library to support this type of program and provides a book prize for the weekly winners.

Literacy-focused Family Nights bring authors and storytellers together with families. The event is further enriched if the librarian plans an interactive component. Here are some options:

- Have a children's author read to the families and share personal experiences that inspired his/her writing. Then offer the following choices of follow-up activities to the families: a small group interaction with the author, games to win copies of the author's book, a workshop where children and parents can outline their own story ideas, or a literature circle where the families can discuss the book.
- Invite a storyteller to share stories and teach families some of the skills of storytelling. Then organize the families into small groups and encourage them to share their own stories with each other.
- Stage a literacy evening where the families have choices to participate in (a) craft workshops including origami (Japanese art of paper folding), paper airplane making, or play dough art; (b) cooking workshops with easy recipes for main courses, snacks and candy; or (c) a newspaper activity to support literacy.
- Coordinate a "making family memories" evening where families revive old favorite holiday activities such as wrapping packages, making simple presents for relatives, or making cards.
- Organize a literary evening where a poem or a paper book is sent home for the families to read together, and then have the families come together like an Oprah Book Club to talk about what they read. Make it a dress-up evening and serve punch and cookies.
- Collaborate with the public librarian on a special night at the local public library. This can be very effective right before summer vacation to introduce the family to what the public library can offer. Create a contest where the class with the highest attendance wins. Provide door prizes for the attendees that support family literacy, such as cookbooks, craft books, or gift certificates to the local bookstore.

CONCLUSION

Reaching the child can make a difference in the moment, but reaching the home can make a difference in the child's and the community's literacy futures. Family literacy research validates the power of working with families, and librarians can engender this power in the school library. The library can bridge the literacy gap by providing resources for communities that lack them. In collaboration with teachers, librarians can design activities that stimulate family literacy in the home. In addition to experiencing literacy opportunities during the school day, children thrive when these opportunities extend to activities with the family in the evenings and on the weekends. In short, the school librarian can assume a dynamic role as a literacy leader, who helps to empower all families to read and learn together.

REFERENCES

Asselin, Marlene. 2001. "Home-School Connections: Children's Literacy Development." *Teacher Librarian* 28, no. 4: 59–61.

Auerbach, Elsa R. 1995. "Which Way for Family Literacy: Intervention or Empowerment." In *Family Literacy: Connections in Schools and Communities,* ed. Lesley M. Morrow. Newark, DE: International Reading Association, 11–27.

Bayley, Joy. 2001. "Learner as a Family Member/Parent." *Literacy Links* 5, no. 3. http://www-tcall. tamu.edu/newsletr/jun01/jun01c.htm (accessed May 18, 2006).

Beaty, Janice J. 2004. *Skills for Preschool Teachers.* 7th ed. Upper Saddle River, NJ: Pearson.

Bus, Adriana G., Marinus H. Ijzendoorn, and Anthony D. Pellegrini. 1995. "Joint Book Reading Makes for Success in Learning to Read: A Meta-Analysis on Intergenerational Transmission of Literacy." *Review of Educational Research* 65 (Spring): 1–21.

DeBruin-Perecki, Andrea., and Scott G. Paris. 1997. "Family Literacy: Examining Practices and Issues of Effectiveness." *Journal of Adolescent & Adult Literacy* 40, no. 8: 596–618.

Edwards, Patricia A. 2003. "Children Have a Right to Reading Instruction That Involves Parents and Communities in Their Academic Lives." In *Promising Practices for Urban Reading Instruction,* ed. Pamela A. Mason and Jeanne S. Schumm, 308–318. Newark, DE: International Reading Association.

Eisenberg, Michael B., and Denise H. Miller. 2002. "This Man Wants To Change Your Job." *School Library Journal* 48, no. 7: 46–50.

Family Lending Library Academy. 2001. *School Renewal through Family Lending Library.* http:// www.schoolrenewal.org/strategies/i-library-hw.html (accessed April 9, 2006).

Griffis, Jennifer. 2003. "Helping Parents Become Their Child's Best Teacher: Family Literacy Programs in School Libraries." *Library Media Connection* 22, no. 1: 30–34.

McGahey, Michelle. 2005. "Hosting a Family Literacy Night at Your School." *Teacher Librarian* 32, no. 5: 28–30.

Mulhern, Margaret, Flora V. Rodriguez-Brown, and Timothy Shanahan. 1994. "Family Literacy for Language Minority Families: Issues for Program Implementation." *NCBE Program Information Guide Series, Number 17.* Washington, DC: National Clearinghouse for Bilingual Education. http://www.ncela.gwu.edu/pubs/pigs/pig17.htm (accessed September 19, 2006).

National Center for Family Literacy. 2003. *Federal Definition of Family Literacy.* http://www.famlit. org/FAQ/About/definition.cfm (accessed May 17, 2006).

Neuman, Susan B., and Donna Celano. 2001. "Access to Print in Low-Income and Middle-Income Communities: An Ecological Study of Four Neighborhoods." *Reading Research Quarterly* 36, no. 1: 81.

North Carolina School Library Media Association (NCSLMA). 2005. *NCSLMA Previous Read2 Succeed Grant Winners.* http://www.ncslma.org/Awards/previousgrantwinners.htm (accessed September 18, 2006).

Oatman, Eric. 2005. "2005 Giant Step Winners." *School Library Journal* 51, no. 6: 38–43.

Piazza, Stephen. 2001. "The Teacher-Librarian As Collaborative Partner in Merging the Understanding of Home and School Cultures." *Teacher Librarian* 28, no. 4: 31–34.

Pitcher, Sharon M., and Bonnie Mackey. 2004. *Collaborating for Real Literacy: Librarian, Teacher, and Principal.* Worthington, OH: Linworth Publishing.

Remsen, Ken. 2004. "Using the Library to Improve Student Literacy." *Teacher Librarian* 31, no. 5: 63.

Rosenfeld, Esther, and David Loertscher. 2006. "Improving Literacy through School Libraries: Evaluation Report." *Teacher Librarian* 33, no. 4: 6–7.

Selwyn, Neil, Stephen Gorard, and Sara Williams. 2001. "Digital Divide or Digital Opportunity? The Role of Technology in Overcoming Social Exclusion in U.S. Education." *Educational Policy* 15, no. 2: 258–277.

Taylor, Denny. 1983 [1998]. *Family Literacy: Young Children Learning to Read and Write.* Exeter, NH: Heinemann Educational Books.

U.S. Department of Education. 2004. *No Child Left Behind: A Desktop Reference.* http://www. ed.gov/admins/lead/account/nclbreference/page_pg5.html (accessed September 15, 2006).

U.S. Department of Education. 2005. *Early Reading First and Reading First.* http://www.ed.gov/ nclb/methods/reading/readingfirst.html (accessed September 15, 2006).

CHILDREN'S BOOKS CITED

Bunting, Eve. 1992. *Fly Away Home.* Illustrated by Ronald Himler. New York: Clarion.

Bunting, Eve. 1994. *Smoky Night.* Illustrated by David Diaz. New York: Harcourt Brace.

Bunting, Eve. 1990. *The Wall.* Illustrated by Ronald Himler. New York: Clarion.

Pollacco, Patricia. 1992. *Chicken Sunday.* New York: Philomel.

Pollacco, Patricia. 1988. *The Keeping Quilt.* New York: Simon & Schuster.

Pollacco, Patricia. 1992. *Mrs. Katz and Tush.* New York: Bantam.

Pollacco, Patricia. 2006. *Rotten Richie and the Ultimate Dare.* New York: Philomel.

Rahaman, Vashanti. 1997. *Read for Me, Mama.* Honesdale, PA: Boyds Mill Press, Inc.

6

Reading the Web: The Merging of Literacy and Technology

Elizabeth Dobler

Imagine, if you will, a scene in a school library in the mid 1970s. An adolescent girl has received an assignment in her world history class to write a research paper about Alexander the Great. She enters the dark, small library and is overcome with the smell of musty books. She gingerly crosses the room with a sense of uncertainty, wondering where she will find the information she needs and how long it will take. Her plan is to find one good book that will answer all of her research questions. An encyclopedia may be used as a last resort, since she cannot check it out to take home. With the assistance of the school librarian, she locates a book, skims the table of contents and index, looking for the required information. The book appears to be old, yellowed, and very thick, and she dreads the time it will take her to read through it and find what she needs.

Now, let your imagination take you forward 30 years. The adolescent girl previously described is now a mother with an adolescent daughter who receives the assignment of researching satellites for science class. Unlike her mother, the daughter does not enter the library to search for a book. Instead, she heads straight to a computer in the school library media center because the World Wide Web is her source of choice for finding information. Her excitement and interest in satellites is high, even though she does not know much about them. Google™ is used as the search engine. Her keyword is satellites, and she easily generates a list of over 95 million websites. Along with factual, content-based information, she also finds websites where she can build a satellite with an interactive construction set, visit a virtual satellite museum, watch the launching of satellites on a video clip, e-mail a NASA scientist with a question about satellites, view a three-dimensional plot of various satellites and their orbits, and use Google Earth™, which applies satellite technology to access an aerial view of her hometown.

These two young women, I and my daughter, experienced reading for information in very different ways. Although our purpose was similar, one of searching for information to complete a school project, the types of information available and the skills needed to acquire this information have changed greatly. These changes are causing educators to rethink what it means to be literate in a technological world. What are the reading skills our students need now, and in their future, to be able to access, understand, and use information? Are we preparing students, like my adolescent daughter described above, to be effective and efficient readers of information text, especially information text found on the Web?

Literacy and technology merge when we read a Web page and use the information to increase our understanding of a concept. We are only just beginning to understand the process of Web reading, and research in this area is in its infancy.[1] Both researchers and educators recognize that when we talk about Web reading, we begin with what we know about the reading process with print text—those skills and strategies that help us effectively understand an informational book or magazine article. To this understanding, we add the additional layers of complexity entailed with reading among the networked, informational spaces of the World Wide Web. These complexities center around the importance of prior experiences with understanding search engines and reading Web pages, the adeptness of navigating between and among websites, and the critical thinking required to evaluate information found on the Web. *Reading on the Web* is not just pointing and clicking, it is *reading, thinking, pointing,* and *clicking,* all of which are done in an instant.

With the complexities of Web reading in mind, this chapter will begin with a focus on the changing view of what it means to be literate in a technological society. This view invites a rethinking of the literacy skills that are crucial for students to be successful now and in their future. The next section draws attention to the role of educators in teaching these valuable literacy skills. In an education system brimming with accountability, who is responsible for teaching the urgently needed Web literacy skills? Following that, the remainder of the chapter will focus on the process of reading as it applies to both print and Web text and will identify strategies that should be taught in order to best prepare our students.

A CHANGING VIEW OF LITERACY

Literacy is the ability to *read and write* in order to understand how the world works socially and culturally. This definition of literacy certainly served us well when our need for and access to information was more limited. Today, however, the World Wide Web provides us with access to a seemingly unlimited supply of information for answering questions and solving problems. Ideas are now presented as text, interactive graphics, icons, sound, and video, all connected with hyperlinks, and all only a mouse click or two away. Literacy remains necessary for creating productive, responsible, and informed members of a society, but how do we define literacy in today's technology-driven and information-rich world? One theoretical perspective, known as the "New Literacies Perspective," takes the view that as new technologies emerge, new literacies emerge:

> The new literacies of the Internet and other ICTs include the skills, strategies, and dispositions necessary to successfully use and adapt to the rapidly changing information and communication technologies and contexts that continuously emerge in our world and influence all areas of our personal and professional lives. (Leu et al. 1572)

Leu argues that "a more precise definition of the new literacies may never be possible to achieve since their most important characteristic is that they regularly change" (Leu in press). Learning to adapt is key to being literate in today's world. Teaching students how to learn, rather than what to learn, gives them the flexibility to adapt to changes in both text and technology.

What does this mean for educators? In short, today's world demands that we now focus on multiple literacies (Lankshear and Knobel 2003). Multiple literacies include how to identify important questions, how to critically evaluate information, how to synthesize information, and how to communicate effectively with others—all of which enable students to gain information from various sources and to communicate using various technologies, while filtering the meaning of information through our own cultural and social lenses. As Leu and Kinzer (2000) describe, reading and writing become even more important in this changing view of literacy, because reading and writing are the foundational skills on which other literacy activities are based. However, while reading and writing are necessary, they are not sufficient. "Those who can access information the fastest, evaluate it most appropriately, and use it most effectively to solve problems will be the ones who succeed in the challenging times that await our children" (Leu and Kinzer 2000, 113).

Reading on the Web, then, is different from reading from a textbook or other informational item. It involves developing a new form of literacy, one that builds on foundational literacy skills (Leu et al. 2004), such as fluency, decoding, and comprehension. To these foundational skills are added skills such as understanding how to evaluate search results, how to navigate within a website, how to determine the accuracy, credibility, and trustworthiness of information, and how to synthesize without copying (Coiro 2003; Coiro and Dobler, 2004; Leu, Leu, and Coiro 2004). Some would argue that this new form of literacy is more complex because the types of text encountered on the Web are more complex (Coiro 2003; Leu 2000; Reinking 1992; Spires and Estes 2002). Today's educators face the challenge of helping students find a balance between the traditional ways of reading for information from books and periodicals, and the new ways of reading for information in an evolving online environment.

A CHANGING VIEW OF TEACHING

Changes in our definition of literacy are reshaping the nature of literacy instruction in library media centers, computer labs, and classrooms, and re-forming the roles of educators. "Literacy educators no longer 'own' the concept of literacy" (Hobbs 2006, 16). Knowing how to access, understand, and use information, once thought to be the realm of reading/language arts teachers, is important in all content areas. Finding the online information for a science report about satellites requires similar reading and navigating skills as does an electronic search for information needed to compare various battles of the Revolutionary War. "Once children are immersed in technology applications in content subjects, their use of literacy is transformed irrespective of the methods and materials with which they interact in 'literacy' classrooms" (McKenna 2006, xiii).

What is the educator's role in preparing students to be successful readers in an online environment? Who is ultimately responsible for teaching students the skills and strategies needed to be effective and efficient readers of Web text? Does the responsibility lie with the classroom teacher, library media specialist, reading specialist, or instructional technology specialist? The classroom teacher has the responsibility of teaching the state standards, which are measured by state assessments. Classroom teachers feel the pressure of time. Some believe that working on the computer is an "extra" or reward for completing other assignments. Others work diligently to integrate computers into instruction and practice.

Library media specialists may follow a curriculum that focuses on the development of research skills or ways to locate information within the library media center, which may or may not include a computer lab. Such a curriculum may include skills for Web searching but may not include important reading strategies such as drawing on previous experiences or creating a mental summary of important ideas. Reading instruction has not typically been in the realm of the library media specialist.

A reading specialist can provide specific instruction about foundational reading skills and those mental strategies important for understanding what is read. However, a reading specialist may or may not be familiar with how to apply these skills to reading on the Web. Often a reading specialist is working with struggling readers who may need to strengthen foundational skills before encountering the complexities of Web text.

An instructional technology specialist typically focuses on the hardware (e.g., using the keyboard), software (e.g., games for practicing skills), and Internet (e.g., e-mail, search engines, websites). A specific curriculum may be available, or the specialist may utilize developmentally appropriate computer activities that match the classroom curriculum. An instructional technology specialist may be able to teach many of the hands-on aspects of Web reading but may not have the background to teach the reading processes necessary to gain meaning.

Clearly, each type of educator brings a specialized knowledge to the learning experience. Each one can add to the development of Web literacy in an important way. The responsibility for teaching students to be effective and efficient Web readers belongs to all educators. A team approach allows students to benefit from the experiences and understandings of varied perspectives and does not place the burden for such a monumental task on the shoulders of any one educator.

Such an all-inclusive view of Web literacy instruction is not always met with open arms. Some educators are resistant to a change from their current role to one that includes teaching Web literacy skills. Library media specialists and instructional technology specialists were the first to embrace these changes and have already begun to include many important Web-reading strategies into their instruction. For classroom teachers, the change has been met with more resistance. A digital divide has emerged between reading/language arts teachers and math and science teachers (Hobbs 2006). Content area teachers have more easily embraced the view of multiple literacies and the importance of gaining information from a variety of sources in a variety of ways. Reading/language arts teachers tend to prefer print to electronic resources. "It is hard for some teachers to consider, yet alone accept, that emerging forms of electronic reading and writing may be as informative, pedagogically useful, and aesthetically pleasing as more familiar printed forms. To consider that electronic forms of text may, in some instances, even be superior is undoubtedly more difficult" (McKenna, Labbo, and Reinking 2003, 325). In effect, the very teachers who have traditionally held the responsibility for traditional literacy instruction tend to be the most resistant to the changing definition of literacy.

Although the team approach to Web literacy is ideal, the reality is that the classroom teacher is still typically responsible for teaching the *reading* skills needed to comprehend Web text. A research study conducted with 23 educators teaching various levels focused on perceptions about teaching Web literacy (Dobler 2004). A majority of these educators believed a team approach was useful for teaching the *technology* skills needed to use the Web, but a majority felt the classroom teacher should be responsible for teaching the *reading skills* needed to use the Web.

THE PROCESS OF WEB READING

The Web provides today's students with instant access to seemingly unlimited sources of information. Along with the opportunities available through the Web come the responsibilities of preparing our students with the new literacy skills needed to locate, understand, and use information found on the Internet. Some educators are hesitant to take on this role because they feel unprepared themselves. While searching for information about the best instructional strategies to enable their students to grow and develop as Web readers, they are also seeking guidance and support in their own growth and development as Web readers.

As noted earlier in this chapter, research in this area is in its infancy. While researchers continue to seek to specifically identify the skills students need to effectively and efficiently read on the Web, for now, educators must rely on what we know from the substantial body of research about the reading process with print text, and add what we know from the limited, but growing, body of Web literacy and our own experiences as Web readers.

Reading on the Web, as with reading any type of text, relies on strong foundational skills. Readers must have a foundation of decoding, vocabulary, and fluency skills. These skills get a reader started, but the real heart of reading lies in comprehension or making meaning. Comprehension is a complex process requiring a reader to "construct meaning by interacting with text through the combination of prior knowledge and previous experience, information in the text, and the stance the reader takes in relationship to the text" (Pardo 2004, 272). Interaction with the text is key to the process and relies on the reader "simultaneously extracting and constructing meaning" (RAND 2002). Fortunately, when it comes to comprehension of print text, the National Reading Panel Report (National Institute of Child and Human Development 2000) and others provide us with a rich history for understanding comprehension. One report, the RAND Reading Study Group (2002), synthesized comprehension research to identify three elements of comprehension: the reader, the text, and the task or process, all of which are influenced by the sociocultural context.

This next section of the chapter will explore the various elements of comprehension and possible ways these elements influence the reading of Web text. Research, when available, and personal experiences will serve to support suggestions for the ways educators can support and encourage growth among the elements of reading.

The Reader

Each reader brings a unique perspective, a set of abilities, and a collection of experiences to the act of reading, all of which prompt the reader to interact with the text in various ways depending on the reader's purpose (RAND 2002). A perspective, or view, depends on the reader's sociocultural background and belief system and colors the way a text is interpreted. A reader's abilities refers to cognitive capacities (e.g., attention, memory, critical thinking skills, and abilities to analyze, synthesize, and evaluate), motivation (e.g., interest, attitude, beliefs), and prior knowledge and experiences (e.g., topic knowledge, vocabulary, decoding, comprehension strategies). Use of these elements varies according to the difficulty of the text and can be developed with more practice and instruction.

Although each of the elements work together to promote effective reading, prior knowledge stands out as being critical to developing an understanding of the text. "What we already have stored in that organized memory helps us make sense of new information that comes to us" (Ulijn and Strother 1995, 128). Background knowledge provides a pegboard on which to hook or connect new ideas. The pegboard, or schema, provides a reader with a structure on which to connect the new pegs. Think of a schema as a mental system for organizing information in long-term memory so it can be recalled easily and quickly. A reader encounters a concept or keyword within a text in the form of a title, heading, or caption. These words trigger the known information to be pulled to the front of the mind to aid in understanding.

A similar process is used to activate prior knowledge when reading Web text. Online readers are more likely to understand the content of a website when they call to mind the information stored in their schema. One big difference for Web readers is that they must rely on additional areas of prior knowledge in order to make meaning (Fidel et al. 1999; Hirsch 1999). Typically, for comprehension of print text, readers draw from prior knowledge of the topic and the text structure or organization of the text. Experiences in both of these areas of prior knowledge provide a reader with a head start when beginning a text. Not only must Web readers rely on these two areas of prior knowledge, but they must also rely on prior experiences with using search engines and reading websites (Coiro and Dobler in press) because searching for information is such an integral part of Web reading. According to Fidel and her colleagues, "being knowledgeable of the topic being searched is necessary for learning how to search the Web, and being somewhat knowledgeable about Web searching is necessary for exploring new topics" (1999, 34). Because Web readers are encountering massive amounts of information in a relatively short time, activating various types of prior knowledge is crucial for the reader to avoid becoming overwhelmed, disoriented, and frustrated.

Teaching Readers

Activating prior knowledge is important for developing an understanding of all types of texts. If students have gaps in prior knowledge, educators can help to fill in these gaps by creating experiences (e.g., field trips, simulations, hands-on activities), providing opportunities for viewing (e.g., videos, DVDs, plays), and encouraging the reading of a variety of texts (e.g., magazines, informational books, websites). Instructional activities that combine information from both print and online sources can also help to build prior knowledge (see Figure 6.1). For example, a graphic organizer can serve as both a tool for assessing prior knowledge and a tool for determining the instruction most needed by the students. Thinking aloud is one way for the teacher to model the thought processes used by skilled readers to activate their own prior knowledge. During a read aloud, pause to orally explain, or think aloud those processes used to activate your own schema and make connections. A think-aloud provides the listener a glimpse into the mind of a skilled reader and demonstrates the mental process that occurs behind the scenes.

The Text

Besides what the reader brings to the reading act, the text itself can help or hinder the process of comprehension. Armbruster (1984) describes the "considerateness" of a text as a text following an organizational structure that helps the reader by providing cues or features that identify important ideas, guide a reader through the text, and enhance comprehension. These features are the tools of the information text reader and often include a title, headings, labels, or bolded words. A title gives the overview of the text and can be used to begin activating the reader's prior knowledge. Headings bring important concepts to the attention of the reader. Labels serve as identification for pictures and other graphics,

Figure 6.1
Instructional Strategies for Developing Prior Knowledge

Type of Prior Knowledge	Instructional Activity
Topic	Combine a class novel unit with Internet activities to build prior knowledge. Use the novel *Zachary Beaver Was Here* by Kimberly Willis Holt, as a part of a literature unit. In the novel, the main character, Zachary, is a sideshow act because he weighs an unusually high amount for a boy. Begin the unit with an Internet study of sideshow acts. Focus on building prior knowledge with a study of the weird and unusual by visiting the *Ripley's Believe It or Not* website at http://www.ripleys.com. To help students understand the concept of people being interested in the unusual, invite the students to visit three predetermined websites about other sideshow acts and to collect important ideas in a journal. Then discuss why people might want to be in a sideshow and why people might want to see a sideshow. Schedule the Web research to occur before and during the reading of the novel, so that students can use their prior knowledge to make connections to the text.
Structure of the Text	Conduct a study of text features. Begin with a social studies textbook, move to a short informational article from *Write Time for Kids* (Prior 2000), and then proceed to websites. Before reading each text, review a list of text features that could possibly be encountered in reading these sources. Then ask students to identify common text features for each text, and develop a text features checklist. With each new text, add features to the list until the group feels the list is all-encompassing. Creating the checklist together will help students to become aware of the individual features in their own reading. Once the checklist is finalized, give students the opportunity to use the checklist on a variety of different texts. Periodically discuss the checklist to determine if revisions should be made and remind students that the goal is for them to develop an understanding of a wide variety of text features and how these features can help in locating and understanding information.
Search engines	Use a search engine comparison activity, where students look for the same information on a variety of search engines. Select two search engines such as Yahooligans at http://www.yahooligans.com, or Ask for Kids at http://www.askforkids.com. Tell students they will be searching for information about cats and will answer the same questions using each website and then compare the answers. Try a broad search: **cat;** How many hits did you get? Try a misspelling: **poplar cat breed;** Did a spellchecker come up? Try keywords: **popular cat breed;** How many hits did you get? Try a question: **What are the most popular cat breeds?;** Which words does the search engine look for? Discuss which website was the most useful for finding information and which one was the easiest to use.
Websites	Use a Subject Sampler to practice reading websites. Subject Samplers are a way to help students become familiar with links, icons, and other navigational features on a website and are similar to a WebQuest in that both provide students with preselected websites as tools for gathering information. A Subject Sampler uses a small number of websites, typically about six, which provides the students with general information about a specific topic. Rather than reading for specific facts, as with a WebQuest, the students are asked to create a personal response to the websites by sharing perspectives, making connections, or responding through oral, written, or visual displays.

99

and bolded words point out key vocabulary necessary for understanding the text. Various studies support the idea that understanding the text structure, or the way the text is organized, helps the reader to be more successful in the process of creating meaning from the text (Afflerbach 1986; Armbruster and Armstrong 1992). Knowledge of such structural cues helps a reader to interpret and use information to construct a mental map of what is being read. In the book, *Exploring Information Texts: From Theory to Practice,* Linda Hoyt and Teresa Therriault (2003) comment on the importance of teaching text structures and features.

> Once students become familiar with the basic organizational structures, they can more easily predict challenges in text, identify language features, and incorporate critical attributes to their own writing. Knowledge of these core structures and signal words provide support to readers so they can better anticipate language and features of each structure during reading. (53)

Although hyperlinks make Web text unique, the reader still encounters many of the same features found in print text. For example, headings, graphics, labels, and even a table of contents or a glossary are found on some websites. Even with the similarities, we do find the structure of websites, the use of hyperlinks, and the unique aspects of reader friendliness make Web text distinctly different, and in some respects, more complex.

One of the complexities of understanding a website structure is that each website appears to be organized with its own structure. Some websites contain an elaborate system of hyperlinks and icons displayed for the reader, while other websites appear to merely be a copy of pages from a book displayed on a Web page with few if any links, icons, or graphics. When taking a closer look at websites, a research study analyzed a sample of 30 websites for textual features, finding many textual features noted in print text to also be found in Web text, such as headings, labels, and captions (Dobler 2003). Although some similarities were found among websites, no two websites in the study contained the same text features. Thus, when a website is encountered, we must reorient ourselves to the organization and features found on that website, much like when we drive a different car and must locate the switches for the lights, windshield wipers, and cruise control. Our past driving experience tells us we should be able to find these switches but does not tell us exactly where they would be found. Because of such varied website structures, we cannot teach students a simple structure to expect each time they encounter a website, but we can teach them common features that will likely be found on a website. A list of text features to look for in a website includes both features from print and Web text (Figure 6.2) and could be made into a checklist and applied to a variety of websites as a way to introduce students to the text features found in Web text.

Websites display a limited amount of information but make additional information available through use of various types of hyperlinks (see Figure 6.3). Hyperlinks can be used to figuratively chain together ideas from various sources including a Web page, image, sound file, or other document. One example of this chaining can be seen through the use of a linking term called "bread crumbs." A website may display the hyperlinks as a reader moves from Web page to Web page within a website, thus providing a hyperlink back to each previous page. The links are displayed horizontally across the top of the Web page with an arrow leading from one link to another. The reader is provided with a

Figure 6.2
Text Features

Organizational Features	Text Features	Graphic Features	Hypertext Features
• table of contents • glossary • index	• bold print • highlighted print • colored print • italics • captions • headings • labels • bullets	• diagrams • tables • charts • timelines • cross section • maps • photographs	• stand alone hyperlinks as icons or highlighted words • hyperlinks embedded within text • hyperlinks to multimedia, including photos, audio and video clips • hyperlinks to definitions with an online glossary • banner heading indicating website host • graphics and icons leading to advertisements

Adapted from: Linda Hoyt, Margaret Mooney, and Barbara Parkes, 2003. *Exploring Information Texts: From Theory to Practice*. Portsmouth, NH: Heinemann.

trail to follow back to the starting point of the website, much like a trail of bread crumbs used by Hansel and Gretel. The website, *Yahooligans,* at http://www.yahooligans.com, displays the path a reader takes as she moves from the homepage, to a section page, then a subsection page. The path for reading about the solar system within Yahooligans is listed as Home > Science > Space > Solar System. The uniqueness of this hypertext feature provides the reader with a visual display of his reading path and provides a visual guide for helping the reader stay on track. Knowledge of how these links are displayed and where the information might lead helps the Internet reader to more efficiently locate information as he makes more accurate predictions about the type of hyperlink and where it leads.

Figure 6.3
Types of Hyperlinks

Type of Link	Description
Stand-alone text link	This link is a word or phrase representing a key idea. These links are often found across the top or bottom, or in a column down the left or right side of the Web page. These links often take the reader to various spots within the website.
Embedded text link	Within the text on the Web page, a word or phrase may appear in a different color, indicating it is a hyperlink. These links may lead to other information found within the website or may link directly to related information on another website. Key vocabulary words within the text may be hyperlinked to a glossary within the website.
Icon links	An icon displays a graphic of where the link will lead the reader. Often an icon is accompanied by a label.

Teaching about the Text

With such varied formats of websites and Web pages, teachers face quite a challenge to provide novice Web readers with specific information about where to find information on a website. When describing print text, we discussed the considerateness of a text when specific features are included that provide a reader with cues about organization and importance. The unique aspects of Web text make these cues *and* additional ones available to the reader depending on the considerateness of the website creator. Features such as a site map, home button, or internal search engine make the task of finding information easier for the reader, thus contributing to the reader friendliness of a website. Figure 6.4 provides Web readers with a checklist for evaluating the "reader friendliness" of a website. When a website is friendly to the reader, information can be found easily, graphics help enhance the information, and navigational clues are distinct. The creator of the website has taken the information and navigational needs of the reader into consideration by providing a sitemap, hyperlinks, and graphics that make locating information easier for the reader. The Reader Friendliness Checklist can provide a useful framework for discussing the helpful aspects of each website. Begin by using the checklist with a well-designed website, such as *StarChild: A Learning Center for Young Astronomers* (http://starchild.gsfc.nasa. gov/docs/StarChild/StarChild.html), created by two middle school teachers and sponsored by NASA. Teachers and students together can discuss various aspects of the website that make it friendly to a reader. Recognizing the reader-friendly qualities of a well-designed website will help readers to know what to expect and look for when encountering other websites. Experienced Web readers recognize the fact that each website they encounter has a distinct way to display and organize information. When encountering a new website, these experienced readers simultaneously look for a familiar feature and rely on their flexible understanding of the way websites are organized. In this way, the uniqueness of each website contributes to the complexities of Web reading.

The Process

Up to this point, the elements of reading have been fairly distinct. The reader brings prior experiences, motivation, and a sense of purpose to the reading task. The text provides structural cues and graphic representations to assist with the organization of ideas. These elements come together during the transaction or the actual act of making meaning from the text. Because of the differences among readers, text, and context, the transaction is unique to each reader and occurs as these various elements merge together in a single point. Rosenblatt (1985) theorizes that the meaning of the text does not merely lie within the words on the page but is only created when a reader interacts with the text. The meaning becomes a new entity based on a combination of what the reader brings and what the author creates. The transactional theory of reading focuses on " the reading act as an event involving a particular individual and a particular text, happening at a particular time, under particular circumstances, in a particular social and cultural setting, and as part of the ongoing life of the individual and the group" (Rosenblatt 1985, 100).

How does this process of transacting differ for Web text? The reader still brings prior knowledge, motivation, and purpose to the reading task, although each of these may be varied or even at a more complex level as described previously in this chapter. The reader encounters the Web text, which contains many of the same structural cues noted in print text but also contains structural cues unique to Web text. The text displayed on a Web page is available to readers, but meaning is only created through the interaction of the reader

Figure 6.4
Reader Friendliness Survey

Identify a website from your inquiry project. Use the Reader Friendliness Checklist to determine if this is a website that will be helpful for finding information.

URL: Yes   No

Does a site map provide hyperlinks to key ideas and display the overarching organization of the website?

Are the hyperlinks easy to distinguish from the rest of the text either by color, size, or shape?

Is there a keyword search function so you can search the site for the specific term you have in mind?

Is the path you have taken through the website listed, so you can easily see where you have come from and how to return?

If you go to another page, is there link to get back to the first page?

Does the title of the page tell you what it is about?

Is there an introduction or welcoming message on the page telling you what is included?

Is each section labeled with a heading?

Is the structure uncluttered and easy to use with space separating ideas?

Is there a lack of annoying features (flashing banners, distracting animated creatures, ugly colors)?

Do the graphics help you to better understand the ideas of the text and do they load easily?

Would you use this website to help you learn more about the topic? Why or why not?

and the text in an active process. With Web text, this active process involves the reader constantly making choices about what to read and then taking action, or navigating, by clicking on hyperlinks or scrolling down or up the page. Through early studies of the process of Web reading, we have begun to realize the important role navigation plays in the complex weaving of decision making and meaning making that occurs during Web reading. In the book, *Teaching with the Internet K–12: New Literacies for New Times* (2004), Leu, Leu, and Coiro describe this evolving definition of navigation.

> Traditionally, Internet navigation connotes the process of moving between one link and another through various webpages. However, we look at navigation within the context of a new literacies perspective. We see the act of deciding which path to follow on the Internet as very tightly woven within a complex process of reading and meaning making. Strategies such as querying search engines, critically evaluating multiple forms of information, weaving through search results, and systematically maneuvering within one website are all important and different aspects of moving between links while making sense of information. . . . It is not simply about how quickly students can move through this online world, but more about how they decide which information is most accurate, relevant, appropriate, and useful for their purposes (37).

Researchers are taking a closer look at the interconnection between comprehension and navigation (e.g. Bilal 2002; Guinee, Eagleton, and Hall 2003; Leu, Kinzer, Coiro and

Cammack 2004; Sutherland-Smith 2002). Web readers have described a mental process of moving between making reading decisions and developing an understanding (Coiro and Dobler in press). This complex, high-level thinking occurs as the readers mentally criss-cross back and forth between comprehension and navigation until the lines are blurred between these processes.

In the Web reading process, navigation becomes the action that facilitates the trans-action between the reader and the text. Navigating among websites and search engines facilitates the Internet reading process as it begins and continues. Navigating makes this transaction visible, especially when the reader has the purpose of searching for informa-tion. For example, a reader wanting to learn the difference between a landfill and a dump must first draw from prior experiences with search engines to locate a useful website such as *Garbage: How Can My Community Reduce Waste?* at http://www.learner.org/exhibits/garbage/intro.html. The reader is then faced with a collection of links with such terms as *introduction, solid waste, hazardous waste, sewage, global effects, the future,* and *related resources.* Before determining a link to select, the reader draws on prior knowledge of landfills and dumps along with knowledge of what these terms mean and how they may be used as headings to indicate more information. Then the reader must recall prior experi-ences with websites to understand that these terms provide an overview of the organization of a website and act as links to access further information. Once a link is selected, the text is read, and important ideas are determined and then synthesized as the reader gathers and comprehends information to answer the question. Throughout this reading process, comprehension and navigation are interdependent on each other, making it impossible to determine which comes first, the navigation or the comprehension, because each one influ-ences the other during the reading transaction.

Throughout the reading process of both print and Web text, proficient readers apply a collection of strategies to support their construction of meaning. Strategies are those in-the-head processes a reader uses to make sense of what is being read. Clay (1991) describes strategies as operations that support comprehension through the manipulation of text in the following ways: interpreting, applying, transforming, reproducing, using, and re-forming. What are the strategies good readers use? How are these same strategies used by Web read-ers? Pearson and colleagues (1992) have developed a comprehension curriculum based around seven comprehension strategies that consistently surfaced in research about strate-gic readers (Figure 6.5). Strategies move comprehension forward and are often used as a collection or bundle, with one strategy enhancing another. These strategies form the basis for an instructional model of the process of reading comprehension and provide educators with a guide for teaching this complex mental process.

Teaching the Process

Within the last 30 years, a strong body of research has been developed to describe the strate-gies used by good readers (see, e.g., Block and Pressley 2002; Pressley and Afflerbach 1995). Good readers are active participants with a clear goal or purpose in mind for their reading. They continually evaluate whether the text and their reading is helping to meet this goal. They move towards repairing comprehension when they realize understanding is not occurring. Since we know what good readers do to make sense of what they read, the next question becomes, can we teach other readers to engage in these same productive behaviors? Researchers have found that explicit instruction in specific strategies such as asking questions (Palinscar and Brown 1984), determining important ideas (Afflerbach and Johnston 1986), and making inferences

Figure 6.5
Comprehension Strategies for Informational Web Text

Strategy	Print Text	Web Text
Activating prior knowledge—drawing on various personal experiences to create a mental connection to new ideas	• Bring to the front of the mind what is known about the topic of the text and the way the text is organized based on personal experiences. • Create mental connections between the text and the reader, other texts, and the world. • Provide a starting point from which to move forward through comprehension process	• Draw from additional experiences of using search engines and reading websites. • Recognize that knowledge of topic and text structure may not guarantee success with Web reading.
Predicting—making a mental guess about the type or location of information	• Make the prediction, gather information to confirm or disconfirm, make judgment about accuracy of prediction. • Making successful predictions leads to a deeper understanding. • Making unsuccessful predictions may cause the reader to feel disconnected or lost.	• Follow similar process of making, confirming, adjusting predictions. • Make navigational predictions about where a hyperlink will lead. • Making accurate predictions about hyperlinks facilitates efficient Web reading.
Questioning—querying yourself during the reading process	• Asking questions helps to activate prior knowledge, clarify ideas, check comprehension, and focus attention. • Generating questions at both higher and lower cognitive levels helps to build a mental structure of the text.	• Generate questions for similar purposes of checking for understanding. • Ask questions that also guide navigating (e.g., Where will a click on this link take me? Did my choice take me to the type of information I thought it would? How can I go back to where I started?).
Inferencing—combining prior knowledge with information from the text to draw conclusions. A best educated guess is used to fill in the missing pieces.	• Search for a chain of related details, and fill in the gaps with inferences. • Read between the lines when text is not clear. • Look for coherence in the text, but may have difficulty filling in the gaps if prior knowledge is limited.	• Use inferences in similar ways, to fill in the gaps when text is not specific. • Make additional inferences about visual cues (e.g., icons, hyperlinks, interactive graphics). • Rely on past experiences with Web reading to guide inferences.

105

(Continued)

Figure 6.5
Comprehension Strategies for Informational Web Text (*Continued*)

Strategy	Print Text	Web Text
Determining important ideas - mentally reducing the text to manageable chunks of key ideas by sorting out the important from the unimportant	• Identifying important ideas occurs throughout the reading process. • Decide *and* remember important details of information text in order to learn something or answer a question. • Rely on text features (e.g., title, heading, bold-faced print) to provide hints about what is important.	• Use similar process of sifting ideas into important and unimportant. • Rely on a wider variety of text features to provide hints about importance (e.g., icons, hyperlinks, bright colors, interactive graphics). • Determine important ideas also from multimedia (e.g., audio clip, video clip, photograph). • Add additional layer of evaluating to determine if information is both true and important.
Visualizing—an active process for understanding information by creating mental images from the text	• Use for building a mental framework to aid in organizing and remembering ideas from the text. • Create mental "pegs" on which information is "hooked" for storage and later retrieval.	• Use a similar process for creating mental framework of information. • Create mental images of the hyperlink path used to locate information. • Use visualization to help store the massive amounts of information encountered in Web reading.
Monitoring and repairing comprehension—checking your understanding throughout the text and figuring out what to do if text does not make sense	• Pause periodically to determine if comprehension is occurring. • Ask yourself questions to check for understanding? (e.g., What was that page about? Do I really understand what this means? What is the most important idea to remember?). • Adjust reading pace for more difficult parts. • Clarify difficult concepts through discussion or further reading.	• Use similar monitoring strategies to check for understanding. • Use Web page tools (e.g., site map, bread crumbs, drop-down menu) to help keep track of where you are in the text in order to monitor understanding of ideas. • Recognize that information is often "hidden" beneath layers of text connected by links.

(Hansen 1981) has improved students' overall comprehension of text. We also know that understanding a strategy is a good starting point, but more effective comprehension occurs when a reader knows when, why, and how to use a strategy (Paris, Lipson, and Wixson 1983).

Teachers recognize the need for quality, explicit instruction of strategies as a way to provide students with the tools needed for constructing a mental framework of the text. A clear description of the strategy is needed, along with the teacher or classmates modeling the strategy in action, possibly through a think-aloud. Pearson and Gallagher (1983) recommend a gradual release of responsibility for strategy instruction, where, at first, the instruction and modeling are done primarily by the teacher. Then the lesson moves into guided practice and scaffolding, which involves shared responsibility between the teacher and the students, then the students take on more responsibility through independent strategy use, while the teacher plays more of a supportive role. When first learning a strategy, students should have opportunities to apply the strategy to texts that are not too challenging in the areas of vocabulary, new concepts, or decoding, so their full attention can be given to applying the strategy, whether reading in a print or online environment.

FINAL THOUGHTS

Understanding the elements of the reader, the text, and the process is a first step in moving towards the idea that we are all teachers of reading. When applying these elements to Web reading, one can see the way a good understanding of the process of reading can help all educators to develop online reading skills. Some of us may feel hesitant, or less than confident in passing on our knowledge of Web reading, both the reading skills and the navigational skills needed to be successful. We know that change is a constant when it comes to technology. If we wait to reach our own comfort level, the technology will likely change again, and our students will be left behind. When we see ourselves as learners, along with our students, we create a learning community where we can rely on the collective knowledge to carry us along this journey of change.

NOTE

1. A growing understanding of new literacies is based on the work of educators and researchers who seek to move beyond traditional definitions and envision the convergence of literacy and technology. Research in this field faces the challenge of trying to keep pace with the changes occurring in technology, and thus it is constantly trying to catch up (Leu et al. 2004; RAND, 2002), which is a concern for educators seeking an evidence base for instructional decisions. However, a small but growing body of research is beginning to form, as researchers study the ways readers comprehend Internet text (Coiro and Dobler in press), the strategies readers use to search for information (Guinee, Eagleton, and Hall 2003; Henry 2006), and the navigational paths readers follow when reading on the Internet (McEneaney 2003). Others have begun to describe the ways teachers are effectively using technology in the classroom (Karchmer 2001; Wepner and Tao 2002) and the ways to create a Web-based curriculum (Eagleton and Dobler 2006). An understanding of the Web-reading process is beginning to take shape based the work of teachers and researchers who seek to link literacy and technology.

REFERENCES

Afflerbach, Peter P., and Peter H. Johnston. 1986. "What Do Experts Do When the Main Idea Is Not Explicit?" In *Teaching Main Idea Comprehension*, ed. James F. Bauman, 49–72. Newark, DE: International Reading Association.

Armbruster, Bonnie. 1984. "The Problem of 'Inconsiderate Texts.'" In *Comprehension Instruction: Perspectives and Suggestions,* ed. Gerald G. Duffy, Laura Roehler, and Jana Mason, 202–217. New York: Longman.

Armbruster, Bonnie, and Jana Armstrong. 1992. *Locating Information in the Text: A Focus on Children in the Elementary Grades.* Champaign: University of Illinois, Center for the Study of Reading, ED 347 502.

Bilal, Dania. 2002. "Perspectives on Children's Navigation of the World Wide Web: Does the Type of Search Task Make a Difference?" *Online Information Review* 26, no. 2: 108–117.

Block, Cathy Collins, and Michael Pressley. 2002. *Comprehension Instruction: Research-Based Best Practices.* New York: Guilford Press.

Clay, Marie. 1991. *Becoming Literate: The Construction of Inner Control.* Portsmouth, NH: Heinemann.

Coiro, Julie. 2003. "Reading Comprehension on the Internet: Expanding Our Understanding of Reading Comprehension to Encompass New Literacies." *The Reading Teacher* 56, no. 5: 458–464.

Coiro, Julie, and Elizabeth Dobler. 2004. *Investigating How Less-Skilled and Skilled Readers Use Cognitive Reading Strategies While Reading on the Internet.* Paper presented at the 54th Annual Meeting of the National Reading Conference, December 1–4, in San Antonio, TX.

Coiro, Julie, and Elizabeth Dobler. In press. "Exploring the Online Reading Comprehension Strategies Used by Sixth-Grade Skilled Readers to Search for and Locate Information on the Internet." *Reading Research Quarterly.*

Dobler, Elizabeth. 2003. *Informational Text and Internet Text: Similarities and Differences among Text Features.* Paper presented at the 53rd National Reading Conference, December 3–6, in Scottsdale, AZ.

Dobler, Elizabeth. 2004. *Exploring Teachers' Perceptions of Their Role in Preparing Students to Read Informational Text on the Internet.* Paper presented at the 54th Annual National Reading Conference, December 1–4, in San Antonio, TX.

Eagleton, Maya B., and Elizabeth Dobler. 2006. *Reading the Web: Strategies for Internet Inquiry.* New York: Guilford.

Fidel, Raya, Rachel K. Davies, Mary H. Douglass, Jenny K. Holder, Carla J. Hopkins, Elisabeth J. Kushner, Brian K. Miyagashima, and Christina D. Toney. 1999. "A Visit to the Information Mall: Web Searching Behavior of High School Students." *Journal of the American Society for Information Science and Technology* 50, no. 1: 501–521.

Guinee, Kathleen, Maya Eagleton, and Tracey E. Hall. 2003. "Adolescents' Internet Search Strategies: Drawing upon Familiar Cognitive Paradigms When Accessing Electronic Information Sources." *Journal of Educational Computing Research* 29, no. 3: 363–374.

Hansen, Jane. 1981. "The Effects of Inference Training and Practice on Young Children's Reading Comprehension." *Reading Research Quarterly* 16, no. 3: 391–417.

Henry, Laurie A. 2006. "SEARCHing for an Answer: The Critical Role of New Literacies While Reading on the Internet." *The Reading Teacher* 59, no. 7: 614–627.

Hirsch, Sandra G. 1999. "Children's Relevance Criteria and Information Seeking on Electronic Resources." *Journal of the American Society for Information Science* 50, no. 14: 1265–1283.

Hobbs, Renee. 2006. "Multiple Visions of Multimedia Literacy: Emerging Areas of Synthesis." In *International Handbook of Literacy and Technology,* ed. Michael C. McKenna, Linda D. Labbo, and Ronald D. Kieffer, 15–28. Mahwah, NJ: Lawrence Erlbaum.

Hoyt, Linda, and Teresa Therriault. 2003. "Understanding Text Structures." In *Exploring Informational Texts: From Theory to Practice,* ed. Linda Hoyt, Margaret Mooney, and Brenda Parkes, 52–58. Portsmouth, NH: Heinemann.

Karchmer, Rachel. 2001. "The Journey Ahead: Thirteen Teachers Report How the Internet Influences Literacy and Literacy Instruction in Their K–12 Classrooms." *Reading Research Quarterly* 36, no. 4: 442–465.

Lankshear, Colin, and Michele Knobel. 2003. *New Literacies: Changing Knowledge and Classroom Learning.* Philadelphia: Open University Press.

Leu, Donald J. 2000. "Our Children's Future: Changing the Focus of Literacy and Literacy Instruction." *Reading Online* (February). readingonline.org/electronic/elec_index.asp?HREF = /electronic/RT/focus/index.html (accessed October 30, 2006).

Leu, Donald J. In press. "The New Literacies: Research on Reading Instruction with Internet and Other Digital Technologies." In *What Research Has to Say about Reading Instruction,* ed. Jay Samuels and Allen E. Farstrup. Newark, DE: International Reading Association.

Leu, Donald J., Deborah D. Leu, and Julie Coiro. 2004. *Teaching with the Internet K–12: New Literacies for New Times,* 4th ed. Norwood, MA: Christopher-Gordon.

Leu, Donald J., and Charles K. Kinzer. 2000. "The Convergence of Literacy Instruction with Networked Technologies for Information and Communication." *Reading Research Quarterly* 35, no. 1:108–127.

Leu, Donald J., Charles K. Kinzer, Julie L. Coiro, and Dana W. Cammack. 2004. "Toward a Theory of New Literacies Emerging from the Internet and Other Information and Communication Technologies." In *Theoretical Models and Processes of Reading,* ed. Robert B. Ruddell and Norman Unrau, 1570–1613. Newark: DE, International Reading Association.

McEneaney, John E. 2003. "A Transactional Theory of Hypertext Structure." In *The 51st Yearbook of the National Reading Conference,* ed. Colleen. M. Fairbanks, Jo Worthy, Beth Maloch, James V. Hoffman, and Diane. L. Schallert, 272–284. Oak Creek, WI: National Reading Conference.

McKenna, Michael C. 2006. "Trends and Trajectories of Literacy and Technology in the New Millennium." In *International Handbook of Literacy and Technology,* ed. Michael C. McKenna, Linda D. Labbo, Ronald D. Kieffer, and David Reinking, xi–xviii. Mahwah, NJ: Lawrence Erlbaum.

McKenna, Michael C., Linda D. Labbo, and David D. Reinking. 2003. "Effective Use of Technology in Literacy Instruction." In *Best Practices in Literacy Instruction,* ed. Leslie M. Morrow, Linda B. Gambrell, and Michael Pressley, 307–331. New York: Guilford.

National Institute of Child Health and Human Development [NICHD]. 2000. *Report of the National Reading Panel. Teaching Children to Read: An Evidence-Based Assessment of the Scientific Research Literature on Reading and Its Implications for Reading Instruction* (NIH Publication NO. 00–4769). Washington, DC: U.S. Government Printing Office.

Palinscar, Annemarie S., and Ann L. Brown. 1984. "Reciprocal Teaching of Comprehension and Comprehension-Monitoring Activities." *Cognition and Instruction* 1, no. 2: 117–175.

Pardo, Laura S. 2004. "What Every Teacher Needs to Know About Comprehension." *The Reading Teacher* 58, no. 3: 272–280.

Paris, Scott. G., Marjorie Y. Lipson, and Karen K. Wixson. 1983. "Becoming a Strategic Reader." *Contemporary Educational Psychology* 8: 293–316.

Pearson, P. David, and Margaret C. Gallagher. 1983. "The Instruction of Reading Comprehension." *Contemporary Educational Psychology* 8: 317–344.

Pearson, P. David, Laura R. Roehler, Janice A. Dole, and Gerald G. Duffy. 1992. "Developing Expertise in Reading Comprehension." In *What Research Has to Say about Reading Instruction,* ed. S. Jay Samuels and Alan. E. Farstrup, 145–199. Newark, DE: International Reading Association.

Pressley, Michael, and Peter Afflerbach. 1995. *Verbal Protocols of Reading: The Nature of Constructively Responsive Reading.* Hillsdale, NJ: Erlbaum.

Prior, Jennifer. 2000. *Write Time for Kids: Nonfiction Reading and Writing Program.* Westminster, CA: Teacher Created Materials.

RAND Reading Study Group [RRSG]. 2002. *Reading for Understanding: Towards an R & D Program in Reading Comprehension.* Santa Monica, CA: RAND. http://www.rand.org/multi/ achievementforall/reading/readreport.html (accessed August 28, 2006).

Reinking, David. 1992. "Differences between Electronic and Printed Texts: An Agenda for Research." *Journal of Educational Multimedia and Hypermedia* 1:11–24.

Rosenblatt, Louise. 1985. "Viewpoints: Transaction versus Interaction—A Terminological Rescue Operation." *Research in the Teaching of English* 19: 96–107.

Spires, Hiller A., and Thomas H. Estes. 2002. "Reading in Web-Based Learning Environments." In *Comprehension Instruction: Research-Based Best Practices,* ed. Cathy C. Block and Michael Pressley, 115–125. New York: Guilford Press.

Sutherland-Smith, Wendy. 2002. "Weaving the Literacy Web: Changes in Reading from Page to Screen." *The Reading Teacher* 55: 662–669.

Ulijn, Jan M., and Judith B. Strother. 1995. *Communication in Business and Technology: From Psychological Theory of International Practice.* Frankfort: Peter Lang.

Wepner, Shelley B., and Liqing Tao. 2002. "From Master Teacher to Master Novice: Shifting Responsibilities in Technology Infused Classrooms." *The Reading Teacher* 55, no. 7: 642–651.

7

Literacy and Learning in a Digital World

Pam Berger

It's 6:30 A.M. Tuesday morning, and Felicia, a junior in high school, wakes up; she has at least an hour before she leaves for school. Still a little groggy from last night's sleep, she rubs her eyes and peers at the computer screen to see how many instant messages and e-mails have appeared. A few classmates tried to reach her. She clicks on her personal Weblog and quickly scans a mix of news, weather, and customized alerts. Her eye quickly goes to the *New York Times* headlines that are displayed on her homepage and she clicks on a link to an article on the greenhouse effect to read the full text. This article might be interesting for her science team that is researching global warming. Almost automatically, Jessica clicks on the "Furl It!" button on her toolbar to save it to the "Global Warming" folder, writes a brief note, and clicks on the save button. It's now archived and a link is sent to her teammates. She scans the rest of the page, smiles as she reads that it's going to be a sunny day since she plans to go to her brother's soccer game after school, and decides the rest of the links can wait till third period, when she has a break in her class schedule.

It's about 6:45 A.M. Felicia moves the books scattered around on her desk to make room for a bowl of cold cereal. She checks her social studies team wiki to see how much progress has been made on their collaborative immigration project; Jessica's team is focusing on nineteenth-century Chinese immigration. She worked on it for a few hours last night using a pathfinder, provided by the school librarian, that guided her through Web sites, subscription databases, online catalogs, search engines, and of course Google™. She was able to identify major legislation and locate a few articles and some primary sources, a few political cartoons, photos, letters, and so on, which she organized, annotated, and posted to the wiki. She updated the list of interview questions the team is planning to use to create MP3 interviews with some senior citizens in Chinatown.

It's getting late. She reads and posts to the Spanish class Weblog, uploads a current Hispanic news assignment she researched using Newseum.org that posts front pages from 552 newspapers from 50 countries every morning, and finishes her morning routine with a quick stop at MapQuest for driving directions to her brother's soccer game. With a few minutes left before she has to jump into the shower, she IMs her friend to tell him to look at the new photos she posted on Flickr and asks if he can meet her third period after science class. With time to spare, she closes her laptop computer, but doesn't log off—she is always connected 24/7.

The latest Pew Foundation research reflects Felicia's reality: youth are leading the transition to a fully wired and mobile nation (Rainie 2005). The majority of teens in the United States, 87 percent of those aged 12 to 17, use the Internet—that's 21 million youth. 75 percent of online teens or about two-thirds of all teenagers use instant messaging and 54 percent know more instant message (IM) screen names than home telephone numbers. The Internet is their primary communication tool: 70 percent use instant messaging to keep in touch and 56 percent of teens online prefer the Internet to the telephone (Rainie 2005). Teens are utilizing the interactive capabilities of the Internet as they create and share their own media creations. Fully half of the teens who use the Internet could be considered content creators (Lenhart and Madden 2005). The number of information tools and resources available to them is extraordinary: instant messages, blogs, RSS Feeds, podcasts, news alerts, wikis, e-mails, search engines, online catalogs, online image archives, digitized scholars' journals, primary sources, collaborative word processing tools, chat, and so on.

Today's secondary and even elementary schools are filled with students like Felicia who are good at multitasking and using technology in multiple ways. A recent Kaiser Family Foundation report, "Generation M: Media in the Lives of 8- to 18-Year-Olds," which surveyed more than 2,000 3rd through 12th grade students, found that almost "one third of young people say they either talk on the phone, instant message, watch TV, listen to music, or surf the Web for fun most of the time they're doing homework" (Rideout and Roberts 2005, 23).

Information and communications technology (ICT) is everywhere. According to Thomas Friedman, author of *The World is Flat,* "Never before in the history of the planet have so many people—on their own—had the ability to find so much information about so many things and about so many other people" (Friedman 2005, 152). Technologies' ubiquitous presence is evidenced in everything we do, including the way we locate information, communicate, write, learn, shop and even socialize. It is having a significant impact on the way we live and even on the notion of an educated person. Competence with ICT is seen as a perquisite for participation in society and the workplace. Considered as essential a life skill as reading and numeracy, knowledge of ICT along with a high degree of competency is required by most employers. According to a report from the Workforce Commission's Alliance of Business, "The current and future health of America's 21st century economy depends directly on how broadly and deeply Americans reach a new level of literacy—'21st Century Literary'" (21st Century Workforce Commission 2000, 8).

There is also a growing international acknowledgment of information and digital literacies. In the latest Pew Foundation research on the Internet, *The Future of the Internet II,* Internet leaders, activists, and analysts placed the highest priority on educating those not currently online (Anderson and Rainie 2006). World summits were held in Dublin and Egypt. The United Nations ICT Task Force global meeting in Dublin, Ireland in April 2005, "Harnessing the Potential of ICT for Education," examined the global crisis in education and proposed how information and communications technologies can provide solutions. Similar issues were addressed at the 2005 Information Literacy Meeting of Experts in Alexandria, Egypt organized by the U.S. National Commission on Library and Information Science and the National Forum on Information Literacy.

On a more grass roots level, a British research team developed and illustrated a nation-wide ICT neighborhood classification tool to profile the level of use and ICT competency ranging from "not at all interested" to "power users" (http://www.spatial-literacy.org/esocietyprofiler). Members of the public can enter their zip codes to find out about the likely use of ICT in their neighborhoods, or of those of their friends. At the same time Britain's National College for School Leadership has targeted administrators for their ICT strategic leadership initiative creating an extensive CD-ROM toolkit with 11 case studies, featuring in-depth interviews from leaders at these schools discussing innovative and practical approaches to sustaining improvement and attainment (http://www.ncsl.org.uk/programmes/slict/slict-sltt.cfm).

It is clear that today's technological environment offers new possibilities not only for teaching and learning, but in a larger arena of political participation, economic development, creation and sharing of content and ideas, and increased communications across continents, languages, and cultures. But it also brings with it fresh demands as we try to keep pace with the skills that must be learned to take advantage of these new opportunities. It is not enough for our students to be able to click and paste, download music files, play video games, and socialize via the Internet. Digital literacy skills go beyond that and incorporate the ability to locate, evaluate, organize, synthesize, and communicate information. School librarians have been teaching these skills for years, but the swift advances in technology have resulted in an abundance of new, often unfiltered text, images, videos, and multimedia information pouring into our schools and homes every day via new tools, software, and services. It is within this context that the meaning of literacy has come under examination. The evolution from a print-based information and communication environment to a digital one predicates an expansion of literacy's traditional definition, leading us to ask, what does it mean to be literate in a digital age?

LITERACY IN THE DIGITAL AGE: WHAT DOES IT MEAN TO BE LITERATE IN A DIGITAL AGE?

The literature abounds with definitions of digital literacy, as does the academic discourse on the digital future. Professionals in fields as diverse as history, philosophy, law, information science, and quantum physics have entered the conversation (see Figure 7.1). Paul Gilster (1997), in his cutting-edge book, *Digital Literacy,* defines it as "the ability to understand and use information in multiple formats from a wide variety of sources when it is presented via computers" (1). As he explains, literacy goes beyond simply being able to read with meaning and to understand. It involves cognition. In turn digital literacy is cognition of what you see on the computer screen and the ability to use this new information in your life. He identifies core competences of locating, evaluating, and organizing networked information and presents a new model that both creates and downloads information, offering new opportunities and challenges.

Kathleen Tyner presents a broader, historical view in her book, *Literacy in a Digital World* (1998), and speaks to the overlapping and confusion among the different literacies such as media literacy, visual literacy, information literacy, computer literacy, and so on. Rather than providing a definition, Tyner attempts to accurately represent literacy in the age of information by organizing these multi-literacies into two groups—tool literacies that encompass computer, network, and technology, and literacies of representation that include information, visual, and media. While each of these literacies has overlapping missions and skill sets, the core constituents of each literacy differ slightly and carry with it different jargon and assumptions (Tyner 1998).

Figure 7.1
The Digital Future

In 2004 and 2005, the Library of Congress's John W. Kluge Center hosted a series of eight (video) discussions to examine how the digital age is changing the most basic ways information is organized and classified. Archived video segments can be viewed at: http://www.c-span.org/congress/digitalfuture.asp.

Speakers included:

- David Weinberger, Research Fellow at the Berkman Center for Internet and Society at the Harvard Law School, and one of North America's best-known experts on "blogging." Weinberger is coauthor of the bestselling book, *The Cluetrain Manifesto* (2000), author of *Small Pieces, Loosely Joined: A Unified Theory Of The Web* (2002), a frequent commentator on National Public Radio's "All Things Considered" and "Here and Now," and has been published in many magazines including *Wired* and the *Harvard Business Review.*

- Brewster Kahle, Digital Librarian, Director and Co-founder of the Internet Archive. Kahle developed the idea and tools to archive the Web. The title of his talk was "Universal Access to Knowledge."

- Juan Pablo Paz, a quantum physicist from Buenos Aires, currently working at Los Alamos. He discussed how quantum computing, now in its development stages, will eventually change the way we collect, store, and distribute information.

- Brian Cantwell Smith, Dean of the Faculty of Information Studies at the University of Toronto and the author of *On the Origin of Objects* (1996). Smith combines degrees in computer science and philosophy and is an expert on the interdisciplinary convergence brought about by digitization. His talk was titled, "And Is All This Stuff Really Digital After All?"

- David M. Levy, professor at the Information School of the University of Washington. Levy, author of *Scrolling Forward: Making Sense of Documents in the Digital Age* (2001), discussed the shift of the experience of reading from the fixed page to movable electrons and the effect that has had on language.

- Lawrence Lessig, professor of law at Stanford Law School and founder of the Stanford Center for Internet and Society, is the author of *Code and Other Laws of Cyberspace* (1999) and an expert on the issues of copyright and "copyleft." He is the inventor of the revolutionary concept and application Creative Commons, which invites the right to use material under specific conditions.

- Edward L. Ayers, Dean of the College and Graduate School of Arts and Sciences at the University of Virginia, is the author (with Anne S. Rubin) of *The Valley of the Shadow: Two Communities in the American Civil War* (http://valley.vcdh.virginia.edu/). Among the questions Ayers addresses are the implications for the creation and distribution of knowledge in today's digital environment.

- Neil Gershenfeld, Director of the Center for Bits and Atoms at the Massachusetts Institute of Technology. Gershenfeld is the author of *When Things Start to Think* (1999). His new concept Internet Zero (0) proposes a new infrastructure for the existing Internet that would give an IP address to all electronic devices—from light bulbs to Internet addresses and URLs—and interconnect them directly, thereby eliminating much intermediating code and server technology. His topic is "From the Library of Information to the Library of Things."

In 2003, a panel of academic librarians, faculty members, and administrators from seven universities, who were the charter members of the Educational Testing Service (ETS) National Higher Education ICT Literacy Project, focused on the cognitive, ethical, and technical abilities necessary to be digitally literate, and defined digital literacy as "the ability to use digital technologies, communication tools and/or networks to solve information problems in an information society. This includes the ability to use technology as a tool to research, organize, evaluate and communicate information and the possession of a fundamental understanding of the ethical/legal issues surrounding the access and use of information" (Brasley 2006, 7).

A similar but shorter definition was developed by the International ICT Literacy Panel: "ICT is using digital technology, communications tools and /or networks to access, manage, integrate, evaluate and create information in order to function in a knowledge society" (International ICT Literacy Panel 2002, 10).

Digital literacy, or for that matter, information literacy, is not without competing terms. Information Fluency, a term that grew out of the 1999 National Research Council (NRC) report, "Being Fluent with Information Technology," is gaining in popularity to describe proficiency in understanding today's information world. "People fluent with information technology (FIT persons) are able to express themselves creatively, to reformulate knowledge, and to synthesize new information. Fluency with information technology (i.e., what this report calls FITness) entails a process of lifelong learning in which individuals continually apply what they know to adapt to change and acquire more knowledge to be more effective at applying information technology to their work and personal lives" (National Research Council 1999, 14). Fluency with information technology requires three kinds of knowledge:

- *Contemporary skills:* The ability to use today's computer applications, which enable people to apply information technology immediately. In the present labor market, skills are an essential component of job readiness. Most importantly, skills provide a store of practical experience on which to build new competence.

- *Foundational concepts:* The basic principles and ideas of computers, networks, and information, which underpin the technology. Concepts explain the how and why of information technology and give insight into its opportunities and limitations. Concepts are the raw material for understanding new information technology as it evolves.

- *Intellectual capabilities:* The ability to apply information technology in complex and sustained situations, which encapsulate higher-level thinking in the context of information technology. These capabilities empower people to manipulate the medium to their advantage, to handle unintended and unexpected problems when they arise, and to engage in more abstract thinking about information and its manipulation.

The Illinois Mathematics and Science Academy's 21st Century Information Fluency Project defines Digital Information Fluency (DIF) as "the ability to find, evaluate and use digital information effectively, efficiently and ethically. DIF involves knowing how digital information is different from print information; having the skills to use specialized tools for finding digital information; and developing the dispositions needed in the digital information environment" (IMSA 2006). In using the term, Digital Information Fluency, IMSA argues that DIF is not as broad a concept as Information Literacy but includes aspects of both Information Literacy and Technology Literacy. They use the term to focus on the knowledge, skills, and dispositions that people need to locate, evaluate, and use digital information efficiently and effectively. They call it "fluency" rather than "literacy" to emphasize that the abilities involved are more than basic abilities (IMSA 2006).

A very different approach to defining digital literacy was taken by the Center for Children and Technology in a one-year research study of children's computer use. They found digital literacy is best viewed as a set of habits children use in their interaction with information technologies for learning, work, and fun. They include the following five dimensions:

- Their *troubleshooting* strategies;
- The range of *purposes* connected to their computing;

- Their skills in *using common tools* such as word processing, email and web searching;
- Their *communication literacy*—how they use email, Instant Messaging, and other tools to talk to peers and adults; and
- Their *web literacy*—how they use the web to find, cull and judge information and their skill at creating web-based materials (Ba, Tally, and Tsikalas 2002, 6).

The ambiguity found in the literature sometimes leads to misunderstandings and misconceptions as some authors restrict the concept to the technical aspects of operating in digital environments and focus on networking, hardware, and software, while others apply it in the context of cognitive and social aspects of work in a digital environment. In most situations, definitions of digital literacy develop depending upon an individual's personal perspective and area of study—media studies, computers and technology, librarianship, and so on. In some education circles, confusion arises from a lack of understanding of the relationship between basic literacy (reading) and information literacy. Traditional information literacy skills—the ability to locate, evaluate, organize, and communicate information—have been repositioned as "new" literacies that students need to read and comprehend information via the Internet (PRNewswire 2006). Not surprisingly, the skills needed for the "new literacies" are the same that we have needed for all information formats, as outlined in the AASL/ AECT Information Power Standards (American Association of School Librarians 1998).

Digital literacy, information literacy, and information fluency (with sub-terms such as media literacy or visual literacy), then, are terms that often overlap, interact, and share common meanings, which is indicative of the newness of this phenomenon. The lack of extensive research related to digital literacy and its impact on the learner helps explain such variations and redundancies. One thing is certain, information and communications technologies are raising the bar on the competencies needed to succeed in the twenty-first century, and they are compelling us to revisit many of our assumptions and beliefs (New Media Consortium 2005).

Within the debate on twenty-first-century literacy there is also agreement on a number of points:

- Individuals, in light of the continual development of digital technology, are required to use a growing variety of technical, cognitive, and social skills in order to perform and solve problems in digital environments.
- Literacy is evolving and the notions of what we think is literacy is changing as a result of the development and use of information and communications technology.
- Literacy, in any form, advances a person's ability to effectively and creatively use and communicate information.

Perhaps in the future it will be understood that the term literacy encompasses all the processes needed to function effectively in a digital environment—with all its complexity. And meanwhile, although confusion between the multiple literacies sometimes creates contention, it also enriches the debate.

LEARNING IN A DIGITAL ENVIRONMENT: HOW IS LEARNING DIFFERENT IN A DIGITAL AGE?

Just as basic literacy means more than just decoding alphabetic symbols, digital literacy involves more than the mere ability to use software or operate a digital device; it includes a variety of technical, cognitive, social, and emotional skills that users need in order to function effectively in a digital environment. In effect, because technology makes the simple tasks easier, it places a great burden on higher level skill (International ICT Literacy Panel 2002). The skills required in this context include the ability to "read" instructions from graphical displays; to navigate effectively; to construct knowledge from a nonlinear, hypertext navigation system; to evaluate the quality and validity of information; to stay focused; and to understand the rules of cyberspace, to name just a few. These have become survival skills for learners to participate in knowledge-construction tasks in a digital environment.

Graphic literacy—thinking visually: The nature of literacy is changing; it includes not only text but also symbols and visual images or icons that make up graphic user interfaces. Students need to learn the language of screen literacy and to develop the skills to understand the instructions and messages represented visually. Research tells us those users who are highly proficient employ a unique form of digital literacy called photo-visual literacy with strong intuitive-associative thinking that helps them to "read" intuitively and freely (Eshet-Alkalai 2004).

Navigation—developing a sense of Internet geography: The hypertext environment of the Internet is a powerful learning environment; however, users are faced with many challenges. "From the educational perspective, the central importance of hypermedia-based environment lies not necessarily in the multitasking capabilities that it offers users, but in the possibility of using such environments for associative, branching and non-linear navigation through different knowledge domains" (Eshet-Alkalai 2004, 99). Hypertext environments provide students with a high degree of freedom in navigating through large amounts of information but also present them with problems arising from the need to construct knowledge from large quantities of independent pieces of information reached in a nonlinear, unorganized manner. Transition from linear to nonlinear environments requires users to develop thinking skills that are characterized by a good sense of multimedia spatial orientation; simply stated—not getting lost when you click from one Web site or page to another.

Often we find that "digital natives" are more intuitive than the "digital immigrants," those who did not grow up with technology (Prensky 2001). "Web-smart kids hone their judgment skills through experience and triangulation as they surf the sheer scope and variety of resources the Web presents, the magnitude of which largely befuddles the non-digital adult" (Brown, 2006, 70). Students, ages 7 to 12, who worked on the International Children's Digital Library (htttp:/www.icdlbooks.org) development team, for example, understood this issue and initiated the design of a screen reader, the Spiral Reader, so that users would have a "sense of place" or visual context while reading a digital book.

Context—seeing the connections: A hypermedia environment encourages nonlinear exploration, but unfortunately it does not provide a context to critically investigate a subject. Unlike a printed book that contains a table of contents and an index to assist the reader to delve deeper and understand the relationships and connections among subtopics, Internet resources are viewed out of context. Students often collect lots of independent pieces of information with no depth to their inquiry. Hypermedia environments encourage broad accumulation of information, but not necessarily deep exploration. Sometimes students link only to resources from one Web site, which might produce the quantity of information needed but could also present a narrow, biased glimpse of a subject.

Focus—practicing reflection and deep thinking: A digital environment offers a multitude of distractions and tends to fragment our attention. When a task is difficult, we naturally tend to succumb to these distractions, and when sitting at a computer they are not only easily available but enticing—checking e-mail, Googling, iTunes, instant messaging, and so on. Deep reading and reflection are necessary for associative thinking, synthesis, and understanding. We need to address these issues and find remedies to guide students to focus and think deeply.

Skepticism—learning to evaluate information: With the rapid growth of information, the ability of users to evaluate and use information competently is a key issue in developing digitally literate students. The need to evaluate information is not unique to the digital age; it has always been part of the information literacy curriculum. Not surprisingly, the criteria needed to determine the quality and credibility of online information are identical to those required for evaluating information found in other forms of communications: accuracy, authority, objectivity, currency, relevance, and coverage of scope (Berger 1998). However, it takes on urgency because of the sheer quantity of information produced daily and the lack of safeguards that publishing houses provide with print media. Students need to develop a sense of skepticism and hone their judgment skills when locating Web-based information to detect erroneous, irrelevant, or biased information. According to Gilster (1997), making educated judgments about what we find on the Internet is the most critical of all the digital-age skills.

Ethical behavior—understanding the rules of cyberspace: Students need to know how to use technology responsibly and thoughtfully, as well as how to protect their safety, security, and privacy online. Ethics and citizenship in cyberspace includes respect for digital property, an understanding of the special privileges and responsibilities of online communication, and the critical thinking and decision-making skills to manage one's actions in cyberspace.

INFORMATION AND COMMUNICATIONS TECHNOLOGY REFORM: HOW IS THE EDUCATION AND LIBRARY FIELD ADDRESSING ICT REFORM?

There is widespread awareness that the advancements in information and communications technology have profound implications for education and that schools must change to meet the needs of the twenty-first-century learners. Policy makers, administrators, and educators all agree that ICT competency is essential for individuals in a democratic society; however, the major thrust of the reform movement has not been initiated from within education, which makes it different in many respects from previous reforms. The impetus to integrate ICT has come from outside the world of education and primarily focuses on economic, social, and pedagogical reasons. The economic focuses on employability asserts that nations embracing ICT will benefit economically; the social aspect argues that facility with ICT is a prerequisite for participation in society and the workplace; and the pedagogical highlights examples of the integration of ICT into schools and curriculum that support the development of higher-order thinking skills, increased motivation, and deeper learning. And although there is growing convergence between these rationales, especially since ICT is needed in our contemporary work lives and leisure activities, as yet there is not a clear understanding of how this reform should take shape. Implementation on the school level is further compounded by the fact that those who are being taught are often more comfortable with the changes than those who are teaching and implementing the changes.

ICT Frameworks and Assessments

In this section, several frameworks, assessments, tutorials, and white papers that have been created by educational coalitions, professional organizations, and universities will be reviewed. Each of these seeks to provide educators with guidelines, strategies, and/or tools that will enable them to infuse twenty-first-century literacy skills across the curriculum.

Framework for 21st Century Learning Skills, developed by the Partnership for 21st Century Skills (http://www.21stcenturyskills.org/index.php), focuses on six primary areas: core subjects, twenty-first-century content, learning and thinking skills, ICT literacy, life skills, and twenty-first-century assessments (see Figure 7.2).

As a leading advocacy organization focused on infusing twenty-first-century skills into education, the organization brings together the business community, education leaders, and policymakers to define a vision for twenty-first-century education to ensure every child's success as a citizen and worker in the twenty-first century. The partnership encourages schools, districts, and states to advocate for the infusion of twenty-first-century skills into education and provides tools and resources to help facilitate and drive change. In addition to the frameworks, they have developed:

Learning for the 21st Century: A Report and MILE Guide for 21st Century Skills, which articulates a collective vision for learning in the twenty-first century and provides a self-assessment tool that assists schools, districts, and states in determining their progress in defining, teaching, and assessing twenty-first-century skills.

Route 21: An Interactive Guide to 21st Century Learning: A Web-based tool that assists education stakeholders in supporting and promoting achievement of ICT Literacy and twenty-first-century skills. As a result, users can develop and implement a plan to support a successful twenty-first-century learning environment.

The Road to 21st Century Learning: A Policymakers' Guide to 21st Century Skills: The report offers specific guidance and policy recommendations to help create a twenty-first-century learning environment. Its aim is to assist state education leaders in crafting visionary education policies.

ICT Literacy Maps: A series of matrices illustrates the intersection between Information and Communication Technology Literacy and core academic subjects including geography, math, English, and science. The maps enable educators to gain concrete examples of how ICT Literacy can be integrated into core subjects.

enGauge 21st Century Skills (http://www.ncrel.org/engauge), a framework and Web-based assessment tool to help schools and districts understand and plan to improve all aspects of the use of educational technology was created by the North Central Regional Educational Laboratory (NCREL). It is composed of Six Essential Conditions for Effective Technology Use and 21st Century Skills. Each skill cluster is further broken down into representative skill sets, which offer guidance on recognizing student performance in developing the twenty-first-century skills (see Figure 7.3).

The 21st Century Information Fluency Project (http://21cif.imsa.edu/), established by the Illinois Mathematics and Science Academy, a pioneering educational institution created by the state of Illinois to develop talent and leadership in mathematics, science, and technology, has developed the Digital Information Fluency (DIF) model to find, evaluate, and use digital information effectively, efficiently, and ethically (see Figure 7.4).

The project also includes a series of tools, tutorials, and resources:

The Wizard Tools are a "one stop shop" to help you become an effective power searcher. The tools are to be used as you move through the main phases of the digital information fluency process and make it easy to teach the essential steps of locating, evaluating, and ethically using digital resources.

The Keyword Blog: A Few Key Words about Searching. This blog, hosted by the 21st Century Information Fluency Project, posts weekly updates about digital information fluency and includes podcasts, resources, and relevant links.

Figure 7.2
Framework for 21st Century Learning Skills

1. **Core subjects.** The No Child Left Behind Act of 2001, which reauthorizes the Elementary and Secondary Education Act of 1965, identifies the core subjects as English, reading or language arts; mathematics; science; foreign languages; civics; government; economics; arts; history; and geography.

2. **21st century content.** Several significant, emerging content areas are critical to success in communities and workplaces. These content areas typically are not emphasized in schools today, and include: global awareness; financial, economic, business and entrepreneurial literacy; civic literacy; and health and wellness awareness.

3. **Learning and thinking skills.** As much as students need to learn academic content, they also need to know how to keep learning—and make effective and innovative use of what they know—throughout their lives. Learning and thinking skills are comprised of:

   - Critical-thinking and problem-solving skills
   - Communication skills
   - Creativity and innovation skills
   - Collaboration skills
   - Contextual learning skills
   - Information and media literacy skills

4. **ICT literacy.** Information and communications technology (ICT) literacy is the ability to use technology to develop 21st century content knowledge and skills, in the context of learning core subjects. Students must be able to use

   technology to learn content and skills—so that they know *how* to learn, think critically, solve problems, use information, communicate, innovate and collaborate.

5. **Life skills.** Good teachers have always incorporated life skills into their pedagogy. The challenge today is to incorporate these essential skills into schools deliberately, strategically and broadly. Life skills include:

   - Leadership
   - Personal responsibility
   - Ethics
   - People skills
   - Accountability
   - Self-direction
   - Adaptability
   - Social responsibility
   - Personal productivity

6. **21st century assessments.** Authentic 21st century assessments are the essential foundation of a 21st century education. Assessments must measure all five results that matter—core subjects; 21st century content; learning and thinking skills; ICT literacy; and life skills. To be effective, sustainable and affordable, assessments must use modern technologies to increase efficiency and timeliness. Standardized tests alone can measure only a few of the important skills and knowledge students should learn. A balance of assessments, including high-quality standardized testing along with effective classroom assessments, offers students a powerful way to master the content and skills central to success.

Source: The Partnership for 21st Century Learning http://www.21stcenturyskills.org/documents/ Frameworkflyer092806.pdf. Reprinted with permission of The Partnership for 21st Century Learning.

Figure 7.3
EnGuage 21st Century Skills

Academic Achievement

Academic Achievement

Digital-Age Literacy

Basic, Scientific, Economic, and Technological Literacies

Visual and Information Literacies

Multicultural Literacy and Global Awareness

Inventive Thinking

Adaptability, Managing Complexity, and Self-Direction

Curiosity, Creativity, and Risk Taking

Higher-Order Thinking and Sound Reasoning

21st Century Learning

Effective Communication

Teaming, Collaboration, and Interpersonal Skills

Personal, Social, and Civic Responsibility

Interactive Communication

High Productivity

Prioritizing, Planning, and Managing for Results

Effective Use of Real-World Tools

Ability to Produce Relevant, High-Quality Products

Academic Achievement

MicroModules Tutorials are self-paced, on-demand learning experiences each tailored to a specific topic. They are designed as 10–15-minute tutorials and some contain audio and/or video segments to communicate key concepts.

Search Challenges Tutorials test your strategies and tactics as you attempt to solve Internet research problems efficiently and effectively. They combine play and performance while you sharpen your power searcher skills.

Syracuse University's Center for Digital Literacy (CDL) (http://digital-literacy.syr. edu/) is an interdisciplinary, collaborative research and development center dedicated to understanding the impact of information, technology, and media literacies on children and adults in today's technology-intensive society. They welcome faculty, students, and organizations within and outside of Syracuse University to work with them on CDL projects and activities. A sampling includes:

Enriching Literacy through Information Technology (E*LIT), organized and managed entirely by Syracuse University students. E*LIT is intended to help children (K–12) in Central New York (and beyond) understand the synergy between technology and literacy. This event has been highly successful in motivating children to read, to work collaboratively, and to use technology in productive ways.

S.O.S. for Information Literacy, a six-year project dedicated to improving the teaching of information literacy and research skills of students at both the K–12 and college levels, through the development of a freely-accessible, Web-based, multimedia database of motivating, tried-and-true lesson plans, contributed by and shared among classroom teachers

Figure 7.4
Digital Information Fluency Model

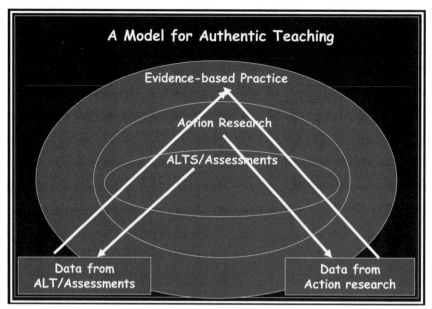

Source: Illinois Mathematics and Science Academy. http://21cif.imsa.edu/resources/difcore/. Reprinted with permission of IMSA.

and library media specialists throughout the world. The project includes a free, online, multimedia magazine called *Educators' Spotlight Digest* (www.sosspotlight.org), which includes articles by national leaders, educators, and graduate students on a variety of topics related to twenty-first-century literacies.

National Educational Technology Standards (NETS) was developed by the International Society for Technology in Education (ISTE). The standards guide educational leaders in recognizing and addressing the essential conditions for effective use of technology to support pre-K–12 education.

> *Technology Foundation Standards for Students* describe what students should know about technology and be able to do with technology.

> *Connecting Curriculum and Technology Standards* provide curriculum examples of effective use of technology in teaching and learning.

> *Educational Technology Support Standards* describe standards for professional development, systems, access, and support services essential to support effective use of technology.

> *Standards for Student Assessment and Evaluation of Technology Use* describe various means of assessing student progress and evaluating the use of technology in learning and teaching.

Educational Testing Service (ETS) Information and Communications Technologies Literacy Assessment (http://www.ets.org) is a fee-based, comprehensive test of information and communication technology proficiency that uses scenario-based tasks to measure both cognitive and technical skills. It measures a student's ability to use critical thinking to define, access, manage, integrate, evaluate, create, and communicate information in a technological environment. Test takers are asked to perform 15 information management tasks—such as extracting information from a database, developing a spreadsheet, or composing an e-mail summary of research findings—in a simulated online testing environment. Currently the test is being marketed to higher education, although it has been field tested in a small number of high schools (see Figure 7.5).

Figure 7.5
Educational Testing Service ICT Information Literacy Assessment

The 75-minute test assesses the following ICT proficiencies:

Define: The ability to use ICT tools to identify and appropriately represent an information need. Activities include:

- Creating an academic research topic to fit a particular information need
- Asking questions to clarify a customer's information need
- Completing a concept map

Access: The ability to collect and retrieve information in digital environments. This includes the ability to identify likely digital information sources and to get the information from those sources. Activities include:

- Searching through databases for information
- Browsing through linked Web sites for information
- Locating information through online Help
- Downloading and installing a (simulated) video player

Manage: The ability to apply an existing organizational or classification scheme for digital information. This ability focuses on reorganizing existing digital information from a single source using existing organizational formats. It includes the ability to identify existing organization schemes, select appropriate schemes for the current usage, and apply the schemes. Activities include:

- Sorting e-mails into appropriate folders
- Re-ordering a table to maximize efficiency in two tasks with incompatible requirements
- Documenting relationships using an organization chart

Integrate: The ability to interpret and represent digital information. This includes the ability to use ICT tools to synthesize, summarize, compare and contrast information from multiple digital sources. Activities include:

- Synthesizing information from IMs into a word-processing document
- Comparing and contrasting information from Web pages in a spreadsheet

Evaluate: The ability to determine the degree to which digital information satisfies the needs of the task in ICT environments. This includes the ability to judge the quality, relevance, authority, point of view/bias, currency, coverage or accuracy of digital information. Activities include:

- Selecting the best database for an information need
- Determining the sufficiency (or lack) of information in a Web site, given the information need
- Ranking Web pages in terms of meeting particular criteria
- Determining the relevance of postings on a Web discussion board

Create: The ability to generate information by adapting, applying, designing or inventing information in ICT environments. Activities include:

- Creating a graph that supports a point of view
- Selecting text and graphics that support a point of view

(Continued)

Figure 7.5
Educational Testing Service ICT Information Literacy Assessment *(Continued)*

Communicate: The ability to communicate information properly in its context of use for ICT environments. This includes the ability to gear electronic information for a particular audience and to communicate knowledge in the appropriate venue. Activities include:

- Formatting a word processing document
- Recasting an e-mail
- Adapting presentation slides
- Preparing a text message for a cell phone

Source: Educational Testing Service (ETS). http://www.ets.org. Reprinted by permission of Educational Testing Service, the copyright owner. However, any other information provided in their entirety by Libraries Unlimited. No endorsement of this publication by Educational Testing Service should be inferred.

Standardized Assessment of Information Literacy Skills (Project SAILS) (http://www.projectsails.org) is a fee-based Web tool created by Kent State University to document information literacy skill levels for groups of student and to pinpoint areas for improvement. It is modeled on the Association of College and Research Libraries (ACRL) standards (http://www.ala.org/ala/acrl/acrlstandards/informationliteracycompetency.htm).

THE ROLE OF THE SCHOOL LIBRARY: HOW CAN SCHOOL LIBRARIANS TAKE A LEADERSHIP ROLE IN PREPARING STUDENTS FOR THE TWENTY-FIRST CENTURY?

Information and communications technology reform is different from other school reforms in that it both underlines a need for curriculum change and provides the means by which the desired change can be achieved. If we view teaching and learning as more than just delivery and consumption of information, then we see a vision of the library as a place that supports learning as a social process that focuses on the learner, interacting with other learners and resources, to create meaning. Information and communications technologies provide school librarians the opportunity to become leaders, advocates, and change agents willing to embrace the digital environment to ensure that students and staff are effective users of ideas and information.

Change has to come from within as a grass roots effort, and school librarians need to lead these efforts as mentors and coaches to the faculty. Competency begins with understanding, and school librarians are in the ideal position as they collaborate with teachers to reflectively question how they can effectively integrate and use new technologies in their teaching and learning. Web 2.0, the term coined for the next generation Web, moves the Internet from being simply Web sites and search engines to a shared network space that offers students a place to publish and broadcast their own writing, collaborate on projects, and engage in conversations. Students with their mobile and non-mobile devices—cell phones, MP3 players, laptops, digital cameras, computers, and so on are always online and connected to one another and to the Web. The first traces of Web 2.0 are appearing in the form of classroom blogs and wikis and Web sites such as Flickr, MySpace, and LibraryThing—displaying the Web 2.0 principles of interactivity, user participation, and collective intelligence. School librarians need to help teachers and administrators understand that the new media "is nothing if not simply another way of viewing our world, of interacting with one another, of opening ourselves to learning in realms of possibilities we never conceived of before" (Jones-Kavalier and Flannigan 2006, 10). Action steps school librarians can use to take a leadership role include:

Action Step 1: Create a shared vision for learning in the twenty-first century with students, faculty, administrators, and parents.

- Create a wiki or a blog to share opinions and encourage discussion.
- Hold a World Café (http://www.theworldcafe.com/worldcafe.html) to encourage dialogue and identify important questions.

Action Step 2: Revisit your information literacy skills curriculum.

- Integrate new technologies into the information literacy skills.
- Recruit the library advisory team to take an active role in integrating ICT into the curriculum and the library program by analyzing where and how the new technologies can be effectively integrated and taught.

Action Step 3: Create an awareness of the need for digital literacy.

- Survey your students' and faculty's perception of their ICT competencies. Compare the findings to the latest research (http://www.pewinternet.org/) and share the results. Use the results to target your instruction and professional development.
- Create a special section on your library Web site to explore digital literacy with links to research, current articles, innovative technology, and so on.

Action Step 4: Ensure equity to all students by providing access to instruction and digital literacy tools.

- Work with the faculty to develop collaborative curriculum units integrating digital literacy skills.
- Work with administrators to help them understand the importance of a flexible schedule, and maintain updated technology in the library for all students to access.

Action Step 5: Support professional development in twenty-first-century skills for teachers, administrators, and parents.

- Organize ongoing workshops for teachers and administrators to integrate digital literacy skills into the curriculum and their practice.
- Recruit and train students to give one-on-one ICT support to teachers and administrators.
- Host a "cybercafé" for parents. Demonstrate the benefits of ICT to the teaching and learning process and share new ICT resources and information.

Action Step 6: Increase your ICT literacy—Embrace emerging technologies yourself!

- Create a library blog to share books.
- Use a wiki with groups of student researchers.
- Hold a podcast forum on a current issue important to the school community.
- Set up an RSS feed on your library Web site to highlight digital literacy issues.
- Use e-mail and instant messaging with students and faculty to support their information needs.
- Purchase audio books and MP3 and DVD players for student and faculty use.

CONCLUDING THOUGHTS

In October 2006, The MacArthur Foundation launched its five-year, $50 million digital media and learning initiative to help determine how digital technologies are changing the way young people learn, play, socialize, and participate in civic life. *Confronting the Chal-*

lenge of Participatory Culture: Media Education for the 21st Century, written by Henry Jenkins, Director of the Comparative Media Studies Program, MIT, the first white paper in a series to be published under the initiative, proposes "to shift the focus of the conversation about the digital divide from questions of technological access to those of opportunities to participate and to develop the cultural competencies and social skills needed for full involvement" (Jenkins 2006, 4). These skills build on the foundation of traditional literacy, research and information literary skills, technology skills, and critical thinking skills—the core skills of the school library program. This initiative is indicative of the growing awareness of the need to understand the impact of emerging technologies on literacy and learning. The conversations will intensify as we wrestle with the questions: What skills do students need to fully participate in the twenty-first century? How can we ensure that they develop these skills? School librarians can be the catalyst to gain a deeper understanding of these issues by taking a leadership role in their schools, actively engaging students, teachers, administrators, and parents in the conversation.

REFERENCES

21st Century Workforce Commission. 2000. *A Nation of Opportunity: Building America's 21st Century Workforce.* Washington, DC: Alliance of Business.

American Association of School Librarians and Association for Educational Communications and Technology. 1998. *Information Power: Building Partnerships for Learning.* Chicago: American Library Association.

Anderson, Janna, and Lee Rainie. 2006. *The Future of the Internet II.* http://www.pewinternet.org/ PPF/r/188/report_display.asp (accessed July 27, 2006).

Ba, Harouna, William Tally, and Kallen Tsikalas. 2002. "Investigating Children's Emerging Digital Literacies." *The Journal of Technology, Learning and Assessment* 1, no. 4: 3–9.

Berger, Pam. 1998. *Internet for Active Learners.* Chicago, IL: American Library Association.

Brasley, Stephanie Sterling. 2006. "Building and Using a Tool to Access Info and Tech Literacy." *Computers in Libraries* 25, no. 5: 6–7, 44–48.

Brown, John Seely. 2006. *Learning in the Digital Age.* http://www.johnseelybrown.com/ learning_ in_digital_age-aspen.pdf. (accessed July 27, 2006).

Brown, John Seely, and Paul Duguid, 2000. *The Social Life of Information.* Boston: Harvard Business School Press.

Eshet-Alkalai, Yoram. 2004. "Digital Literacy: A Conceptual Framework for Survival Skills in the Digital Age." *Journal of Educational Multimedia and Hypermedia* 13, no. 1: 93–106.

Friedman, Thomas L. 2005. *The World Is Flat: A Brief History of the Twenty-First Century.* New York: Farrar, Straus and Giroux.

Gershenfeld, Neil A. 1999. *When Things Start to Think.* New York: Henry Holt.

Gilster, Paul. 1997. *A Primer on Digital Literacy.* Mississauga, Ontario: John Wiley & Sons.

Illinois Mathematics and Science Academy (IMSA). 2006. *DIF FAQ.* http://21cif.imsa.edu/resources/ difcore/dif_faqs.htm (accessed April 10, 2006).

International Information and Communication Technologies (ICT) Literacy Panel. 2002. *Digital Transformation: A Framework for ICT Literacy.* Princeton, NJ: Educational Testing Services. http://www.ets.org/Media/Tests/Information and Communication (accessed April 10, 2006).

Jenkins, Henry. 2006. *Confronting the Challenge of Participatory Culture: Media Education for the 21st Century.* http://www.digitallearning.macfound.org (accessed November 15, 2006).

Jones-Kavalier, Barbara R., and Suzanne Flannigan. 2006. "Connecting the Dots: Literacy of the 21st Century." *Educause Quarterly* 29, no. 2: 7–10.

Lenhart, Amanda, and Mary Madden. 2005. *Teen Content Creators and Consumers.* Pew Internet & American Life Project. http://www.pewinternet.org/PPF/r/166/ report_display.asp. (accessed May 13, 2006).

Lessig, Lawrence. 1999. *Code: And Other Laws of Cyberspace.* New York: Basic Books.

Levine, Rick, and David Weinberger. 2000. *The Cluetrain Manifesto: The End of Business As Usual.* Cambridge, MA: Perseus Books.

Levy, David M. 2001. *Scrolling Forward: Making Sense of Documents in the Digital Age.* New York: Arcade Pub.

National Research Council. Committee on Information Technology Literacy. 1999. *Being Fluent with Information Technology.* Washington, DC: National Academy Press.

New Media Consortium (NMC). 2005. *A Global Imperative: The Report of the 21st Century Literacy Summit.* http://nmc.org/pdf/Global_Imperative.pdf (accessed April 10, 2006).

Prensky, Marc. 2001. "Digital Natives, Digital Immigrants." *On the Horizon* 9, no. 2: 1–6.

PRNewswire. 2006. *A New Type of Literacy For Children of the Digital Age.* http://biz.yahoo.com/prnews/060815/nyfnsh12.html?.v = 1 (accessed August 15, 2006).

Rainie, Lee. *The Internet at School.* 2005. Pew Internet & American Life Project. http://www.pewinternet.org/PPF/r/163/report_display.asp (accessed June 20, 2006).

Rideout, Victoria, and Donald F. Roberts. 2005. *Generation M: Media in the Lives of 8- to 18-Year-Olds.* Kaiser Family Foundation. http://www.kff.org/entmedia/upload/Executive-Summary-Generation-M-Media-in-the-Lives-of-8–18-Year-olds.pdf (accessed June 20, 2006).

Smith, Brian Cantwell. 1996. *On the Origin of Objects.* Cambridge, MA: MIT Press.

Tyner, Kathleen. 1998. *Literacy in a Digital World.* Mahwah, NJ: Lawrence Erlbaum Associates.

Weinberger, David. 2002. *Small Pieces, Loosely Joined: A Unified Theory of the Web.* New York: Perseus Books.

Part IV

Serving Diverse Student Populations

8

Special Education and Inclusion: Opportunities for Collaboration

Mary Jo Noonan and Violet H. Harada

Since the passage of the Education for All Handicapped Children Act of 1975 (PL 94–142), students with disabilities in the United States have been provided with special education in the public schools. The special education law, renamed the Individuals with Disabilities Education Act (IDEA) in 1990, defines special education as "specially designed instruction, at no cost to parents, to meet the unique needs of a child with a disability" (U.S. Government 1997). Special education is made available to school-aged students, ages 3 to 21, who meet the eligibility criteria associated with one of 13 disability categories *and* need special education and related services to benefit from their education. The disability categories are autism, deaf-blindness, deafness, emotional disturbance, hearing impairment, mental retardation, multiple disabilities, orthopedic impairment, other health impairment, specific learning disability, speech or language impairment, traumatic brain injury, and visual impairment including blindness. *Related services* are additional supports, such as speech therapy, physical therapy, or counseling, that are necessary in order for a student to benefit from education.

Approximately nine percent of children ages 3–21 receive special education (U.S. Department of Education, Office of Special Education and Rehabilitative Services, Office of Special Education Programs 2005), and about 90 percent of these students have *mild to moderate* disabilities, such as speech or language impairments, learning disabilities, or mild mental retardation. During the school day, they may stand out from their peers because they learn more slowly or need special teaching techniques to be successful learners. Outside of school, however, many of these students appear to be typically developing children and are virtually indistinguishable from their age peers. A small percentage of students receiving special education have more noticeable and severe disabilities, such as severe mental retardation, multiple disabilities, deaf-blindness, or autism. Their special needs are more significant and affect all areas of development.

Regardless of the nature or severity of a student's disability, IDEA requires that special education be provided in the *least restrictive environment (LRE)*. The LRE provision states that students with disabilities may only be removed from the general education classroom if they are unable to benefit from instruction in that environment, even with the use of supplemental supports (such as modified educational materials or special instructional strategies). The intent is that the majority of students are educated with peers who do not have disabilities. Recent amendments to IDEA have emphasized that special education should be viewed as a set of services, *not* a place. Specifically, IDEA now clarifies that students with disabilities should have access to the general education curriculum. The implication of LRE and access to the general education curriculum for library media specialists is that students with disabilities participate with their nondisabled peers in library activities and can be taught the associated skills. This chapter provides an overview of special education reform and describes logistics and strategies for including students with disabilities in library media activities and instruction.

THE INCLUSION REFORM

Despite a legal mandate that students with disabilities be educated with their nondisabled peers and have access to the general education curriculum, it has been all too common for special education to be provided in *self-contained* classes—separate special education classes taught by special education teachers. The result is that students with disabilities have limited opportunities to socialize with their nondisabled peers. Furthermore, students in self-contained classrooms usually experience an atypical curriculum that is limited in scope, addressing primarily the goals from the students' Individualized Education Plans (IEPs). In some cases, the logic is that separate classes provide intensive instruction and prepare students for success in general education settings. Data indicate to the contrary, however: Once a student is placed in a special education setting, the likelihood of returning to the general education setting is slim (Edgar, Heggelund, and Fischer 1989).

In response to the continued segregation of students receiving special education, the *inclusion* reform emerged. *Inclusion,* sometimes referred to as *full inclusion,* means that *all* students receive *all* of their education in the general education setting (Lipsky and Gartner 1997). *Pull-out* for special services (as in *mainstreaming*) does not occur in the full inclusion model. Instead, all special education and related services are provided in the general education classroom. In addition to providing access to the general education curriculum, major rationales for the inclusion reform are:

1. *New knowledge and skills are best learned in the context where they are needed.* This addresses the concern that many students with disabilities have difficulty generalizing what they've learned from the instructional setting to natural settings where the skills are needed.

2. *Inclusion with nondisabled peers provides opportunities for observational learning.* General education classrooms provide competent peer models for students with disabilities. Research on imitation indicates that individuals tend to imitate others who are (a) perceived as more competent; (b) observed receiving reinforcement; (c) thought to have status; and (d) viewed as similar to them.

3. *Students with disabilities benefit socially from interactions with nondisabled peers.* Many students with disabilities also have social skill needs. The inclusive setting provides occasions

for observational learning of social skills as well as opportunities to form relationships with socially competent peers.

As the inclusion model becomes more prevalent, library media specialists will encounter students with a range of disabilities and educational needs as members of general education classrooms. The challenge, and opportunity, is for library media specialists to provide appropriate and effective resources, services, and instruction for this diverse student population.

SPECIAL EDUCATION SUPPORTS FOR INCLUSION

As discussed in the introduction to this chapter, to be eligible for special education services, students with disabilities must need specialized instruction or supports to benefit from their instruction. The goal is to provide an effective learning experience for the students with disabilities. Two types of supports for inclusion are curricular and instructional.

Curricular Supports

Curricular supports modify or change instructional content to increase a student's participation and learning. They make the content easier or more aligned with a student's learning style (e.g., adding pictorial cues may support a student who has a predominantly visual learning style). Modifications can simplify content or accentuate features of the curriculum. If a student is not reading on grade level, for example, a shorter reading assignment may simplify the activity. Another support to simplify the assignment would be to provide another version of the reading assignment with less complex grammar and easier vocabulary. A curricular support that changes the assignment might require that a student listens as a passage is read aloud and writes key words after each paragraph is read. Or instead of working with the same reading material as the rest of the class, a conceptually easier book on the same topic may be provided to the student with disabilities.

Instructional Supports

These supports are specialized teaching methods that have been effective in helping students with disabilities learn. Three instructional supports that have wide applicability across content areas and can be used with students of all ages and types of disabilities are (a) task analysis, (b) direct instruction, and (c) time delay. In *task analysis,* the skill or activity is broken down into its component steps. Teaching a skill or activity in a step-by-step manner makes a complex task achievable (Gold 1980). Think of a task analysis as an *instruction manual* or *recipe.* In applying task analysis to instruction, it might first be demonstrated as the student observes. In the library media center, a peer might explain the use of a video camera, step-by-step, to the student with disabilities. Next, the peer prompts the student with a few key words for each step of the task. This procedure is followed each time the student uses the camera. An alternative would be to provide the student with a written and/or pictorial list of the steps. In this way, the student self-instructs using the task analysis.

If a task analysis is very lengthy or complex, it may be taught (*chained*) one step at a time. In *forward chaining,* the student learns the first step and a teacher or peer completes the rest of the task. In backward chaining, all but the final step is provided, and the student is taught the final step first. As each step of the task analysis or chain is learned, the next is taught (progressing either forward or backward) and the student is required to perform the new step along with ones previously learned.

The second instructional support for including students with disabilities is *direct instruction* (Noonan 2006). In direct instruction, the student is provided with one or more prompts and is then expected to demonstrate the correct response. *Prompts* are anything that help a student respond correctly. Common types of prompts are verbal (*"Sound out each letter"*), gestural (a teacher points where the student should begin the task), visual (word, highlight, drawing, photograph), physical (hand-over-hand assistance), and auditory (audio-recorded directions). It is sometimes helpful to combine prompts, such as a verbal description while demonstrating a response. Good prompts are ones that are effective in helping a student demonstrate a correct response. If frequent errors occur, a different or additional prompt should be used. If the student responds incorrectly or partially, a correction procedure follows. A correction procedure is one or more additional prompts that virtually guarantee that the student will make a correct response. A correct response is followed by praise or positive feedback to ensure that the student recognizes that the response is correct.

Direct instruction procedures are implemented in exactly the same manner each time the skill or activity is taught. Consistent instruction is critical to the success of direct instruction. Student learning is monitored through data collection and the procedures are modified if the student doesn't make adequate progress.

Time delay, the third instructional support, is an instructional procedure that is designed to be error-free (Snell and Gast 1981; Touchette 1971). It is a form of direct instruction. In its simplest application, a *natural prompt* (the librarian's instructions to the group) is provided. If the student doesn't respond within four seconds, an *instructional prompt* that is highly likely to result in correct responding is provided. When a correct response occurs (either before or after the instructional prompt), the student is given praise or positive feedback. If the student doesn't know the correct answer, the student will wait for the prompt because the correct response is reinforced. As learning occurs, the student will anticipate the instructional prompt and respond prior to it (as in a *beat the clock* game). A benefit of time delay is that the special instructional procedure is automatically faded as the student learns to respond to natural prompts.

The three instructional supports just described—task analysis, direct instruction, and time delay—represent just a few of empirically demonstrated techniques that can be used to create an effective learning environment for students with disabilities in library media settings. Some additional instructional support strategies include the following:

- *Oral readings* help to uncover story structure.
- *Related or themed readings* allow children to improve their recall levels because of the repetition or sameness. It helps them build vocabulary.
- *Illustrated storybooks* allow focusing on pictures and narrowing of the avenue of referents.
- *Directive scaffolding,* sometimes referred to as IRE (initiation-response-evaluation), helps develop concepts and communication competence. Directive scaffolding is a series of questions asked in a reliable order. The inquiries provide cloze questions (reader pauses for the child to provide a response), binary choices (is it this or that), expansions (reader elaborates on child's response), and constituents, or wh-questions (who, what, where, when).
- *Interaction and movement* (songs, music, finger plays, stories) provide interesting, fun, and engaging situations for learning.

SUPPORTING SPECIAL EDUCATION STUDENTS: STRATEGIES FOR THE SCHOOL LIBRARY MEDIA SPECIALIST

Both the inclusion movement and school library reform efforts embrace similar visions: to provide all students with maximum access to learning and resources. The Information

Literacy Standards for Student Learning (AASL and AECT 1998) promote the importance of core skills that all students need to succeed in the digital information age. These skills include the ability to locate, retrieve, evaluate, and use information and ideas in meaningful ways. Library media specialists are essential partners in designing and implementing learning experiences that encourage special education students to practice these skills with their peers.

As teaching colleagues, library media specialists contribute valuable experiences in working with faculty across grade levels and departments. They are familiar with school-wide curricula and with a global network of resources to support various programs. In order to include students with disabilities in a meaningful way, many aspects of library activities should be considered, including instructional strategies, materials selection, and positive peer interaction. To address the numerous student, curriculum, and instructional factors associated with planning and implementing inclusion, a collaborative team approach, involving the general education teacher, special education professionals, and the library media specialist, is vital.

Collaborative Planning

A central requirement of IDEA is that each student who receives special education must have an IEP that delineates instructional objectives to meet his or her special learning needs. The majority of students in special education have *unique needs* in select areas (e.g., reading comprehension) rather than across the entire curriculum. It is critical for library media specialists to become informed of students' unique needs so they might assist students in mastering specific skills. For example, many areas of information literacy that are directly addressed in the library media center can be aligned with reading, writing, and oral communication skills. Collaborative planning to develop the IEP and provide instruction, therefore, is essential for integrating information literacy skills with the IEP goals so that the library media specialist can support and reinforce learning.

Collaborative planning for the IEP. When a student with disabilities has unique needs related to information literacy skills, the library media specialist should recommend incorporating the skill into an existing IEP goal or the creation of a new goal. For example, the library media specialist observes an elementary student with disabilities having difficulty using the online catalog to locate a book. She brings this to the attention of the team for discussion and inclusion in the student's IEP. Or the special education teacher observes that regularly occurring library activities, such as group assignments, would be a valuable context for addressing a student's skill need in language arts and thus suggests an IEP objective integrating language arts and information literacy skills.

An IEP goal should be stated as a measurable behavioral objective, such as, *When in the library media center, Lisa will use the online catalog to locate a book on the classroom's science topic. She will demonstrate this skill three times.* Behavioral objectives have three components: condition (*When in the library media center*), behavior (*Lisa will use the online catalog to locate a book on the classroom's science topic*), and criterion (*she will demonstrate this skill three times*). The condition describes the situation in which the skill must be demonstrated. The behavior is an observable response that is the focus of instruction. And the criterion describes the standard to which the skill must be demonstrated.

The keys to effective collaboration for IEP planning are three characteristics of the transdisciplinary team model (Lyon and Lyon 1980): *joint functioning, continuous staff development,* and *role release. Joint functioning* means that the team members work together whenever possible. In developing a goal related to information literacy for an IEP, the team members (including the student, parents, teachers, and library media specialist) construct the goal together by providing input from their various perspectives. For example, the general education teacher contributes information on the unit themes planned for the school year; the library media specialist informs the team of information retrieval skills that will be covered; the parent describes the student's related interests and information retrieval skills demonstrated on the home computer; and the special education teacher suggests two IEP objectives integrating the contributions of the team members. This is in contrast to other team models where the team members work independently and one professional synthesizes team member contributions.

In *continuous staff development,* team members assist one another in learning new skills. The library media specialist, for example, might instruct the special education teacher on how to develop a goal using digital video as an alternative communication mode for a student who has difficulty writing, and the special education teachers might assist the library media specialist in developing short term objectives that will lead to independence in using the digital video.

Finally, *role release* occurs when professionals assist team members in performing tasks that are typically associated with their discipline. For example, after participating on several IEP teams, the library media specialist might formulate and suggest an IEP objective—a task that is typically the responsibility of the special education teacher.

Collaborative planning for instruction. The transdisciplinary team model—including joint functioning, continuous staff development, and role release—is applicable to all collaborative teaming. When planning for instruction, the focus is on (a) addressing IEP objectives, (b) modifying curriculum, (c) identifying instructional strategies, (d) selecting and/or developing materials, (e) promoting full participation, and (f) facilitating peer interaction, rather than on developing the IEP objectives. Although the purpose of collaborative planning differs from developing IEP objectives, the way the team works together is the same.

Embedding. In addressing IEP objectives, the first concern in planning for instruction is usually accomplished by *embedding.* Embedding is providing specialized instruction targeting the IEP objective in the context of the general education lesson. Planning entails identifying (a) *when* instruction will occur; (b) *who* will provide the instruction; and (c) *how* the instruction will be provided.

In deciding *when* instruction will occur, the team discusses the lesson plan and identifies times where it seems to fit logically. Instruction is embedded several times, rather than once, so that a sufficient amount of teaching is provided. If enough opportunities for instruction do not seem to be naturally available, additional ones must be created or *engineered.* In planning to embed a communication objective *to request assistance when needed* during the library period, the team must identify times that the student is likely to need help (e.g., locating information in an online encyclopedia; understanding the Dewey Decimal arrangement of nonfiction resources). To engineer additional instructional opportunities, the team discusses how they might create the need for the student to request assistance (e.g., including a research question that requires use of an online encyclopedia; providing students with call numbers to locate nonfiction titles).

There are numerous options for *who* will provide the instruction: the library media specialist, the general educator, the special educator, an educational assistant, a related service specialist (e.g., a therapist), a peer, or the student (using self-instruction strategies). Returning to the example of *requesting assistance,* if the library media specialist is leading the lesson and students tend to look to her for direction, the team might decide that the library media specialist will provide the instruction. Another approach would be to teach two of the peers in the student's group to provide the instruction when it appears that assistance is needed.

Planning *how* instruction is provided involves delineating the teaching strategy that will be used for the embedded teaching opportunities. In the example discussed here, the special education teacher or speech pathologist may recommend research-supported teaching strategies designed specifically to teach students how to request assistance. If the focus of the IEP objective is an information literacy skill, the library media specialist may have an instructional strategy to suggest. As the teams' collaboration experience cumulates, role release may occur with team members suggesting strategies they have learned from other disciplines represented on their team.

Modifying curriculum. The second focus of collaborative planning is on modifying curriculum. Curriculum modification involves individualizing and altering what is taught so that it is at the appropriate instructional level for a student with disabilities. An appropriate instructional level is one that is challenging and attainable: it means that the content is neither too simple nor too difficult for the student to learn. Curriculum modifications are accomplished by simplifying a task, breaking it down into steps (task analysis) or changing the task. For example, while most students in the class are expected to write three paragraphs summarizing what they learned from their research activity, the student with disabilities is required to write one paragraph (simplification) or dictate a paragraph to a peer who types it (task change). In collaborating on curriculum modification, the library media specialist contributes expertise on the skills that she teaches and insures that modifications still address the objectives.

Identifying instructional strategies. In this third focus of collaborative planning for inclusion, the team works together to individualize teaching methods for students with disabilities who are likely to have difficulty learning through the teaching strategies selected for the overall lesson. For example, some students with disabilities can follow a sequence of directions if they are written down and accompanied by illustrative photographs. Other students may need the instruction presented in a totally different manner, such as observing a peer perform the task competently several times, or responding to step-by-step prompts provided by an adult assistant.

Selecting and developing resources. The fourth area of collaborative planning is selecting and/or developing materials. Materials are a critical component of teaching: they can influence student participation and include prompts to promote skill acquisition. For example, a high-interest low-readability book replete with detailed illustrations can engage a student who is a struggling reader and provide access to content that is otherwise beyond the student's understanding. While the special education teacher may be the team member who is most familiar with a student's special learning needs, the library media specialist can make valuable contributions in materials selection and development. The increasing range and availability of multimedia contributes significantly to options for instructional materials.

Promoting full participation. The fifth area of collaborative planning, promoting full participation, is essential to full inclusion. Also known as *engagement,* educational participation has been shown repeatedly to be a strong predictor of learning (Anderson 1976; McWilliam 1991; Walker and Hops 1976). Research indicates that the greater the amount of engaged time (or time on task), the greater the amount of learning. In collaborative planning, the team should always ask, "How can we ensure that *all* students fully participate in the lesson?" With full participation as the goal, library media specialists and teachers must observe and identify the types of activities, materials, teaching strategies, and learning arrangements associated with high levels (and low levels) of participation for each student with disabilities. This information can then be used in collaborative lesson planning. For example, the library media specialist observes that the student with disabilities remained engaged throughout the previous week's library activity when working on the computer. She suggests for the next week's lesson that this student complete an assignment using the computer, rather than paper and pencil, as a means for promoting engagement. In some cases, student response requirements will be individualized to promote engagement; in other cases, the overall lesson structure will be effective in keeping all students engaged. Many group activities, especially *cooperative learning group* structures, are effective in engaging diverse student groups.

Facilitating peer interaction. This sixth and final component of collaborative planning refers to instructional arrangements that encourage students without disabilities to communicate and work with their peers who have disabilities. Peer interaction can foster positive social relationships and support learning. Two ways to facilitate peer interaction are peer tutoring and collaborative learning groups. In peer tutoring, students teach one another, usually in dyads. Students generally enjoy working with their age-mates and may prefer peer tutoring to the more typical teacher-lecture format. An obvious arrangement in the inclusive setting is to have a peer without disabilities tutor a student with disabilities. For a student with severe disabilities, it may be necessary to teach the peer without disabilities to provide specific instructional prompts (Kohler and Strain 1997). Other arrangements can also be effective. For example, students working at the same level may tutor one another. Do not discount the possibility of a student with a disability tutoring a peer without disabilities. Oftentimes students with disabilities have areas of high competence related to their individual interests. Providing tutoring to their peers places them in the position of being *helpers* rather than *helpees*. Emphasizing a student's competence through peer tutoring arrangements not only contributes to learning, but also builds self-esteem.

Collaborative learning groups (Johnson and Johnson 1975, 1986; Putnam et al. 1989), the second strategy for promoting peer interaction, are a group instruction format with four essential elements:

1. *Positive interdependence:* Group members work together to achieve a common goal. Methods for facilitating positive interdependence include mutual goals; divisions of labor; materials, resources, or information divided among group members; role assignments; and joint rewards.

2. *Face-to-face communication:* Group members must interact and communicate with one another to accomplish their task. The task is structured so it is not possible for students to divide up responsibilities and then work independently.

3. *Individual accountability:* Each student is responsible for learning the assigned work and contributing to the group's effort. Individual accountability is usually ensured through individual grading (e.g., quiz) in addition to a group grade.

4. *Group process:* Students are taught and evaluated on their use of interpersonal and small-group skills, such as sharing and negotiating.

In planning cooperative learning groups, the first step is to decide on a theme or topic that will be the focus of the activity. Often this is a unit theme that the class is targeting. Next, clear academic and cooperative skill objectives are delineated. These will be the focus of instruction and evaluation in the lesson. A lesson plan is then developed. The plan describes the activity, what the students will do, and what the teachers and library media specialist will do to teach and support the activity. Students are then assigned to small groups and provided with an explanation of the lesson objectives and activity. If group members are assigned roles, the expectations of each role should be described. It is helpful to discuss the cooperative skill objectives in detail and with demonstrations. For example, if *negotiation* is an objective, it should be defined and discussed. The students can generate examples of the skill from home and their community. And finally, the teachers and students can role-play how negotiation might occur during the cooperative learning group activity. While the group activity is conducted, the teachers and library media specialist circulate among the groups and monitor that students are on task and using the cooperative skill. Following the activity, the class debriefs on the success of the activity and their experience with the cooperative skill. Individual and group performance is evaluated as specified in the lesson plan.

Collaborative Teaching

The library media specialist, general education teacher, and special education teacher should work together to provide instruction for students with disabilities. A collaborative approach with joint planning is important for several reasons. First, the team members have unique information—the library media specialist knows the information search process and the teaching techniques used with general education students, the general education teacher knows the grade level curriculum, and the special education teacher knows the individual students and the teaching accommodations that may facilitate learning. Second, the team members can promote generalization by assisting students to apply a skill to another setting or situation. Third, the library media specialist becomes one more adult with whom the special education student can interact and develop appropriate social skills. Several collaborative teaching models have been identified (Friend 2000; Friend and Cook 1996; Reinhiller 1996); two are particularly useful for including students with disabilities in library media activities. These are the co-teaching and consultation models.

Co-teaching

In the co-teaching model, the professionals conduct the lesson jointly. They take turns teaching and providing directions. If the professionals are new to teaming (or new to the particular partnership), they might script out their lesson in detail, specifying which professional conducts which parts of the lesson. As they gain experience as a team, they may plan and execute their roles more loosely, observing one another and stepping in to add clarity, an example, or an elaboration. Experienced co-teachers seem to teach together seamlessly.

Co-teachers each assume full responsibility for all students during the lesson. This means that the special education teacher does not focus solely on the students with disabilities, and the general education teacher and library media specialist do not focus solely on the general education students. *Role release,* described earlier in the discussion on professional collaboration, is essential for successful co-teaching.

Consultation

The second collaborative teaching model, consultation, occurs when one professional provides direct service and the other offers expertise. In the case of teachers and a library media specialist collaborating, each has expertise and could assume the role of consultant. In the classroom, for example, the library media specialist observes language arts instruction and suggests literature at varied reading levels to enrich the lesson. Or in the library media center, the special education teacher models *time-delay,* a special teaching strategy, to reduce a student's dependence on continuous teacher assistance.

Providing Resource Support

To ensure that special education students have appropriate access to a range of resources, the library media specialist must work in partnership with colleagues to review materials in a variety of formats and determine what might be appropriate for special education students. Materials should be selected in all types of formats: videos (both signed and closed captioned), audiocassettes, books, toys, games, computer software, puppets, magazines, and the appropriate equipment to make these materials accessible.

Considerations:

- Books: large-print, taped books, wordless picture books, big books, signed stories, books in Braille to meet the varying interests and skills levels of those with different abilities. Books to read aloud should include a good deal of figurative language (e.g., onomatopoeia), repetitive language, dialogue, and predictable plots. For the young, picture books with simple story structures and concise language make fiction easy to understand and enjoyable.

- Manipulatives: The specific learning need may suggest use of a manipulative item, such as a game, toy, or puppet, for development of fine motor skills, for social skills development, or as an aid to self-expression.

In general: Look for high-interest materials on popular topics. Materials should have clear pictures and photos, clean type, and plenty of white space on the page. Students with reading difficulties will require high-interest–low-vocabulary resources.

Assistive Technology

Assistive devices include portable amplifiers and assistive listening devices, captioned videos (for hearing impaired students), descriptive videos (for visually impaired students), and TV sets equipped to decode these captions. High-tech and low-tech devices for students with vision impairment include audiocassette recorders, magnifiers, braillers, and print-enlarging computers.

Issues of Access

Common concerns about technology and electronic accessibility in the library arise in terms of physical, sensory, and cognitive access for students with disabilities.

Physical access: Wheelchair accessibility is commonly addressed first in making libraries barrier-free. Other barriers such as space, architectural features, and furnishings also need attention. Motor impairments influence locomotion within the library and the ability to operate equipment such as the standard computer keyboard. Through a cooperative team approach, the proper seating and positioning of the student along with the appropriate computer access method (e.g., keyguard, alternative or expanded keyboard, touch screen, touch tablet/pad) can be designed to meet the student's needs.

Sensory access (vision and hearing): Many students need alternatives to conventional print. From infancy through early childhood years, toys and books for promoting sensory stimulation and physical activity are appropriate. For older students, nonprint displays of information (e.g., photos) are useful. For a visually impaired student, the optimal strategy includes a speech recognition system that enables access by voice commands and in which

Table 8.1.
Special Education Reform—Change Agent Strategies for School Library Media Specialists

Learning and Teaching

Collaborate with special education professionals and general education teachers to address IEP objectives, modify curriculum, and identify instructional strategies.

Collaborate with special education professionals and general education teachers to develop IEP goals related to information literacy and technology use.

Select and develop resources that meet the needs of special education students.

Facilitate peer interaction through the development of cooperative learning groups and peer tutoring programs.

Guide and assist teachers, students, and parents/guardians in the use of assistive technologies and media for teaching and learning.

Information Access and Delivery

Provide resources in a variety of formats.

Provide assistive technologies.

Establish and maintain ties with information resources and services in the community that can help meet the information needs of special education students.

Program Administration

Maintain an environment that meets the information needs of special education students through appropriate physical adaptations.

Collaborate with teachers and others to develop policies and procedures that provide appropriate access to services for special education students.

---

the information on the computer screen is accompanied by speech. For a hearing impaired students, multimedia applications that include information by both sound (e.g., music, narration) and pictures (art, maps) and those that are interactive, might be considered.

Cognitive access: Two challenges in using computer technology effectively are attention (creating an inability to follow screen prompts and commands, difficulty with multi-step procedures and busy screens, and difficulty with large amounts of computer speech or multimedia applications) and memory (creating difficulties with menus and recalling computer symbols or commands, inabilities in sequencing steps to complete commands, generalizing operations and procedures, and locating and recalling files).

Fostering Relationships

The library media specialist, in collaboration with the classroom teacher, may employ strategies to enhance informal peer support and friendships for students in integrated settings. Students who feel a sense of belonging and acceptance will have a better chance of success in all their educational pursuits.

Possible activities might target the following: sensitization activities (awareness of disabling conditions, respect for individual differences), direct instruction of social skills, and cooperative learning activities.

CONCLUSION

The focus of this chapter was special education reform, specifically inclusion. We described the rationale for inclusiveness and the strategies that help special education students acquire the cognitive and social skills for success in school and the future workplace. We then provided strategies school library media specialists can use to support special education students (see Table 8.1).

Library media specialists are in a strategic position to enrich the inclusive learning opportunities for special education students. By planning and working collaboratively with special education teachers, general education teachers, and additional personnel, they transform the library media center into an exciting laboratory for guided learning where special education students truly succeed.

REFERENCES

American Association of School Librarians, and Association for Educational Communications and Technology. 1998. *Information Power: Building Partnerships for Learning.* Chicago: American Library Association.

Anderson, Lorin W. 1976. "An Empirical Investigation of Individual Differences in Time to Learn." *Journal of Educational Psychology* 68, no. 2: 226–233.

Edgar, Eugene, Michael Heggelund, and M. Fischer. 1989. "A Longitudinal Study of Graduates of Special Education Preschools: Educational Placement after Preschool." *Topics in Early Childhood Special Education* 8, no. 3: 61–74.

Friend, Marilyn P. 2000. "Myths and Misunderstandings about Professional Collaboration." *Remedial and Special Education* 21, no. 3: 130–132.

Friend, Marilyn P., and Lynne Cook. 1996. *Interactions: Collaboration Skills for School Professionals.* 2nd ed. New York: Longman.

Gold, Marc W. 1980. *Try Another Way: Training Manual.* Champaign, IL: Research Press.

Johnson, David, and Roger Johnson. 1975. *Learning Together and Alone: Cooperation, Competition, and Individualization.* Englewood Cliffs, NJ: Prentice Hall.

Johnson, David, and Roger Johnson. 1986. "Mainstreaming and Cooperative Learning Strategies." *Exceptional Children* 52, no. 6: 553–561.

Kohler, Frank W., and Phillip S. Strain. 1997. "Merging Naturalistic Teaching and Peer-Based Strategies to Address the IEP Objectives of Preschoolers with Autism: An Examination of Structural and Child Behavior Outcomes." *Focus on Autism and Other Developmental Disabilities* 12, no. 4: 196–206.

Lipsky, Dorothy K., and Allen Gartner. 1997. *Inclusion and School Reform: Transforming America's Classrooms.* Baltimore, MD: Paul H. Brookes.

Lyon, Steve, and Grace Lyon. 1980. "Team Functioning and Staff Development: A Role Release Approach to Providing Integrated Educational Services for Severely Handicapped Students." *Journal of the Association for the Severely Handicapped* 5, no. 3: 250–263.

McWilliam, R. A. 1991. "Targeting Teaching at Children's Use of Time: Perspectives on Preschoolers' Engagement." *Teaching Exceptional Children* 23, no. 4: 42–43.

Noonan, Mary Jo. 2006. "Instructional Procedures." In *Young Children with Disabilities in Natural Environments: Methods and Procedures,* ed. Mary Jo Noonan and Linda McCormick, 119–150. Baltimore, MD: Paul H. Brookes.

Putnam, JoAnne W., John E. Rynders, Roger Johnson, and David Johnson. 1989. "Collaborative Skill Structure for Promoting Positive Interactions between Mentally Handicapped and Nonhandicapped Children." *Exceptional Children* 55, no. 6: 550–557.

Reinhiller, Noelle. 1996. "Coteaching: New Variations On a Not-So-New Practice." *Teacher Education and Special Education* 19, no. 1: 34–48.

Snell, Martha E., and David L. Gast. 1981. "Applying Time Delay Procedure to the Instruction of the Severely Handicapped." *Journal of the Association for Persons with Severe Handicaps* 6, no. 3: 3–14.

Touchette, Paul E. 1971. "Transfer of Stimulus Control: Measuring the Moment of Transfer." *Journal of the Experimental Analysis of Behavior* 15: 347–354.

U.S. Department of Education, Office of Special Education and Rehabilitative Services, Office of Special Education Programs. 2005. *25th Annual (2003) Report to Congress on the Implementation of the Individuals with Disabilities Education Act* (vol. 1). Washington, D.C.: U.S. Department of Education. http://www.ed.gov/about/reports/annual/osep/2003/25th-vol-1-front.pdf (accessed May 17, 2006).

U.S. Government. 1997. "Individuals with Disabilities Education Act Amendments of 1997, Pub. L. No. 105–15, §602." http://thomas.loc.gov/cgi-bin/query/z?c105:H.R.5.ENR: (accessed May 17, 2006).

Walker, Hill, and Hyman Hops. 1976. "Increasing Academic Achievement by Reinforcing Direct Academic Performance and/or Facilitative Nonacademic Responses." *Journal of Educational Psychology* 68, no. 2: 218–225.

9

Language, Culture, and the School Library

Denise E. Agosto and Sandra Hughes-Hassell

You can't erase what you know. You can't forget who you are.

—Sandra Cisneros

Although students with limited English proficiency, called English-language learners (ELLs), have been a significant population in the U.S. education system since its onset, two recent phenomena have brought issues related to teaching ELLs closer to the educational forefront than ever before. First, the number of ELLs in U.S. primary and secondary schools has risen dramatically over the past 15 years:

In 1991, the number of students classified as ELL's was just over two million; today, more than five million ELL students attend schools in the United States. Native speakers of 460 languages attend our schools, but the vast majority of ELL's, some 80 percent, are Latinos. (McElroy 2005, 8)

This substantial increase in ELL student enrollment means that school library media specialists and teachers at all levels of the education system and in most school districts across the nation must devote increased time and resources to supporting education for students with limited English skills. Language limitations affect student performance in all academic disciplines, from language arts, to science, to math, and so on, and they also affect social skills and other non-academic areas of student learning. There has been a similar increase in native English-speaking students from minority backgrounds, and these students face many of these same educational issues.

Second, the federal No Child Left Behind (NCLB) legislation has mandated that schools begin testing ELLs' English-language skills more frequently and in more depth than previously required. As of the spring of 2006, 44 U.S. states and the District of Columbia had implemented the use of new in-depth testing for ELL English language proficiency in order to comply with NCLB requirements (Zehr 2006, 22). At this point, most states had also implemented new or newly revised standards for directing and measuring the ELL student language-learning progress.

As is true of many of the requirements of NCLB, the use of these new, more comprehensive English-language learning tests is quite controversial. Those in favor of the tests feel that more developed standards and increased testing will lead to improved ELL education, as it can be difficult to assess students' English-language proficiency without formal testing. One reason is that students who are fairly adept in conversational English can have far greater difficulty with more formal, more complex, academic English:

> Teachers often assume that because students can converse well in English, they should also be able to complete academic tasks and assignments. Conversational ability is acquired relatively quickly (taking one to three years), but academic proficiency—the ability to read with comprehension, analyze materials, and draw conclusions in English—is what students need for success in school and is more complex, taking between five and nine years to develop completely. (Echevarria 2006, 18–19)

Proponents of the new, more in-depth tests argue that they can better reveal students' real levels of language proficiency.

On the other hand, those opposed to the use of the more comprehensive testing for ELLs object to classroom instruction time being diverted to test preparation and administration, resulting in a loss of precious instruction time. The new tests take as long as six hours for students to complete, whereas the previous English-language skills tests that most states used took just 20 to 30 minutes to complete (Zehr 2006, 22). Test administration time for the new, longer tests combined with necessary test preparation time can mean the loss of the equivalent of two or even three complete days of instruction. As most ELLs are at an educational disadvantage due to language limitations, this significant loss of classroom instruction time can become an additional impediment to learning.

Since the NCLB testing requirements are new, the true impact on ELL learning remains to be seen. What is known for sure and has been known for some time is that language and culture strongly affect student learning in a number of ways. This chapter will discuss the major issues relating to language, culture, and learning, and offer suggestions for ways that school library media specialists can support and enhance the education of ELLs, and of native-English-speaking students from minority backgrounds as well.

LANGUAGE, CULTURE, AND LEARNING

Language and culture shape student learning in a variety of areas. Most significantly, students' linguistic and cultural backgrounds affect educators' assessments of student skills, student comprehension of information resources, and student socialization.

Language, Culture, and Student Assessment

The ability to use language to express one's ideas is a necessary component of nearly all areas of the curriculum, from math, to science, to history, and so on. Limited English language skills can cause educators to misinterpret students' English-language limitations as more widespread educational difficulties. For example, an English-speaking science teacher might think that a student who cannot describe the process of photosynthesis in

English does not understand it, when in fact the student simply lacks the English skills necessary to demonstrate her understanding. Valenzuela and colleagues (2006) found dramatic proof of this unfortunate consequence of limited English skills in their study of ELLs enrolled in a large Southwestern school district. They found ELLs to be disproportionately enrolled in special education programs for the academically disadvantaged, when in fact they should have been receiving additional English language instruction, not special education instruction.

It is important to keep in mind that students who lack reading, writing, and oral expression skills in English might be highly developed in these areas in their home languages. In cases in which students underperform in both their home languages and English, then special attention is crucial to supporting student learning. As Echevarria (2006) explains, students who have had limited formal schooling in their first language and consequently have below grade-level literary skills in all languages are most at risk for educational failure. Thus, whenever possible the first step in assessing ELLs' educational needs should involve testing in students' primary languages to prevent assessors from confusing language difficulties with knowledge gaps.

Many native English-speaking students also face linguistic barriers due to variance between the form of English that they use at home and the kind of academic English needed for success in school. As Morrow (2005) explained:

> Any given group may contain children using words, syntax, and language patterns quite different from those of standard English. Particularly in the United States, there are many different forms of English usage. There are, for example, distinct grammars in rural New England, Appalachia, and some African American communities. (56)

In most cases students will need to learn "standard" English in order to achieve their academic potentials. However, it is important to recognize that these different forms of English are legitimate languages with their own grammatical structures and usage rules. Educators should teach children "standard English" while still showing respect for their home dialects and for the family members who speak them. As Morrow (2005) points out, "children are not to be degraded or viewed as less intelligent for speaking different dialects" (84).

Language, Culture, and the Comprehension of Information Resources

Just as limited English-language proficiency is a strong influence on student learning, cultural background also plays a significant role in the learning process. In today's diverse world, the term "culture" refers to much more than just racial, ethnic, or linguistic background. It can refer to a person's "ethnic, racial, linguistic, religious, gender, disability, political, geographic, age, or socioeconomic status" (Agosto 2001a, 20). Beyond mere language comprehension, students' linguistic and cultural backgrounds influence their understanding and interpretation of library resources, such as books, Web sites, databases, magazine, and DVDs. Each time students read or listen to or view information resources, they relate them to their wider social and cultural knowledge. This means that although other factors also influence the construction of meaning from information resources, students' cultural and linguistic backgrounds create frameworks through which they interpret information.

When ELLs and other minority students are taught to read using resources representing unfamiliar cultural events, images, and concepts, they are faced with the doubly-demanding task of trying to interpret unfamiliar English words while trying to comprehend unfamiliar cultural elements (Agosto, 2001b). That is, variance between their family cultures and "mainstream" U.S. culture can create an additional learning disadvantage for students with limited English skills, and also for native English-speaking students from minority backgrounds. Helping minority students learn English through culturally relevant texts greatly reduces this learning obstacle and enables them to focus more directly on the primary task at hand: learning to read.

For example, the picture book *Fourth of July Mice* (by Bethany Roberts, illustrated by Doug Cushman, Clarion, 2004) is well-suited for use in teaching reading to many kindergarten and first-grade students. The text uses simple words, short phrases, and a large-typeface, and the illustrations provide clear visual clues to help in deciphering unfamiliar words. The story follows a group of mice who celebrate the Fourth of July with a baseball game, a parade, a picnic, and fireworks, familiar cultural images for many U.S. students. However, a student born in Mongolia might first need to become familiar with the concept of "the Fourth of July" (and perhaps baseball, parades, picnics, and fireworks as well) before being able to understand the context of the story and before being able to use contextual clues to help him decipher unfamiliar words in the text.

As a result, to facilitate the literacy process, "titles that spring from the students' cultures are ideal in providing familiarity for ease of comprehension as well as for identifying with story characters" (Vardell, Hadaway, and Young 2006, 736). This is not to suggest that ELLs and other minority students should be restricted to learning from resources that reflect their own cultural backgrounds, but rather to point out that *some* of their learning materials should be culturally relevant. It follows that school libraries should be well-stocked with resources representing a wide variety of cultures and that school library media specialists should collaborate with teachers to identify ways to use them in their classes.

Carroll and Hasson (2004) offer a framework for helping ELLs connect to literature, even literature representing unfamiliar cultures. They suggest that educators use literature as three types of lenses for learning: mirrors, microscopes, and telescopes. Using literature as a mirror for learning entails "helping students to enter and connect the text world by finding themselves and their world in it" (22).

For example, school library media specialists can assist students with locating materials containing settings and/or characters reflecting their own cultures to foster personal connections. Or, as another example, if students in an English class are about to read an assigned text that does not reflect their home cultures, such as a novel dealing with the relationship between a white, native, English-speaking girl and her mother, the school library media specialist, working collaboratively with the teacher, can turn the text into a mirror by guiding students though a free writing project about their own relationships with their mothers, before, during, or after the assigned reading period. In this way, students can make personal connections to the material, even if it represents a foreign culture or an unfamiliar way of life.

Using literature as a microscope for learning entails "helping students better understand the discrete and interrelated elements of literary art, thus teaching them to read a text as if they are looking at it under a microscope" (Carroll and Hasson 2004, 22). For example, a school library media specialist could ask a group of ELLs to keep a list of unfamiliar words or phrases as they read a text. Then periodically throughout the reading, the school library media specialist could direct students in small groups to collaborate to determine the meaning of these words or phrases. They could look up the unfamiliar English words in bilingual and monolingual dictionaries and use context clues to interpret phrases. As the students work with the other group members they could discuss how the sentences that contain the new words or phrases relate to and bring meaning to the broader text. In this way, students can use close examination of selected parts of a resource to create a fuller understanding of the resource as a whole.

Using literature as a telescope for learning entails "helping students learn to extend the ideas that emerge from the text and to apply them to broader considerations, such as social issues and universal values" (Carroll and Hasson 2004, 22). For example, if a class is studying the environmental significance of the Amazon rainforest, the teacher and the school library media specialist could employ Banks's (1999) transformational approach to curriculum design. With this approach "the curriculum is changed to enable students to view concepts, issues, events, and themes from the perspective of diverse ethnic and cultural groups" (Banks 1999, 31).

Examining the economic impact on developing countries of using disappearing rainforest lands as nature preserves from the locals' perspective, not just the perspective of outsiders from developed countries, would show students that creating land preserves can prevent impoverished countries from being able to fully develop their land and from being able to establish badly needed agricultural and industrial concerns. In this way, the school library specialist and teacher help students to understand that social, environmental, and political issues usually have cultural components as well, and that the side of a controversial topic that a person supports often reflects his/her cultural background.

Language, Culture, and the Student Socialization Process

Of course, students gain more than just academic knowledge at school. Schools serve as social microcosms, enabling students to learn how to navigate the social world that exists outside of school. Students from linguistic and/or minority groups often face added learning barriers when it comes to learning social norms and proper behaviors. For many minority students, the characteristics that define their minority status (such as being a non-native English-speaker, or having been born in another country) set them apart socially and emotionally from the majority of the other students in their classrooms and schools. This prevents them from being able to gain full access into the school culture and restricts their experiences within the social microcosm of the school. As a result, it is often more difficult for ELLs and other minority students to learn important social rules and expected social behaviors than it is for non-minority students.

Similarly, the school library serves as a social microcosm of the school and of the wider community in which it is situated. School library media specialists need to be sure that library collections mirror their students' backgrounds as much as possible to create an accurate representation of the student body and of the broader community as well. Likewise, they need to make sure ELL students see themselves and their language in visual displays such as posters, artwork, and photographs. If students do not see people and characters similar to themselves in the school library, they are likely to feel as if they are not a valued part of the school culture, further isolating them from the rest of the student body and further restricting their healthy social development.

IMPLICATIONS FOR PRACTICE

Keeping these issues in mind, how can school library media specialists support the healthy academic and social development of ELL students and of native English speakers from minority cultures? The following sections outline strategies that school library media specialists and other educators can use to support ELL and minority student learning and socialization within the school library and throughout the school. Table 9.1 provides a summary of the suggested strategies.

Table 9.1.
Strategies School Library Media Specialists Can Use to Support English Language Learners

Learning and Teaching

Promote the use of multicultural and bilingual resources across the curriculum.

Help English language learners make personal connections to library resources representing unfamiliar cultures.

Facilitate the language acquisition process for English language learners.

Collaborate with teachers to plan instructional units that integrate content and language learning for English language learners.

Encourage learning partnerships between English language learners and English-language proficient students.

Information Access and Delivery

Create a culturally diverse library collection.

Establish and maintain ties with information resources and services in the community that can help meet the information needs of English language learners.

Introduce English language learners to the library and the library's resources.

Program Administration

Create a culturally diverse library environment.

Collaborate with teachers, students, and parents to develop a library policy that promotes equity and respect.

Supporting ELL and Minority Student Learning

Strategy 1: Create a Culturally Diverse Library Collection. The first method of supporting ELL and minority student learning is through the creation of a culturally diverse library collection. The familiar cultural concepts and visual images in multicultural materials give ELLs and minority students a sense of security, familiarity, and confidence that encourages them to want to learn to read and write. And, in view of the crucial connection between cultural background and textual understanding, culturally familiar resources make the English-language learning process easier for ELLs. The most responsive collections include not only multicultural books, but a wide range of materials including newspapers from the student's countries of birth; bilingual books, videos, and music; English-language translations of stories from students' countries/cultures of birth; and digital resources, including links to Web sites that are culturally relevant and, if available, written in their native languages.

Feger (2006) offers classroom support for this idea. When teaching English to ninth- and tenth-grade ELLs, she initially used standard English-language grammar textbooks. However, she found that "once [the] students acquired a sufficient command of English grammar to participate in classroom lessons, the books did little to engage them, much less develop their literacy" (18). Since most of her students had come from the Caribbean and Central and South America, she began replacing the standard textbooks with books representing these cultures. She soon found that: "The more [she] had incorporated culturally relevant literature and non-fiction into the curriculum, the more [her] students' engagement in reading had increased" (18).

A well-balanced collection can also teach non-minority students about the true nature of our diverse world. It can show students that there are many other viewpoints than theirs in our world, and it can teach them to value and respect these other points of view. A culturally diverse library collection also encourages student interest in learning about traditions, behaviors, and other aspects of human life in other parts of the world.

Developing an age-appropriate culturally diverse collection, or improving one that already exists, requires effort and commitment. Begin by identifying the stakeholders in the learning community who can best help you locate, evaluate, and select resources. Obvious partners include ELL teachers, parents, students, and representatives from the local public library. Seek out other qualified individuals from the community, as well, such as representatives from cultural organizations.

Gather detailed data about the ELL students in your school. All ELL students won't have the same resource needs. The daughter of migrant workers from Mexico, for example, may have less familiarity with the English language than the daughter of a foreign diplomat from a European country where English is taught as a second language in most schools.

Take into consideration family background, years in this country, prior exposure to and experience with the English language, learning styles and learning differences, and so forth when determining the types of resources needed.

Locate professional resources that feature reviews of multicultural and foreign language materials. Examples include: *Criticas,* an all-Spanish periodical with articles and book reviews; *Multicultural Book Review,* a journal focused on race, ethnicity, and religious diversity that provides reviews of books and other media with multicultural themes and topics; and the Barahona Center for the Study of Books in Spanish for Children and Adolescents (http://www.csusm.edu/csb/), a comprehensive, bilingual database by national expert Isabel Schon for books published in Spanish-speaking countries and/or translated into Spanish from other languages. Become familiar with distributors such as Libros sin Fronteras, Asia for Kids (http://www.afk.com/), and Books without Borders (http://www.bookswithoutborders.com/). Monitor book awards that recognize distinguished books about various cultural groups, such as the Tomas Rivera Mexican-American Children's Book Award given annually for the most distinguished book for children and young adults about Mexican Americans. Take a look at the electronic books available free from the International Children's Digital Library at the University of Maryland (http://www.icdlbooks.org/). The collection includes 1,562 books in 37 languages. Finally, utilize your local community resources. School library media specialists in the Philadelphia area, for example, have a wealth of resources at hand, including the Multicultural Resource Center, Taller Puertorriqueno Julia de Burgos Book and Craft Store, Keepers of the Culture, and the Asociación de Móscicos Latino Americanos.

Strategy 2: Promote the Use of Multicultural and Bilingual Resources across the Curriculum. It is important to move beyond simply collecting multicultural library resources to taking an active role in promoting their use in all areas of the school. Within the school library, librarians can also use methods such as reading or telling multicultural or bilingual stories, promoting multicultural materials through readers' advisory, and inviting guests to the library to tell stories, read books, or present programs that represent minority cultures and languages. In his book *Holler If You Hear Me* (1999), Gregory Michie provides a powerful example of the impact these kinds of activities can have on students. After recording interpretive readings of the stories in *The House on Mango Street* in an after-school drama club, the "Mango Girls" (the five inner-city Mexican American girls who made up the club) wrote a letter to Sandra Cisneros inviting her to visit their school. To Michie's surprise Cisneros agreed. Michie describes the girls' meeting with Cisneros this way:

> After the assembly, I looked on from the sidelines as Cisneros met with the Mango Girls in the library, where she chatted with them, signed their books, and answered their questions. But the girls didn't act as if they were meeting a celebrity. It was more as if they were welcoming home an aunt or an older friend who they hadn't seen in years–a soul sister, *una hermana del alma*. They weren't awestruck, just filled with a deep sense of appreciation and respect. For someone who knew what it was like to be in their *chanclas*. Someone who hadn't forgotten. (Michie 1999, 65)

Outside of the library, school library media specialists can encourage teachers to incorporate multicultural and bilingual materials into their lessons, thereby broadening their impact on minority and non-minority students. School library media specialists can also encourage students to take these materials home and to use them for leisure reading and exploration.

Strategy 3: Introduce ELL Students to the Library and the Library's Resources. Many ELL students may have little knowledge of libraries, particularly school library media centers. If your school has separate ELL classes, invite them to the media center for their own private orientation. Plan the orientation in collaboration with the ELL teacher, who can offer strategies for making the visit a successful one. Introduce the staff and explain their responsibilities. Discuss basic information, such as the types of resources available, how the library is arranged, how to locate resources, and so on. Make sure to explain that all of the media center's resources and services are free—again this may be an unfamiliar concept to some of the students.

Consider working with the ELL teacher and a group of ELL students to develop a virtual tour of the library for the library's Web site. A project like this would allow the students to apply their new knowledge about school library media programs, practice their language and communication skills, and learn video and Web production skills in the context of creating a useful product.

Strategy 4: Help Students Make Personal Connections to Library Resources Representing Unfamiliar Cultures. Educators must remember that students' cultural backgrounds affect their interpretations of the information resources with which they interact, and that helping students make personal and cultural connections to information increases the engagement and learning of all students, minority and non-minority alike (Agosto 2002). Whenever possible, teachers and school library media specialists should guide students in their use of library resources to ease their struggles with culturally unfamiliar concepts. Discussion groups, literature circles, and other discussion-based techniques are especially effective student guidance methods, especially when educators use these techniques for helping students find personal connections with resources.

For instance, Esmeralda Santiago's autobiography *Almost a Woman* (Reading, MA: Perseus Books, 1998) details the author's teen years, including her move from Puerto Rico to Brooklyn. In a class of students studying the book, few would have made that same move, but most will have shared the author's more universal teenage experiences:

feeling that like an "outsider" at school, the growing desire to gain independence from one's parents, an increasing interest in the opposite sex, and so on. By examining these universal experiences through class discussions, school library media specialists and teachers can help students connect their own life experiences to the author's experiences, thereby increasing most readers' interest in and understanding of the text and the culture it describes.

Strategy 5: Encourage Learning Partnerships between Minority and Non-Minority Students. Another useful technique for increasing minority student learning involves pairing ELLs with English-language proficient students, and native English-speaking minority students with students from non-minority backgrounds. As Fitzgerald (1993) explains, "Literacy is more likely to develop through activities that create relationships between English learners and English speakers representing various literacy levels" (645). Pairing bilingual and monolingual children for projects increases the literacy skills and confidence of all children, and pairing minority and non-minority students helps minority students become better integrated into the school culture.

Strategy 6: Facilitate the Language Acquisition Process for ELLs. The school library media specialist is in a unique position to help ELL students with their language development. Vardell, Hadaway, and Young (2006) explain how to make literature play a critical role in supporting ELL language acquisition. In addition to suggesting the use of "read-alouds, book talks, story retellings, literature circles, book buddies, author studies, and other reading response projects" (734), the authors stress the importance of selecting materials that are age-appropriate and interesting to ELLs while keeping in mind language comprehension limitations. In many cases, picture books best meet these criteria, as there are an ever-increasing number of picture books suited to older children's developmental needs and interests, and the language used in picture books is often more straightforward than in longer written works. Picture books also provide visual clues that can help ELLs decipher unfamiliar English words, phrases, and concepts. Poetry is another genre that offers benefits to English-language learners. As Vardell, Hadaway, and Young (2002) explain, listening to the spoken word is an important step in learning any language. Poetry is ideal because of its rhythm, repetition, rhyme, and brevity.

Vardell, Hadaway, and Young (2006) propose four essential elements to consider when selecting resources for ELLs: *Content accessibility, language accessibility, visual accessibility, and genre accessibility* (735). To assess *content accessibility,* school library media specialists should consider whether the story or topic is likely to be within the students' knowledge base. If specific knowledge about national, state, or local culture is necessary to comprehend the content, school library media specialists should take care to provide context, as in a video set during a presidential campaign, an event that might be foreign to many ELLs. To assess *language accessibility,* school library media specialists should determine if the vocabulary and sentence structure are relatively straightforward, or if terminology, similes, metaphors, complicated sentence construction, and so on are likely to cause comprehension difficulties. To assess *visual accessibility,* school library media specialists should consider whether the pictures or graphics are likely to clarify the content, or if they are primarily decorative. Pictures that explain and clarify the text are preferable, as they provide comprehension assistance. To assess *genre accessibility,* school library media specialists should provide a variety of genres (fiction, nonfiction, poetry, etc.) to expose ELLs to a wide range of English-language patterns.

Morrow and Gambrell (2004) suggest a number of additional strategies for helping ELLs learn English. While they were writing specifically with preschool students in mind, most of their suggestions can be used with a wider range of students in school library and classroom settings. These suggestions include:

1. Providing materials in students' home languages.

2. Providing English-language translations of stories from students' countries/cultures of birth.

3. Using a few key phrases from students' home languages in the classroom.

4. Assigning bilingual students to serve as buddies for ELLs with limited English proficiency.

5. Speaking slowly when speaking to a group of ELLs, repeating important phrases; also using gestures and visual cues.

6. For each ELL student, making "a book filled with photos or drawings of different parts of the classroom"; also creating drawings of daily routine activities "to help make the child feel safe and confident in the classroom." (7)

7. Repeating the use of the same books with ELLs until they can master them.

8. Showing students the illustrations when reading illustrated materials aloud.

9. Discussing stories after reading them aloud.

10. Asking children to retell stories that they have heard.

Finally, any good techniques for teaching reading and writing are likely to be good for supporting English-language learning. As Morrow (2005) explains, "most good strategies for teaching early literacy development for native English speakers . . . are also good strategies to use with ELL" students (85).

Strategy 7: Collaborate with Teachers to Plan Instructional Units That Integrate Content and Language Learning for ELLs. Support for integrated language and content instruction can be found in the literature on ELLs (Langer and Applebee 1987; Mohan 1990; Penfield 1987). Using this approach, the classroom teacher, ELL teacher (or language specialist), and school library media specialist agree on target outcomes and goals for each area (subject or content, language, and information literacy) and develop language-sensitive ways to support ELL students' work on tasks (Hurren 1993; Mohan 1990). The classroom teacher brings extensive experience with the curriculum and the background knowledge the students are likely to have. The school library media specialist, who is experienced in collaborative planning and teaching at all levels, brings expertise in information literacy skills, resources, and teaching strategies that worked with similar groups of students. Finally, the ELL teacher knows how best to support language learning.

Supporting ELL and Minority Student Socialization

Strategy 1: Make the Library a Welcoming Place for All Students. The school library should be a welcoming, supportive place. It is important to create a library atmosphere that shows an appreciation for students' cultural backgrounds, as social acceptance figures strongly in self-motivation for educational success. Meltzer and Hamann (2006) explain that "a supportive environment is necessary to encourage the participation of ELL's who may be shy or embarrassed about speaking, writing, or reading in English" (34), and the same is true for students from other minority backgrounds. If minority students know that the school library media center is a place where their differences are welcomed and celebrated, they will want to visit it and to use its resources, and they will want to participate more actively in the school culture.

Strategy 2: Create a Culturally Diverse Library Collection. Probably the most effective method of creating the culturally tolerant and acceptant school library environment discussed previously is through the integration of multicultural resources into the collection and curriculum. A school library collection that represents the perspectives of a wide range of cultures can serve as a form of advocacy on behalf of students from minority backgrounds by making them feel included in the classroom and school environments. As López-Robertson (2006) explains, striving to make students' home languages, family backgrounds, and native cultures a part of the school culture leads to higher levels of self-esteem and greater openness to learning. In addition, school libraries should also contain a variety of materials in the home languages of all students so that ELLs can improve their literacy in their primary languages as well as in English.

Including multicultural and bilingual resources in the school library also benefits minority and non-minority students by enabling students from all types of ethnic and cultural backgrounds to experience lives different from their own. Exposure encourages acceptance and appreciation, meaning that providing multicultural materials in the school library fosters a more accepting school culture. Not only does the use of multicultural materials increase children's positive attitudes toward human differences in general, but without education and intervention, negative attitudes toward people from "other" cultural groups actually increase as children mature (Wham, Barnhart, and Cook 1996).

Strategy 3: Establish a Library Policy That Promotes Equity and Respect. In many cases, students have never directly faced ideas of cultural and ethnic insensitivity and intolerance. Work with students and members of the library advisory committee to establish a library policy that promotes equity and respect. Post a large-print copy in the library's main entranceway and on the library's Web site. Read and discuss it in library orientations at the beginning of each school year. Call parents' attention to the policy at the same time through newsletters, parent meetings, or other means. Review the policy with newcomers throughout the year. Tolerance.org, an online resource sponsored by the Southern Poverty Law Center, provides guidelines for developing these types of policies, as well as examples of school-wide policies that could be adapted to the library.

Open discussions about diversity issues can also bring equity and respect into student consciousness and help students to work toward cultural sensitivity. For example, if a school library media specialist overhears a student comment that "All Asians are good at math and science," he can turn a culturally insensitive comment into a teachable moment by leading a discussion of racial and ethnic stereotypes. The school library media specialist could explain that even though comments such as these might seem at face value to express positive images, they are untrue generalizations that can hurt people. Bringing students to discuss diversity issues such as these helps them to understand the importance of cultural sensitivity and empathy for all, an important part of the socialization process.

Strategy 4: Create a Culturally Diverse Library Environment. Finally, one easy method of showing that the school library supports student diversity is by creating a visually diverse library environment. Placing objects that represent different student cultures around the library sends a strong visual message to minority and non-minority students, telling them that the library celebrates the diversity of its student body. School library media specialists should make a special effort to include items representing as many student cultures and language groups as possible, such as posters, artwork, photographs, and other cultural objects. Inviting students to bring items from home to combine into a library bulletin board or library display is a good way of gathering culturally authentic items, and it can open up student discussions about their family backgrounds. Translating library signage into multiple languages can also have a beneficial impact. Not only will it help ELL students navigate the library, but it will also provide language learning opportunities for native English speakers.

Finally, efforts to create a culturally diverse library environment should extend to the library's Web site. If the school serves a diverse population, visitors to the library Web site should be able to tell this at a glance from the images, photographs, language, and recommended resources included. Parents of ELL students may also be visitors to the library's Web site. Keep in mind that many of them may have limited English proficiency and will be learning English along with their children. Consider providing resources for them such as links to adult literacy programs, naturalization and immigration services, and cultural institutions that offer programs for adult immigrants.

CONCLUSION

Echevarria (2006) explains that "there is a shortage of teachers who have been prepared to work effectively with ELLs" (16). The same is true of school library media specialists, and the same is true of educators working with English-speaking minority students. In order to overcome this lack of formal education relating to language, culture, and student learning, school library media specialists should be familiar with the major ways in which language and culture impact student learning and socialization, as discussed in this chapter, and they should strive to support ELL and minority student development in as many of the ways detailed here as possible. Most importantly, school library media specialists should strive to make the school library a sanctuary for all students, a place where students from all linguistic and cultural backgrounds can feel welcome, appreciated, and valued.

REFERENCES

Agosto, Denise E. 2001a. "Bridging the Culture Gap: Ten Steps Toward a More Multicultural Youth Library." *Journal of Youth Services in Libraries* 14, no. 3: 20–23.

Agosto, Denise E. 2001b. "The Cultured Word: Cultural Background, Bilingualism, and the School Library." *School Libraries Worldwide* 7, no. 1: 46–57.

Agosto, Denise E. 2002. "Facilitating Student Connections to Judith Ortiz Cofer's *The Line of the Sun* and Esmeralda Santiago's *Almost a Woman*." *ALAN Review* 29, no. 3: 40–43.

Banks, James A. 1999. *An Introduction to Multicultural Education.* 2nd ed. Boston: Allyn and Bacon.

Carroll, Pamela Sissi, and Deborah J. Hasson. 2004. "Helping ELL's Look at Stories through Literary Lenses." *Voices from the Middle* 11, no. 4: 20–26.

Cisneros, Sandra. 1994. *The House on Mango Street.* New York, Knopf.

Echevarria, Jana. 2006. "Helping English Language Learners Succeed." *Principal Leadership* 6, no. 6: 16–21.

Feger, Mary-Virginia. 2006. "'I Want to Read': How Culturally Relevant Texts Increase Student Engagement in Reading." *Multicultural Education* 13, no. 3: 18–19.

Fitzgerald, Jill. 1993. "Literacy and Students Who Are Learning English As a Second Language." *Reading Teacher* 43 (May): 638–648.

Hurren, Patti J. 1993. "Expanding the Collaborative Planning Model to Meet the Needs of ESL Students." *Emergency Librarian* 20, no. 5: 8–12.

Langer, Judith A., and Arthur N. Applebee. 1987. *How Writing Shapes Thinking.* Urbana, IL: National Council of Teachers of English.

López-Robertson, Julia. 2006. "The Making of a Bilingual Educator." *Language Arts* 83, no. 5: 388–389.

McElroy, Edward J. 2005. "Supporting English Language Learners." *Teaching PreK–8* 36, no. 3: 8.

Meltzer, Julie, and Edmund T. Hamann. 2006. "Literacy for English Learners and Regular Students, Too." *Education Digest* 71, no. 8: 32–40.

Michie, Gregory. 1999. *Holler if You Hear Me: The Education of a Teacher and His Students.* New York: Teachers College Press.

Mohan, Bernard A. 1990. *LEP Students and the Integration of Language and Content: Knowledge Structures and Tasks.* Paper presented at the National Symposium on Limited English Proficient Students Research Issues. Washington, DC: United States Department of Education, Office of Bilingual Education and Minority Languages Affairs.

Morrow, Lesley Mandel. 2005. *Literacy Development in the Early Years: Helping Children Read and Write.* Boston: Pearson.

Morrow, Lesley Mandel, and Linda B. Gambrell. 2004. *Using Children's Literature in Preschool: Comprehending and Enjoying Books.* Newark, DE: International Reading Association.

Penfield, Joyce. 1987. "ESL: The Regular Classroom Teacher's Perspective." *TESOL Quarterly* 21, no. 1: 21–29.

Valenzuela, J. S. de, Susan R. Copeland, Cathy Huaqing Qi, and Miwha Park. 2006. "Examining Educational Equity: Revisiting the Disproportionate Representation of Minority Students in Special Education." *Exceptional Children* 72, no. 4: 425–441.

Vardell, Sylvia M., Nancy L. Hadaway, and Terrell A. Young. 2002. "Choosing and Sharing Poetry with ESL Students." *Booklinks* 11, no. 5: 51–56.

Vardell, Sylvia M., Nancy L. Hadaway, and Terrell A. Young. 2006. "Matching Books and Readers: Selecting Literature for English Learners." *The Reading Teacher* 59, no. 8: 734–741.

Wham, Mary Ann, June E. Barnhart, and Gregory L. Cook. 1996. "Enhancing Multicultural Awareness through the Storybook Reading Experience." *Journal of Research and Development in Education* 30 (Fall): 1–9.

Zehr, Mary Ann. 2006. "New Era for Testing English-Learners Begins." *Education Week* 25, no. 42: 22, 28–29.

Part V

Building Professionalism

10

The Real Thing: Authentic Teaching through Action Research

Carol A. Gordon

WHY PERCEPTIONS ARE NOT ENOUGH

A teacher asks, "What can I do to motivate my students to read more?" A principal wonders, "How can we raise the test scores of our low-achieving students?" A technology director puzzles, "How can I demonstrate that technology helps students learn better? A school librarian asks, "How can I improve the level of collaboration with teachers to design more challenging projects for students?"

What we often view as problematic may be a research situation. When practitioners become practitioner-researchers, they create opportunities to gain new perspectives, discover insights, and solve problems. Although practitioners are continuously taking in information from observation, their reflections are extemporaneous and their conclusions are based on perceptions. So, why aren't perceptions enough?

Sarah, a school librarian in a diverse suburban community, collaborates with the members of the English Department to produce a Web-based summer reading program. Students select three books for summer reading from 12 reading lists that do not designate grade levels. The lists include titles students and staff recommended in a survey. Students choose a reading response activity for each of the books they read and bring their projects to school when they return in September. Responses include nontraditional tasks such as creating a menu for a dinner party for the characters of a book, and technology-based activities such as blogging. Students can link to library catalogs, Amazon.com, and commercial bookstores from the Web site to borrow or purchase books. They can read excerpts from the books and reviews by students and staff. Sarah immediately begins to form perceptions about the program. Its features address student feedback about prior summer reading lists. Students are enthusiastic about the book titles on the new lists. They are

161

coming to the library to check out books. Parents are complimentary about the Web site. Teachers are using the list for their own reading. In fact, the school board has awarded Sarah a *Hat's Off* certificate for the initiative. All indicators point to a successful reading program. Sarah, however, wants to know how she can revise the Web-based program for next summer.

When classes resume in September, Sarah conducts a survey and interviews to find out what students and teachers thought about the program. The questions are designed to determine whether the Web-based summer reading program affected their attitudes toward reading and motivated them to read more. When she analyzes the data she find that students grouped in "average" classes were very favorably affected by the program but not so the low-achieving students. These students almost unanimously wrote comments such as: "Why do we have to read in the summer?" "I hate to read." "I don't have a computer so I used the list my teacher printed for me." These students comprised 25 percent of her student population. These students were reading below grade level. These students were failing standardized tests. These were the students dropping out of school. The data contradicted Sarah's perceptions; the summer reading program was not helping those students who were most needy. This is called "disconfirming information."

> Disconfirming information is not enough . . . because we can ignore the information, dismiss it as irrelevant, blame the undesired outcome on others or fate, or as is most common, simply deny its validity. In order to become motivated to change, we must accept the information and connect it to something we care about. The disconfirmation must arouse what we call "survival anxiety" or the feeling that if we do not change we will fail to meet our needs or fail to achieve some goals or ideals that we have set for ourselves. (Schein n.d., 5)

Equity is an important value for Sarah; she wants all students to have opportunities to read and learn. Raising the annual yearly progress of minority and special needs students is a survival anxiety for Sarah's school administrators. Had she not collected data, her perceptions would have been dominated by what was working, rather than what was not. She would have implemented the summer reading program for a second year without addressing the needs of poor readers and aliterate students. When Sarah collected data through a survey of students she discovered evidence did not support her perceptions. She became a practitioner-researcher in the world of action research.

WHAT IS ACTION RESEARCH?

Action research is a systematic approach to problem-solving and understanding phenomena in depth that can be woven into the fabric of everyday work patterns and routines. There is an abundance of definitions for action research, many of which distinguish action research from formal research. According to Ziegler (2001) ". . . action research is an intentional systematic method of inquiry used by a group of practitioner-researchers who reflect and act on the real-life problems encountered in their own practice" (3). Boomer (1987) defines action research as a "deliberate, group or personally owned and conducted, solution oriented investigation" (8). Anderson, Herr, and Nihlen (1994) describe action research as "insider research done by practitioners using their own site as the focus of their study . . . it is oriented to some action or cycle of actions that practitioners wish to take to address a particular situation" (2). Action research is problem focused, context specific, and future oriented and aims at improvement and involvement (Hart and Bond 1995).

The "action" in action research refers to the application of findings to the workplace and it is this action plan that distinguishes action research from formal research. There are many commonalities, however, between the two. Action research employs the same methodologies as formal qualitative research: interviews, focus groups, surveys, observations, and journaling. Action research must meet the same standards of validity and reliability required for formal research, although findings are not usually generalizable from sample to population because sample sizes are generally small.

ORIGINS OF ACTION RESEARCH

Kurt Lewin, a scientist who emigrated to the United States from Prussia, is recognized as the founder of modern social psychology. He contributed terms such as "feedback," "participant observation," and "cognitive aids" to this discipline. Lewin articulated his field theory, which enabled him to apply psychology to the problems of society. He defined a field as "the totality of coexisting facts which are conceived of as mutually interdependent" (Lewin 1951, 240). He attributed differences in human behavior to the tensions between perceptions of the self and of the environment. The "lifespace," or psychological field in which people acted, had to be understood as a whole to understand the behavior. Three premises underlie Lewin's theory: (1) Behavior is a function of the field that exists at the time the behavior occurs; (2) Analysis begins with the situation as a whole from which are differentiated the component parts; and (3) The concrete person in a concrete situation can be represented mathematically (Hall, Lindzey, and Campbell 1978).

Lewin founded the Center of Group Dynamics at the Massachusetts Institute of Technology to study group productivity, communication, social perception, inter-group relations, and group membership. He worked in real life situations to understand and remedy the effects of gang behavior, discrimination, and immigration. He argued that social problems should serve as the locus of social science research and coined the term, "action research."

> The research needed for social practice can best be characterized as research for social management or social engineering. It is a type of action-research, a comparative research on the conditions and effects of various forms of social action, and research leading to social action. Research that produces nothing but books will not suffice. (Lewin 1948, 202–203)

While Lewin is credited by some as the founder of action research (Coughlan and Brannick 2004) others offer contrary explanations for its origins. McKernan (1991) maintains that action research evolved from the Science in Education movement of the late nineteenth century, which applied the scientific movement to education. There is also evidence that social reformists such as Collier in 1945, Lippitt and Radke in 1946, and Corey in 1953 used action research prior to Lewin (Masters 1995). What is clear is that Lewin's work in social psychology was a conceptual framework for action research, and that his work applied these methods to education.

Lewin (1948) defined action research as "proceeding in a spiral of steps, each of which is composed of planning, action and the evaluation of the result of the action" (206). Figure 10.1 illustrates this model whereby identifying a problem, fact-finding, planning, action, and evaluation begins a spiral of activity that is iterative: every amended plan of action regenerates the process (Smith 2001).

The application of action research in American education is rooted in the experimentalist and progressive educational work of John Dewey "who applied the inductive scientific

Figure 10.1
Action Research As Conceived by Kurt Lewin

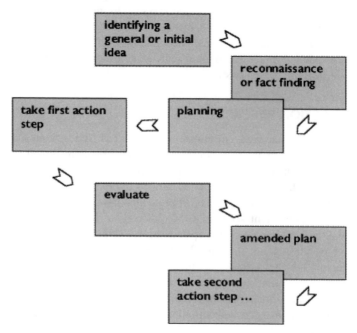

Source: Smith, Mark. 2001. "Kurt Lewin: Groups, Experiential Learning and Action Research." http://www.infed.org/thinkers/et-lewin.htm
(accessed October 24, 2006). Reproduced from *The Encyclopaedia of
Informal Education.* http://www.infed.org.

method of problem solving as a logic for the solution of problems in such fields as aes-
thetics, philosophy and education" (McKernan 1991, 8). Allport (1948) points out the
similarities between Dewey and Lewin.

> Both agree that democracy must be learned anew in each generation, and that it is a far more
> difficult form of social structure to attain and to maintain than is autocracy. Both see the inti-
> mate dependence of democracy upon social science. Without knowledge of, and obedience to,
> the laws of human nature in group settings democracy cannot succeed. And without freedom
> for research and theory as provided only in a democratic environment, social science will
> surely fail. Dewey, we might say, is the outstanding philosophical exponent of democracy.
> Lewin is its outstanding psychological exponent. More clearly than anyone else he has shown
> us in concrete, operational terms what it means to be a democratic leader, and to create demo-
> cratic group structure (6).

In post–World War II America action research was applied to education as "a general
strategy for designing curricula and attacking complex problems, such as inter-group
relations and prejudice through large curriculum development projects" (McKernan
1991, 10). Noted researchers included Corey, Taba, and Brady and Robinson. In the
1950s action research was discredited as expert educational research and development
laboratories emerged. Stringer (1999) attributes the decline of action research during
the 1960s to its association with radical political activism. Twenty years later Stenhouse

engaged in the Humanities Curriculum Project that led to the teacher-researcher movement in the United Kingdom (Masters 1995). Stenhouse's work focused on the idea that teaching is based upon research and that teachers should engage in research and curriculum development. Action research has since become a tradition in improving classroom practice, as pioneered by Stephen Corey in 1949. Many models of action research have emerged as it has identified with community-based, participatory action research. It is disputed, however, that action research must be collaborative, although it often is. A useful action research model for educators (Figure 10.2) illustrates the components of reflection, inquiry, and action as well as its recursive nature (Patterson and Shannon 1993).

Action research may originate with an observation, a feeling of dissatisfaction, or an unexpected outcome. Reflection may result in a question, hypothesis, or desire to understand the situation. This "situation" is where the fieldwork takes place. The action researcher uses qualitative methods to collect evidence that s/he analyzes. Unlike traditional research, this analysis results in new action that addresses the situation sparking the reflection. The new action becomes the context for another spiral of action research. The cyclical process alternates between action and reflection. In later cycles, research methods, data, and interpretation are continuously refined in light of the understanding that develops in the earlier cycles. Initially an exploratory stance is adopted, where an understanding of a problem is developed, observations and plans are made for some form of intervention, and the cyclic process repeats, continuing until a sufficient understanding of, or solution for the problem is found. However, McTaggart (1996) cautions that it is a mistake to think that following the action research spiral constitutes "doing action research" (248). Action research is not a "method or a procedure for research but a series of commitments to observe and problematize through practice a series of principles for conducting social enquiry" (McTaggert 1996, 248).

Figure 10.2
Action Research: Reflection, Inquiry, Action

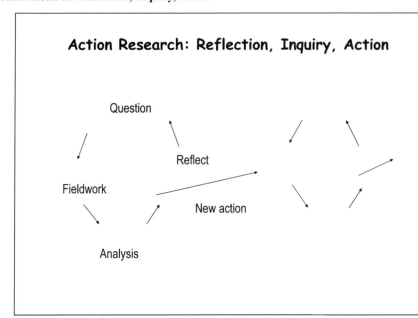

ACTION RESEARCH AND THE SCHOOL LIBRARY PROGRAM

Action research is a tool of evidence-based practice ". . . where day-by-day professional work is directed toward demonstrating the tangible impact and outcomes of sound decision making and implementation of organizational goals and objectives" (Todd 2003). Evidence-based practice offers six key benefits:

1. It provides evidence at the local school level that library initiatives make a visible contribution to learning, and that administrators, teachers and parents can see the real impacts;

2. It convinces administrators and community funders that the money invested in the school library is worth it;

3. It demonstrates the librarian's commitment to learning outcomes;

4. It helps librarians plan more effective instructional interventions and information services;

5. It contributes to job satisfaction; and

6. It moves beyond anecdotal, guess work, hunches, advocacy, and touting of research findings (Todd 2003).

These benefits of evidence-based practice provide three goals for the school librarian's action research agenda:

1. To develop and refine pedagogies of inquiry that enrich the knowledge base and deepen understanding. Action research can engage educators in examining the effectiveness of their methods when they have identified an area of concern or interest and use systematic research procedures to gather evidence.

2. To establish the school librarian as a leader in teaching and learning. Reflection helps practitioners understand what they are currently doing, why they are doing it, whether it is what they want to do, and what they should do in the future (Patterson 1996). Reflection identifies weaknesses and strengths and validates decision-making inherent in the teaching process.

3. To demonstrate to the community the value that school libraries bring to learning and achievement. Reporting results of action research can provide the vicarious experiences related by narrative accounts from schools and classrooms, which educators find more helpful than formal educational research (Anderson, Herr, and Nihlen 1994).

Action research is well suited to the school library program. The strong qualitative tradition of research in the social sciences and the development of action research as a tool for the practitioner have contributed methodologies that are easily integrated with everyday work. The field is the school library and the classroom. A holistic view of the learning situation is balanced by studying individual learners in structured learning environments. The collaborative nature of the classroom teacher/library media specialist relationship in planning and instruction is ideal for the collaborative tendencies of action research.

Action research also suits the collaborative nature of guided inquiry and information literacy instruction as it has evolved as a process approach. Increasingly, teacher education programs use action research to promote inquiry, reflection, and self-analysis so it is becoming increasingly familiar to educators. Therefore, it can be common ground for collaborations between school librarians and classroom teachers. As a tool for professional development, it offers school librarians opportunities to model the research process to their colleagues in the course of reflective practice as they refine their skills in data collection and analysis.

Additionally, action research incorporates many of the qualities of an ideal staff development program.

It is individualized and can be used by a teacher at any developmental level. It assumes teachers are knowledgeable and gives them power to make decisions. It can be carried out collaboratively. It is an on-going process and for that reason can be more effective than a typical one day in-service presentation. One of the more significant qualities of action research is that it puts the teacher in the position of accepting more responsibility for her (his) own professional growth. (Wood 1988, 16–17)

When school librarians incorporate action research into their teaching and share action research with colleagues, collaboration becomes the context for leadership and change.

While action research can be applied to all facets of the library program, it has profound implications for the pedagogy of school librarians.

In order for school libraries to play a key role in the Information Age school, I believe there needs to be a fundamental shift from thinking about the movement and management of information resources through structures and networks, and from information skills and information literacy, to a key focus on knowledge construction and human understanding, implemented through a constructivist, inquiry-based framework. (Todd 2001)

Implicit in this paradigm shift from an information-centered to a knowledge-centered instructional program is the teaching and application of formal research methods for students. "The research assignment acts as a reporting exercise when student involvement is limited to information gathering, which is usually demonstrated by reading, taking notes, and writing a summary. Reporting has masqueraded as researching for so long that the terms are used interchangeably" (Gordon 1999).

In a study that interviewed ninth graders as they worked through a research assignment, students revealed that their perception of doing research was writing a grammatically correct report that was well presented and provided other peoples' answers to someone else's question. The research process was not internalized in the school library; it was perceived as an extension of classroom practice. Students talked about it as though it was a test; creativity and inquiry were not perceived as part of the process and grades were perceived as the most important measure of success (Gordon 1996).

In another study, which piloted an "authentic research" project that required students to engage in data collection and analysis, as well as information searching and use, students were asked, "How was this research assignment different from what you have done in the past?" They responded positively, "Longer, more depth, more detailed, more demanding" (Gordon 1999). Student-generated comments mentioned precise instructions, format, and regulation as an unpleasant aspect of the assignment, but the same number of comments revealed that they felt more independent. "In the past I was given full instructions on the essay. Now I had to do it by myself." When asked what the best aspect of the project was, one student wrote, "That we stood on our own two feet!" (Gordon 1999). Comments also reflected an appreciation for the distinction between reporting and research: "I never did proper research before. It was the first real serious research I have done. It was much longer and more difficult than previous papers. It was also much more interesting and more fun as well" (Gordon 1999).

The methodology of authentic research for students promotes higher-order thinking skills and knowledge construction. Raising the bar for students, however, requires that the school librarian know how to do research and how to teach students to do it. For this reason, action research is especially relevant to the teaching content of librarians: the methods of inquiry for action research and authentic research for students are similar. Through action research school librarians refine their own research skills, gaining confidence to rescue student research assignments that are stuck in a "reporting" mode. Through action research educators can elevate the academic climate of a school by creating a community of learners in which everyone does research.

GETTING STARTED WITH AUTHENTIC LEARNING TASKS

Educators do not have to be expert researchers to start doing action research. Authentic, or performance-based assessments are formative in intent, seeking to provide feedback to the teacher about a student's progress (Wiggins 1993). Journals, rubrics, and portfolios are commonly used strategies that generate evidence that can inform the teacher's instructional decisions to meet individual student needs. Through the eyes of a researcher, these authentic assessments become instruments of data collection that elicit evidence about what is working and what is not. Authentic assessments of student work that are self-evaluative or peer reviewed shift responsibility for assessment from teachers to learners, who develop evaluative abilities as they work towards becoming their own best critics. Table 10.1 displays the criteria for content, methodology, and design of these tasks (Gordon 2007).

Any given authentic task is not characterized by every descriptor in Table 10.1, but it is characterized by many of these criteria. Authentic learning tasks offer learners the opportunities not only to assume real-life roles, but to use the tools of the expert. For example, Irina, a third grader, is an astronaut planning her flight to Mars. She trains in the library, gathering information on her pressurized astronaut suit and life without gravity. She uses tools of the scientist, such as the telescope and photos from NASA. She tastes astronaut food and learns how her space ship works. She keeps a journal of her preparations, which is the formative assessment that generates data for the teacher and librarian. It contains drawings, photos, and daily written entries that track Irina's "journey." Her entries are structured by writing prompts designed to provide data about her progress, understanding, and knowledge construction. The school librarian and classroom teacher monitor these "teachable moments" and offer appropriate interventions. Taking the broad point of view, the authentic learning task is the assessment. Figure 10.3 shows how an authentic learning task looks different from a traditional project-based assignment that tends to be product-, rather than process-, oriented (Gordon 2007).

Table 10.1
Criteria for an Authentic Learning Task

Content	Methodology	Design
The task	The learner	The teacher
• is meaningful, academic	• uses prior knowledge, experiences	• includes clear expectations and outcomes
• relates to internal and external learning standards	• applies information to new situations	• provides exemplars
• uses tools of the expert	• uses divergent, critical thinking	• identifies resources
• requires problem solving, decision making	• engages in a variety of tasks	• offers assessment tools appropriate for the task
• culminates in a summative assessment based in whole or part on display, presentation, and/or sharing of outcomes	• has choices	• includes learners in the development of the assessment
	• uses ongoing formative assessments that offer opportunities for self-evaluation, peer review, and revision	• includes input from learners and teachers for task evaluation and revision
	• has opportunities to work in groups	

Source: Gordon, Carol A. 2007. "A Study of a Three-Dimensional Action Research Training Model for School Library Programs." *School Library Media Research.* http://ala.org/ala/aasl/aaslpubsandjournals/slmrb/slmrcontents/volume9/actionresearch.htm.
Reprinted with permission of School Library Media Research.

Figure 10.3
Projects vs. Authentic Learning Tasks

Projects	Authentic Learning Tasks
Assume role of students	Assume role of historians, writers, scientists
Focus on content of curriculum	Focus on inquiry driven by academic questions
Choose from presented options	Create responses
Are assessed through recall, recognition, minimal competencies	Are assessed through performance, problem-solving
Are assessed summatively	Are assessed formatively as well as summatively
Depend on authority	Students are critics

Source: Gordon, Carol A. 2007. "A Study of a Three-Dimensional Action Research Training Model for School Library Programs." *School Library Media Research.* http://ala.org/ala/aasl/aaslpubsandjournals/slmrb/slmrcontents/volume9/actionresearch.htm. Reprinted with permission of School Library Media Research.

Assessment of projects tends to focus on the products that students create rather than on processes such as higher-order thinking skills of application, analysis, synthesis, and evaluation (Bloom 1956). When students are doing authentic research, which is a specialized type of authentic learning task; they are focusing on inquiry driven by questions that are essential to the structure of the discipline in which the assignment is nested. They are no longer expected to be students operating in the artificial learning environment of school, but to think and respond as historians, or mathematicians, or scientists, or writers as they learn the distinct structures of these disciplines. This is a structuralist approach to learning: one cannot understand a discipline until one understands its structure. "The curriculum of a subject should be determined by the most fundamental understanding that can be achieved of the underlying principles that give structure to that subject" (Bruner 1960, 31). This structure of an academic discipline dictates unique methods of inquiry that researchers use to expand knowledge in the discipline. These knowledge structures open doors to discovery.

> Mastery of the fundamental ideas of a field involves not only the grasping of general principles, but also the development of an attitude toward learning and inquiry, toward guessing and hunches, toward the possibility of solving problems on one's own. Just as a physicist has certain attitudes about the ultimate orderliness of nature and a conviction that order can be discovered, so a young physicist student needs some working version of these attitudes if he is to organize his learning in such a way as to make what he learns usable and meaningful in his thinking. To instill such attitudes by teaching requires something more than the mere presentation of fundamental ideas. . . . it would seem that an important ingredient is a sense of excitement about discovery. (Bruner 1960, 20)

For example, what does it look like when a student becomes a historian? A tenth grader researches whether the power of kings really derived from God. His research is framed by the essential historical questions: "What was it like to live in the past?" "What really happened?" He explores primary documents and artifacts that provide evidence to answer these questions. He is concerned with attribution and citation in order to confirm the evidence. He looks for bias and distortion of facts. These are the literacies of historical inquiry. Authentic research cannot be guided solely by information literacy. Instead, school librarians, in collaboration with teachers who are content area experts, instruct students in the structure of the academic disciplines and use that structure as the framework for guided inquiry. Thus the integrity of the academic subjects is preserved in terms of their structure. There is a lot of work to be done in this area to provide school librarians with the mentoring and materials that will ensure effective interventions that will motivate, guide and remediate learners.

The use of authentic learning tasks and authentic assessments, when used concurrently with action research methodologies, as shown in figure 10.4, constitutes authentic teaching whereby the evidence-based context generates data from authentic learning tasks and assessments, as well data collection methods appropriate to the academic discipline in which the inquiry is nested (Gordon 2007).

The practitioner researcher can add the dimension of action research to any instructional unit that is authentic assessment-based by posing the question, "How can I do it better next time?" Data are gathered from students who fill out a survey as shown in Figure 10.5 (Gordon 2007). The survey is designed to elicit student ratings about the support they were given for a research paper (questions 1–10) as well as their sustained comments to more general questions about the assignment (questions 11–15). It can be adapted for any assignment and grade level by adjusting the language, by replacing numerical ratings with graphics, and by oral, rather than written explication.

USING QUALITATIVE DATA COLLECTION METHODS

When school librarians and classroom teachers become practitioner-researchers, they experience the same cognitive stages, feelings, and behaviors as their students who are

Figure 10.4
A Model for Authentic Teaching

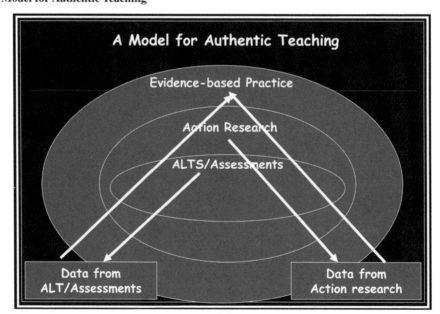

Source: Gordon, Carol A. 2007. "A Study of a Three-Dimensional Action Research Training Model for School Library Programs." *School Library Media Research.* http://ala.org/ala/aasl/aaslpubsandjournals/slmrb/slmrcontents/volume9/actionresearch.htm. Reprinted with permission of School Library Media Research.

Figure 10.5
"How Can I Do It Better Next Time?" Student Survey

Circle number 1 if you strongly disagree, number 2 if you disagree, number 3 if you agree, and 4 if you strongly agree.

1. Timelines were reasonable.	1	2	3	4
2. Instructions were clear.	1	2	3	4
3. Library resources were adequate.	1	2	3	4
4. I could get help when I needed it.	1	2	3	4
5. I felt well-prepared to search for information.	1	2	3	4
6. Bibliography charts were helpful.	1	2	3	4
7. Graphic organizers for note taking were helpful.	1	2	3	4
8. The list of key words was helpful.	1	2	3	4
9. Grading (50% for information literacy/research skills and 50% for content) was fair.	1	2	3	4
10. Now I understand the difference between the Internet and a library.	1	2	3	4
11. What were the best things about this project?				
12. What would you change?				
13. What was the most difficult task? Why do you think it was difficult?				
14. How was this project different from others you have done?				
15. Do you think this project was worth the class time allotted? Why? / Why not?				
Other comments:				

Source: Gordon, Carol A. 2007. "A Study of a Three-Dimensional Action Research Training Model for School Library Programs." *School Library Media Research*. http://ala.org/ala/aasl/aaslpubsandjournals/slmrb/slmrcontents/volume9/actionresearch.htm. Reprinted with permission of School Library Media Research.

engaged in research. As shown in figure 10.6, Kuhlthau's Information Search Process (1983) captures these complexities.

Practitioner-researchers should be aware of their own progress through the model as they conduct action research. For example, the focus stage of the Information Search Process is difficult: it requires knowledge of the subject being researched to formulate a focus, but it is situated early in the process before information collection. It is evident that practitioner-researchers, like their students, need support and intervention. In a study that resulted in an action research training model, instruments were developed to accomplish this. The proposal template (figure 10.7) is a focusing instrument that requires researchers to read, without note taking, to formulate a focus, and to generate a short list of pertinent resources (Gordon 2007). The proposal template helps the practitioner-researchers to focus their action research as well as plan their authentic learning task. The guiding question for developing the survey is, "How can you change your teaching to help students perform better?"

WHAT DOES ACTION RESEARCH LOOK LIKE?

Two school librarians collaborated with a fifth grade teacher to investigate whether their students could distinguish between ethical and unethical use of information. To find out,

Figure 10.6
The Information Search Process

Kuhlthau's Model of the Information Search Process

Stages	Feelings	Thoughts		Actions
Task Initiation	uncertainty	ambiguity		seeking
		i	i	relevant
Topic Selection	optimism	n	n	information
		c	t	
Pre-focus exploration	confusion	r	e	
		e	r	
Focus formulation	clarity	a	e	
		s	s	
Information Collection	confidence	e	t	
		d		
Search closure	relief	specificity		seeking
				pertinent
Starting writing	satisfaction/dissatisfaction			information

Note: Figure 10.6 represents the information search process developed by Carol C. Kuhlthau (1983).

they designed a survey, "Is This Okay? Is This Not Okay?" The school librarians and teacher proposed a rationale for administering the survey to their students.

> With this generation's easy access to information, ethical use questions have arisen. This action research project was developed to survey the ethical use, knowledge, practices of fifth grade students. . . . The survey results indicated areas of misunderstanding with regard to what constitutes plagiarism, copyright infringement, and what are "fair" or "unfair" practices with regard to use of information (Parker, Sand, and Skoropowski 2004).
>
> They wondered whether there would be a difference in students' responses to the survey before and after they taught the class about ethical information use in the context of thematic units of instruction in social studies and science. The timeline ranged from November to May of the school year. Students could respond in one of three ways to each question: Fair, Unfair, Not Sure. Samples of survey questions appear in column 1 of table 10.2 (Parker, Sand, and Skoropowski 2004).

To address the concerns in column 2 of the table, the librarians and teacher taught lessons on note taking, using bibliography cards, and what it meant to plagiarize. Instruction also addressed copyright; a lawyer/parent was invited to talk to the class. The post-survey listed in column 3 showed substantial improvement. Additionally the practitioner-researchers asked students the following questions when they administered the post-survey (Parker, Sand, and Skoropowski 2004).

1. What is plagiarism?
2. Why would someone be tempted to plagiarize?

Figure 10.7
A Template for Practitioner Researchers' Proposals.

PROPOSAL FOR ACTION RESEARCH SUBMITTED BY: (Practitioner Researcher)

1. Research question or hypothesis stated as a question

2. Area of Investigation (e.g., Instruction, Library Management, Public Relations....)

    a. Topic _____

    b. Teacher collaborator (if needed) _____

    c. Timelines

        Start: _____

        End: _____

    d. Description of the project or unit. Please include information, such as what is suggested below, to provide enough information so that someone could replicate your unit. For example, Student product? Information/research skills stressed/assessed? Assessments? Lessons taught? Support materials used?

How will this investigation improve your practice?

3. Data Collection

Two types of evidence (e.g., interviews, surveys, grades, observation/journal entries, photographs, student products/projects)

Source: Gordon, Carol A. 2007. "A Study of a Three-Dimensional Action Research Training Model for School Library Programs." *School Library Media Research.* http://ala.org/ala/aasl/aaslpubsand journals/slmrb/slmrcontents/volume9/actionresearch.htm.
Reprinted with permission of School Library Media Research.

3. Draw the copyright symbol.

4. Explain some things you can do to make sure you do not plagiarize and violate copyright laws.

The results are summarized in Table 10.3.

So what did the action research team learn from their experience of conducting action research? Their findings can be categorized as follows (Parker, Sand, and Skoropowski 2004):

1. What did we learn that surprised us?

    • Students didn't know how much help is okay.

    • Students didn't see the librarian as a resource.

    • Copying CDs, software, videos was thought to be okay.

    • Students showed honesty in their responses on the survey and in questions posed during classroom lessons.

2. How will this project change or inform our practice?

    • We need to make students aware that their school librarian is a resource to assist them with research.

    • We need to introduce ethical use practices/knowledge as an information literacy skill at a younger age. Currently ethical information use is addressed in 7th grade.

    • This year our research centered around 5th grade classrooms, two from each school; we determined that a copyright dos and don'ts lesson would be beneficial to 5th graders next year.

Table 10.2.
Is This Okay? Is This Not Okay? Survey and Results

Is this okay? Is this not okay?	Pre-survey	Post-survey
1. John goes to the library and asks the librarian to help him search the Internet for information for his report on hurricanes.	31% thought this was Fair or Not Sure	10% thought this was Fair or Not Sure
2. Lindsey copies 2 complete sentences from a Web site and includes them in her report without using quotation marks.	34% thought this was Fair or Not Sure	3% thought this was Fair or Not Sure
3. Jane needs 3 sources of information for her report on New Hampshire. She has used only 2. She lists a source she did not use in her bibliography so she will have the 3 she needs.	44% thought this was Fair or Not Sure	14% thought this was Fair or Not Sure
4. Will cuts and pastes a chart for his hurricane report from a Web site and doesn't include the Web site in his bibliography.	30% thought this was Fair or Not Sure	3% thought this was Fair or Not Sure
5. Ben downloads copyrighted music from the Internet.	32% thought this was Fair or Not Sure	16% thought this was Fair or Not Sure
6. Alex uses a video he bought to make copies for his friends.	38% thought this was Fair or Not Sure	2% thought this was Fair or Not Sure
7. Mary has new software for her computer. She lets her friend, Madison, install the software on her computer too.	80% thought this was Fair or Not Sure	12% thought this was Fair or Not Sure
8. Sean burns a CD for his friend with his favorite songs from his CD collection.	81% thought this was Fair or Not Sure	20% thought this was Fair or Not Sure
9. Jillian lets her friend photocopy a guitar music book so her friend will not have to buy it.	47% thought this was Fair or Not Sure	26% thought this was Fair or Not Sure

Table 10.3
Student Responses to Additional Post-Survey Questions

Research Question	Student Responses
What is plagiarism?	*83% correctly defined "plagiarism."*
Why would someone be tempted to plagiarize?	*Don't want to buy something. (33%)* *Quick, easy, saves time. (28%)* *Get good grade. (11%)* *Need more information. (9%)* *Well written. (5%)* *Help a friend. (5%)* *Time pressure. (4%)* *Don't know the law. (2%)* *Friends think it's cool. (2%)* *Other people do it all the time (1%)*
Draw the copyright symbol	*74% of students were able to draw the copyright symbol correctly.*
Explain some things you can do to make sure you do not plagiarize and violate copyright laws.	*Use your own words (23%)* *Bibliography (21%)* *Use quotation marks (19%)* *Take notes (15%)* *Don't steal CDs, movies, etc. (14%)* *Do the right thing (7%)* *Don't copy (7%)* *Get permission to copy (6%)* *Study copyright law (5%)* *Buy CDs (5%)* *Ask an adult (2%)* *Other (2%)*

3. How would we teach differently next time?

   - We would spend more time on note taking and bibliography lessons. We discovered that students were not familiar with note-taking strategies or the benefits of taking good notes. A review of good note-taking practices should be offered at the onset of each research project.

   - Lessons on highlighting pertinent information from a source should be offered to students.

   - A follow-up lesson on copyright laws would be welcomed by students. They had a lot of questions and were very interested. Our copyright attorney was a wonderful resource and she was willing to answer any questions the students posed.

   - If time permitted, individual student interviews would have been a nice addition. It would have been beneficial to document their response to questions such as these: What did you learn that you didn't know before? Has this knowledge changed your attitude or practices with regard to what is "fair" and "unfair" use of copyrighted materials?

4. What were some of the most difficult aspects of doing this action research?

   - Scheduling time to meet with students. Our 5th grade teachers have many curriculum requirements to meet, so it was difficult scheduling class time to teach these additional lessons.

   - Trying to answer students' questions and realizing that we were not familiar enough with the interpretations of copyright laws. It is one thing to know the laws, but interpreting them is a different matter.

5. What were some of the most rewarding or helpful aspects of doing this action research?

   • The students' eagerness to hear and discuss ethical use dos and don'ts with us.

   • Receptivity of the students to the subject.

   • The post survey results, which demonstrated the change in attitude and student understanding of the material presented.

WHAT DO SCHOOL LIBRARIANS AND TEACHERS THINK ABOUT ACTION RESEARCH?

The author has worked with school librarians and teachers in Londonderry, New Hampshire, who are in their sixth year of action research. After their first year, the practitioner-researchers reported the following reactions to the process.

> [Action research] . . . caused me to think about the disconnect between the teacher's and my perception of the usefulness of technology in the writing process and some of the students' perceptions. The most difficult aspect of doing action research was ". . . making sure the action research blended well with the teacher's objectives." (Gordon 2007)

At the midpoint of the project the Londonderry Director of Library, Media and Technology noted, "They do not know their own power even though they have carte blanche in their buildings and their principals are very supportive" (Gordon 2007).

By the end of the project, school librarians experienced more confidence in collaborating with teachers, even when their collaboration was not initially successful.

> I feel I have concrete data, and common discussion points, to bring to the Freshman House teachers . . . to improve students' performance. I think the Social Studies and Science teachers can see how information skills affect their curriculums . . . The reading teacher is working to improve skills we identified as weak and I would like to increase the degree of collaboration with the teachers. The reading teacher would like to enlist me as a compatriot in teaching skills of reading non-fiction. (Gordon 2007)

A factor in helping school librarians gain ownership and confidence was their ability to make the leap from reflection generated by their action research to the action plan. There were many journal entries and comments like this one:

> Note taking—kids are on target—have lots of sources, but we need to consider revising our "Trash or Treasure" review—need to present on overhead—then give each student a researchable question and the paragraph on which to take notes instead of completing it as a group exercise. All students would still have the same paragraph and question, but would be accountable for their own notes. (Gordon 2007)

Action research was a powerful intervention that empowered the school librarians with hard evidence for improvement of the instructional unit, and consequently, with a sense of ownership.

The way that school librarians felt about the action research was a key indicator of their confidence levels and, in turn, their feelings about collaboration. One explained the most rewarding aspect of her action research: "It raised my awareness and caused me to think differently about assumptions and making decisions" (Gordon 2007). Although they were excited about their projects and research findings at the end of the action research project, it was not until after their presentations at the state conference that they seemed to find their voices as leaders. They exhibited energy, enthusiasm, and confidence that were transformational. They had clarified their personal teaching theories, explored their sense of self and their role as teachers, and gained awareness of their students' perspectives and needs.

CONCLUSION

Action research anchors the school library in the teaching and learning context of the school, enhancing its instructional role and breaking down barriers between classroom and library. It bolsters school librarians' confidence and transforms their perceptions of their role from one of support to one of leadership. As one librarian stated, engaging in action research entails taking risks, but risks with rewards.

> Reflective thinking is always more or less troublesome because it involves overcoming the inertia that inclines one to accept suggestions at their face value; it involves willingness to endure a condition of mental unrest and disturbance. Reflective thinking . . . means judgment suspended during further inquiry; and suspense is likely to be somewhat painful . . . To maintain the state of doubt and to carry on systematic and protracted inquiry—these are the essentials of thinking. (Gordon 2007)

REFERENCES

Allport, Gordon W. 1948. "Introduction." In *Resolving Social Conflicts: Selected Papers on Group Dynamics.* Kurt Lewin, ed. Gertrud W. Lewin, 1–7. New York: Harper & Row.

Anderson, Gary K., Kathryn G. Herr, and Ann Nihlen. 1994. *Studying Your Own School: An Educator's Guide to Qualitative Practitioner Research.* Thousand Oaks, CA: Corw2007.

Bloom, Benjamin S. 1956. *Taxonomy of Educational Objectives: The Classification of Educational Goals.* New York: McKay.

Boomer, Garth. 1987. "Addressing the Problem of Elsewhereness: A Case for Action Research in Our School." In *Reclaiming the Classroom: Teacher Research as Agency of Change,* ed. Dixie Goswami and Peter Stillman, 4–13. Portsmouth, NH: Boynton/Cook Publishers.

Bruner, Jerome S. 1960. *The Process of Education.* Cambridge, MA: Harvard University Press.

Coughlan, David, and Teresa Brannick. 2004. *Doing Action Research in Your Own Organization.* Beverly Hills, CA: Sage Publications.

Gordon, Carol A. 1996. "Is Fish a Vegetable? A Qualitative Study of a Ninth-Grade Research Project." *School Library Media Quarterly 25,* no. 1: 27–33.

Gordon, Carol A. 1999. "Students as Authentic Researchers: A New Prescription for the High School Research Assignment." School Library Media Research 2. http://www.ala.org/ala/aasl/asslpubsandjournals/slmrb/slmrcontents/volume21999/vol2gordon.htm (accessed October 24, 2006).

Gordon, Carol A. 2007. "A Study of a Three-Dimensional Action Research Training Model for School Library Programs." *School Library Media Research.* http://ala.org/ala/aasl/aaslpubsandjournals/slmrb/slmrcontents/volume9/actionresearch.htm (accessed January 19, 2007).

Hall, Calvin S., Gardner Lindzey, and John B. Campbell. 1978. *Theories of Personality.* New York: John Wiley & Sons.

Hart, Elizabeth, and Meg Bond. 1995. *Action Research for Health and Social Care: A Guide to Practice.* Buckingham, PA: Open University Press.

Kuhlthau, Carol C. 1983. *The Library Research Process: Case Studies and Interventions with High School Seniors in Advanced Placement English Classes Using Kelly's Theory of Constructs.* PhD diss., Rutgers University.

Lewin, Kurt. 1948. Resolving Social Conflics: Selected Papers on Group Dynamics. Ed. Gertrud W. Lewin. New York: Harper and Row.

Lewin, Kurt. 1951. *Field Theory in Social Science: Selected Theoretical Papers.* Edited by Dorwin Cartwright. New York: Harper & Row.

Masters, Janet. 1995. "The History of Action Research" In *Action Research Electronic Reader,* ed. Ian Hughes. http://www.scu.edu.au/schools/gcm/ar/arr/arow/rmasters.html (accessed October 20, 2006).

McKernan, James. 1991. *Curriculum Action Research: A Handbook of Methods and Resources for the Reflective Practitioner.* London: Kogan Page.

McTaggart, Robin. 1996. "Talk for a Chautauqua: Issues for Participatory Action Researchers." In *New Directions in Action Research,* ed. Ortrun Zuber-Skerritt, 234–255. London: Falmer Press.

Parker, Marie, Jean Sand, and Stella Skoropowski. 2004. *Is This Okay? Is This Not Okay? Do 5th Grade Students Know the Difference Between Ethical and Unethical Use of Information?* Londonderry, NH: Londonderry School District.

Patterson, Leslie. 1996. "Reliving the Learning: Learning from Classroom Talk and Texts." In *Research in the Classroom: Talk, Texts, and Inquiry,* ed. Zoe Donahue, Mary Ann Tassell, and Leslie Patterson, 3–9. Newark, DE: International Reading Association.

Patterson, Leslie, and Patrick Shannon. 1993. "Reflection, Inquiry, Action." In *Teachers Are Researchers: Reflection and Action,* ed. Leslie Patterson, Carol Minnick, Kathy G. Short, and Karen Smith, 7–11. Newark, DE: International Reading Association.

Schein, Edgar H. n.d. *Kurt Lewin's Theory in the Field and in the Classroom: Notes toward a Model of Managed Learning.* http://www.a2zpsychology.com/ARTICLES/KURT_LEWIN'S_CHANGE_THEORY.HTM (accessed October 5, 2006).

Smith, Mark. 2001. "Kurt Lewin: Groups, Experiential Learning and Action Research." In *The Encyclopedia Of Informal Education.* http://www.infed.org/thinkers/et-lewin.htm (accessed October 24, 2006).

Stringer, Ernest T. 1999. *Action Research.* Thousand Oaks, CA: Sage Publications.

Todd, Ross J. 2001. "Transitions for Preferred Futures of School Libraries: Connections, Not Collections; Actions, Not Positions; Evidence, Not Advocacy." Paper presented at the annual meeting for the International Association of School Librarianship in Auckland, New Zealand, July 9–12, 2001. http://www.iasl-slo.org/virtualpaper2001.html (accessed October 24, 2006).

Todd, Ross J. 2003. "Learning in the Information Age School: Opportunities, Outcomes, and Options." Paper presented at the annual meeting for the International Association of School Librarianship, Durbin, South Africa, July 7–12, 2003. http://www.iasl-slo.org/conference2003-virtual-pap.html (accessed October 24, 2006).

Wiggins, Grant. 1993. *Assessing Student Performance: Exploring the Purpose and Limits of Testing.* San Francisco: Jossey-Bass.

Wood, Patricia. 1988. "Action Research: A Field Perspective." Paper presented at the annual meeting for the American Educational Research Association in New Orleans, LA, April 1988.

Ziegler, Mary. 2001. "Improving Practice Through Action Research." *Adult Learning* 12, no. 1: 3–4.

11

Professional Development in Communities of Practice

Joyce Yukawa, Violet H. Harada, and Daniel Suthers

As discussed in earlier chapters, improving practitioner quality requires a broad program of strategic recruitment and changes in school context. Within this broader program, in-service professional development plays a critical role. How can professional development contribute to effective school reform? In addition to the No Child Left Behind (NCLB) focus on ensuring that teachers have sufficient content knowledge in core academic subjects, it is also critical to assist educators in improving their skills as reflective practitioners. This chapter discusses how reflective practice can be fostered by a program of professional development that emphasizes learning in communities of practice. We introduce the concepts of reflective practice and communities of practice, describe how we have implemented these concepts in a course involving inquiry partnerships between teachers and library media specialists, and conclude with guidelines for professional development.

REFLECTIVE PRACTICE

Reflective practice (Schön 1983) has been clearly established as a key component of practitioner growth and effectiveness (NCATE 2001). Reflective practice is valuable not only for the sustained growth of individual practitioners but also for school and district improvement and educational reform. York-Barr and colleagues (2006) describe a "reflective practice spiral" that begins with individual reflection and then extends to reflection with partners, reflection in small groups and teams, school-wide reflective practice, and beyond these to broader social groups and systems. A reflective educator is one who "is committed to continuous improvement in practice; assumes responsibility for his or her own learning; demonstrates awareness of self, others, and the surrounding context; develops the thinking skills for effective inquiry; and takes action that aligns with new understandings" (York-Barr et al. 2006, 10). Two important personal capacities that promote reflection are building trusting relationships and expanding thought and inquiry.

Similarly, Robb (2000) redefines school staff development as inquiry-based professional development within a school that "creates a teacher-centered learning environment that recognizes and respects the differences in teachers' theoretical backgrounds, prior knowledge, familiarity with [content areas], classroom experiences, and expertise" (2). Her alternative to the typical one-day teacher training—one-size-fits-all presentation with minimal administrator support and lack of follow-up support—is a program of peer coaching, lead teachers, and study groups. Key ingredients are supportive administrators and support networks among teachers to create a climate for change. Among the conditions that contribute to change are personal commitment, collaboration, risk taking, reflection and evaluation, and feedback.

Osterman and Kottkamp (1993) argue that top-down reform fails to create change because change begins with practitioners. They believe that reflective practice has the greatest potential to create educational improvement because it is "situation specific and places the professional in the very center of the attempt to create improvement" (187). Their reflective practice model posits that change comes via self-awareness and that it is not only rational but also emotional, social, and cultural. They provide an important caveat—that the means and ends of reflection cannot be formulaic or predetermined: "We cannot reach an externally produced, preordained end through genuine reflective practice processes. Because reflective practice leads individuals to improve their own performance, the process ultimately enriches the organization's ability to achieve goals, but it is an unwritten assumption that through reflection many alternative and effective paths to the same goal will emerge" (Osterman and Kottkamp 1993, 187).

Levin (2003) conducted a rare 15-year longitudinal study of four student teachers as they matured into professionals. She found that three major factors influenced the development of their pedagogical understandings over their careers: (1) ongoing support in order to continue to develop and to remain in the classroom; (2) opportunities that encouraged and allowed them to continue to be learners; and (3) reflective and metacognitive thinking about teaching, learning, behavior, and development.

Thus, we see that effective professional development reflects the following attributes: (1) personal commitment; (2) building trusting relationships through collaboration; (3) opportunities and ongoing support for continuous learning; (4) inquiry-based, practice-based learning within school settings; (5) respect for differences in practitioners' theoretical backgrounds, prior knowledge, experiences, and expertise; (6) risk taking; and (7) evaluation and feedback.

PROFESSIONAL DEVELOPMENT FOR REFLECTIVE PRACTICE

How well do current professional development efforts reflect these attributes? Typical professional development activities are often: (1) focused on individual learning; (2) one-time events (e.g., lecture or workshop) or formal classroom instruction (e.g., semester-long course); (3) conducted away from school; (4) based on artificial exercises or independent practice without guidance; (5) focused on action rather than reflection; and (6) focused on answers rather than inquiry.

Based on expert findings and the experiences we describe in this chapter, we believe that a practice-based approach within communities of practice offers an effective means to achieve sustainable school reform through professional growth for individuals and schools. The practice-based approach to professional development (PD), advanced by Ball and Cohen (1999), uses authentic records and tools for teaching and learning with the aim of creating a common ground for individuals and teams to work, co-reflect, explore alternatives, and support each other. Activities are grounded in participants' ongoing efforts to design units of instruction and strategies for assessing student learning. This approach recognizes that curriculum reform involves "just in time" learning focusing on immediate problems of practice as well as problems of greater complexity. It acknowledges that the processes of teaching and learning are ambiguous, complicated, and nonlinear. The curriculum centers on the tasks, questions, and problems situated in practice. Instead of definitive answers and preordained solutions, participants focus on possibilities, methods of reasoning, and alternative conjectures. Importantly, this inquiry-oriented stance is a collective endeavor where professionals learn from one another.

Learning collaboratively through relationships formed in practice is the age-old means of learning in community articulated by Dewey (1897) a century ago and rearticulated for our time as communities of practice (CoPs). Since the 1991 publication of *Situated Learning* by Jean Lave and Etienne Wenger and Wenger's later elaboration (Wenger 1998), the CoP concept has achieved wide-ranging resonance with practitioners, primarily in education, health care, knowledge management, and computer-supported collaborative learning, but also in such diverse areas as sociolinguistics, geography, engineering, anthropology, religious education, and gender studies.

COMMUNITIES OF PRACTICE

What are communities of practice? CoPs are groups of people who share similar goals and interests and collaborate over time to share ideas and find solutions (Lave and Wenger 1991; Wenger 1998; Wenger, McDermott, and Snyder 2002). What holds them together is a common vision, a sense of purpose, and a real need to know what each other knows. In pursuit of these goals and interests, they employ common practices, work with the same tools, and express themselves in a common language. Through such activity, they come to hold similar beliefs and value systems. They collaborate directly, use one another as sounding boards, and teach and learn from each other. They are colleagues committed to jointly developing better practices. Increasingly, these communities are found online. We describe a model of learning in communities of practice (adapted from Wenger 1998) that involves relationship building, three modes of participation, and three creative tensions that influence participation in online professional development communities (see Figure 11.1).

Building Trusting Relationships

In a CoP, one learns and comes to know by doing, reflecting, and co-reflecting in trusting relationships with other practitioners (Dufour and Eaker 1998, Lave and Wenger 1991; Spraker 2003; Wenger 1998). CoPs create opportunities for learning through building these relationships in a shared practice with a vision and goals for achieving the vision. Trusting relationships support all activity within a community of practice and constitute the binding force for the community.

Participation

Trusting relationships are built through participation. Three modes of participation in a CoP provide opportunities for learning: engagement, imagination, and alignment.

Figure 11.1
Learning in Communities of Practice

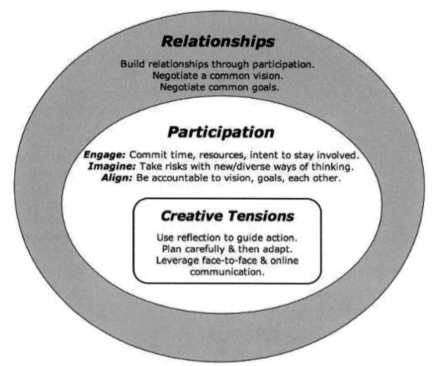

Engagement is a process of getting and staying involved. This is the most basic way of participating. When we participate through sustained, long-term involvement, we build relationships, learn who is good at what, and come to know how we can contribute best. We create a shared history and shared practices through engagement.

Imagination involves considering new or diverse ways of thinking related to our practice and our situation. This is a deeper type of participation than engagement. We use imagination when we brainstorm, try to see things from others' points of view, get outside advice, and exchange ideas with other communities. Because we consider new or diverse ways of thinking, conflict is inevitable. Trusting, respectful, strong relationships provide support for open and honest exploration through imagination (Grossman, Wineburg, and Woolworth 2000).

Alignment is achieving consensus on and consistency of vision, goals, and action among community members. This is the deepest form of participation and at its best is a harmony of ideas, values, and practices. There are diverse means by which alignment can be achieved, ranging from individual and community initiatives to those that are externally imposed by law. Harmony is challenging to achieve but, in the long run, more effective and efficient because community members work together from desire rather than directives that do not have enthusiastic support. If a whole community is behind an effort, the effort has sustainability because it will be carried on even if some community members leave.

Creative Tensions

Tensions are inherent to social participation. While tension is commonly thought of as the stress or conflict that arises from competing choices, a *creative tension* involves two elements that are always involved, interact, and take different forms and degrees. The focus is not on choosing one element or the other but on understanding the interaction between them and using this effectively. Three creative tensions are fundamental to participation in a professional CoP: (1) reflection and action, (2) the planned and the emerging, and (3) face-to-face and online communication.

In the context of professional development, the creative tension of *reflection and action* is best understood as reflective practice—using reflection to guide our actions. This involves collaborative learning and using best practices under the complex, ambiguous, and often time-scarce conditions of daily teaching. The power of this inquiry-learning process is that ideas and questions are tested through experience. Best practices are the basis for future action, providing goals and concepts that interact with experience. In a professional development community, this process creates a history of shared experience and collaboratively created tools, such as curriculum maps and assessment strategies that strengthen the community and sustain reform efforts.

The creative tension of *the planned and the emerging* refers to the need for both careful planning and adaptation to the changing or unpredictable conditions of actual practice. Planned structure interacts with emerging structure, for example, practitioners' knowledge of curriculum standards interacts with a growing awareness of the needs of students with differing abilities and potential. Uncertainty exists between a plan and realizing it in practice, since practice is not the result of a plan but a response to it.

The creative tension of *face-to-face and online communication* (added to CoP theory by Barab, MaKinster and Scheckler 2003) refers to leveraging the communication strengths of each of the modes and compensating for their respective weaknesses. In professional development that is based on face-to-face communication, facilitators and participants have a wide range of communication resources to draw from to convey meaning. They share the same physical environment, see each other, hear each other, and engage in conversation using implicit social rules for taking turns (Clark and Brennan 1991). Because these features are generally missing from online communication, communicators must consciously adopt compensatory strategies. A clear advantage of using online media is the ability to communicate at any time from anywhere, enabling interaction that might not otherwise take place. In addition, written communication, the predominant medium in online environments, has several advantages (Clark and Brennan 1991). Communicators can review each other's messages as often as they desire, because the messages are permanently recorded. This encourages reflection and co-reflection. Communicators can also revise messages for each other before sending them, potentially avoiding embarrassment or conflict.

The remainder of this chapter focuses on a course designed to develop the notion of reflection in a professional community of teachers and library media specialists.

DESIGNING FOR LEARNING IN A COMMUNITY OF PRACTICE

A yearlong professional development course, "Inquiry Learning through Librarian-Teacher Partnerships," was conducted in 2005–2006. Jointly sponsored by the Hawaii Department of Education's (HIDOE) School Library Services (SLS) Division and the University of Hawaii's (UH) Library and Information Science (LIS) Program, the course was designed on CoP principles.

The course development team included three facilitators/mentors (called "mentors"), as well as research and support staff from HIDOE and UH. The lead developer and mentor was a professor in the LIS Program with expertise and many years of experience teaching and facilitating workshops. A second senior mentor was a retired library media specialist, an experienced practitioner and skilled facilitator, who had collaborated on professional development activities with the lead mentor for many years. The third mentor was an SLS staff member skilled in the use of technology for learning and a former student of the lead mentor. Thus, the mentor team began the course with the fundamentals of a CoP in place: trusting relationships in a shared practice with a vision and goals for achieving the vision.

The participants in this four-credit, fee-based course were nine K–12 school teams of library media specialists and teachers as curriculum partners who designed and implemented inquiry-focused instruction, and three library media specialists who participated without teacher partners. The practitioners varied widely in experience, from relatively new professionals to veterans with over 30 years of experience. The library media specialists, most of them former students of the lead mentor, took the lead in forming their own teams to participate in the course.

The collaboration histories of the teams ranged from those newly formed for the course to teams working together for many years. Among some of the experienced teams, strong friendships had developed, with brainstorming and planning taking place during Friday night pizza dinners or Saturday morning exercise sessions. While many of the library media specialists had known each other from previous LIS courses or through participating in state library associations, most of the teachers did not know any of the other participants except their team partner.

Both face-to-face and online media were used for course communication. Online communication was conducted via e-mail, as well as workspaces and discussion spaces available on the Hawaii Networked Learning Communities Web site (www.hnlc.org).

The learning outcomes required school teams to design and implement units that integrated content standards with information literacy skills. Specifically, the teams were guided to address these key concepts and course objectives:

Objective 1: Determine essential questions through:

- Focusing on a generative theme or problem.
- Identifying one or more essential questions that drive the project.
- Transforming standards into clearly stated learning criteria.

Objective 2: Foster the inquiry process through:

- Defining student performance tasks that clearly measure the learning goals.
- Incorporating strategies that motivate student curiosity.
- Incorporating strategies that challenge students to generate higher-level questions.
- Incorporating strategies that help students investigate their theme or problem effectively and efficiently.
- Incorporating tasks that assist students in creating personal knowledge from collected information and data.
- Requiring final products that challenge their students to effectively communicate their knowledge.

Objective 3: Achieve assessment-driven decision making through:

- Collecting and compiling formative and summative assessment data.
- Analyzing the data to inform instruction.

STRUCTURES FOR PARTICIPATION

The course was designed to provide face-to-face and online opportunities for engagement, imagination, and alignment (see Table 11.1).

Table 11.1.
Course Schedule and Requirements

Time	Activity
June	Summer Institute to introduce key concepts and plan for school-based implementation and ongoing mentoring (face-to-face, 3 days)
August–April	Onsite curriculum development and implementation by school teams
August–April	Online mentoring by mentors
Sept–March	Monthly individual logs sent via e-mail to mentors
Sept–March	Monthly team reports posted in the community discussion space
Sept–March	Responses posted in the discussion space by "buddy teams" assigned to each other by the mentors
Sept–April	Site visits by mentors on request by teams
January	Midpoint reunion to explore and clarify assessment strategies (face-to-face and videoconferencing)
February	Presentations by each team about their work at the annual Hawaii Department of Education E-School Conference
April	Learning portfolios consisting of unit and lesson plans, student samples with critiques, and cumulative team reports and individual logs

Initial Face-to-Face Engagement Activity

The initial three-day, face-to-face summer institute was a critical engagement activity. The mentors introduced the key concepts: (1) determining essential questions, (2) fostering the inquiry process, and (3) assessment-driven decision making. The mentors engaged the teams in intra- and inter-team discussions to share and reflect on their past experiences, thus connecting prior teaching activity with the key concepts through co-reflection. They also provided models and demonstrations, putting the concepts into action to support reflection and understanding.

The teams also began the work of collaborative curriculum planning. Many noted that this was a precious opportunity to work together that was difficult to find at their schools, due to the pressures of time, scheduling, and school priorities. Collaborative planning was also the means for relationship building. For first-time collaborators, it was a chance to define identities, learn who is good at what, discover how to engage with each other, and begin to establish trust and respect. Veteran teams explored new ideas in the context of their shared experiences, negotiated the meaning of the key concepts, and redefined the purpose of their collaboration for a new curriculum project. It was also an important time for participants to share across teams. All teams began to create a unit plan that would be the artifact they used throughout the year to interact, discuss, brainstorm, plan, implement, and assess their understanding of best practices. In short, the unit plan was the focus of collaborative reflective practice in both emerging and established CoPs.

The mentors introduced a general process for designing and implementing a unit, supported by monthly individual and team reflections and yearlong mentoring. Each team was assigned a buddy team with whom to co-reflect throughout the year. Monthly buddy team responses were required, but teams were encouraged to freely respond to other teams in the online discussion spaces. The culminating activities and celebrations included submission of an individual learning portfolio and team presentations at an annual state educators' conference.

Building Teams: School-Based Planning and Implementation

At their respective schools, the teams continued their collaboration. Because the institute occurred in June, working together during the remainder of the summer allowed them more time for collaboration than is normally possible during the academic year. Teams focused on understanding and assimilating new concepts and continued to develop their unit plans. Most teams revised their units, some extensively. One team wrote: "We have revised, revised, and revised our unit (via face-to-face meetings, email, phone) trying to ensure that it has all the components shared at our workshop. We then developed the related inquiry lessons and are currently in the midst of implementing. Although we have begun implementing, we are still dialoging about strategies to guide our students to make the critical connections/generalizations between science, technology, and society [that is] one of our target Science Standards of the unit."

While the teams were diverse in the grade levels, subject areas, and activities and strategies used, the team members valued the synergy and support available through partnering. As partners, they were able to share the load, bring together different skills, complement each other's working styles, act as sounding boards for each other, provide emotional support, and help each other preserve their sanity under the pressures of practice and meeting school priorities. All of these activities contributed to the development of a professional CoP around each team.

Through engagement and imagination, the team members were able to leverage their strengths. Teachers knew their subject areas and students, while library media specialists had broader knowledge of the curriculum and the research process. For one teacher, the collaboration changed her image of her library media specialist: "It was a wonderful partnership. I was never this much involved with the library before. How could I have survived all these years without the library? We're content oriented. Librarians have such a wealth of information. Talking to [my librarian partner] gave me so many ideas."

Partnering focused on the key components of the course also resulted in higher levels of achievement for both practitioners and their students. For one teacher new at her subject, inquiry "really opened up my eyes, and it took me to the next level. It helped me work with the standards and break them down. I never worked with essential questions before. This I had to learn with the kids at the same time. Working with essential questions opened up a whole lot." For one veteran team, the CoP learning design encouraged deeper critical thinking: "I see the course as helping us have deeper conversations." The team members struggled to define essential questions and their relationship to student inquiry, ultimately achieving a higher-level understanding of course concepts and alignment with each other about best practices for their students: "We addressed the essential questions as part of the background building, and the students' own questions as the inquiry." The partnering also helped another team take student achievement to a higher level: "Working together with [my librarian partner], I've spiraled my kids far above the second-grade level standards."

The importance of reflection was evident in the learning reported by this participant: "When we did our unit plans, we got the students do to their activities based on essential questions. Our curriculum coordinator told me, 'This [essential questions] is what I've been telling you all along.' But it didn't make sense until I took this class."

Along with increased competence came growing self-esteem for some: "At the first workshop, I was totally impressed with all the other teams. Everyone was so smart. Then I realized, 'Well, you're smart too.' This [class] is where I really developed my self-esteem as a teacher. This class has helped me, especially the encouragement of the mentors. They were always so positive. This showed me how to be more positive, and I was more positive with the kids."

Through imagination and alignment, several teams connected their work to school priorities and reform efforts, such as reading and writing programs, standards, and curriculum mapping. For one special education team, the course helped them move significantly toward meeting the requirements of NCLB: "NCLB raises my expectations of my SPED kids. Special Education can get very lax and just be comfortable with what the kids are learning and doing. NCLB has set my levels high, and with this class even higher." A number of teams extended their efforts to other teachers in their grade level or department, other grade levels or departments, and other support personnel such as the curriculum coordinator and technology resource teacher.

The time available to meet varied greatly by team. While some teams met weekly to plan, brainstorm, reflect, and do formative assessments, other teams were able to meet only briefly and irregularly due to school schedules. School environments also varied from strong school-wide learning communities under the leadership of the principal to more fragmented environments influenced by staff changes. Veteran teams tended to come from strong school-based learning communities.

To summarize, the real work of relationship building and community building came in the teams' work in their schools. The course design and structure provided learning opportunities but did not dictate how each team should use these opportunities. Reflective practice helped the teams develop their own understandings of best practices through testing them. Each team was also challenged to achieve its own balance of the creative tensions of reflection and action, the planned and the emerging, and face-to-face and online communication.

The competence and collaboration experience that the teams brought to the course influenced the nature of their participation and the depth of community building. One of the mentors observed that teams who were new to collaboration seemed to spend more time "tweaking their relationships and adapting to each other's styles" while veteran teams "had all the extras built into their relationships"—knowledge of each other's strengths and weaknesses, knowledge of school resources, collaboration skills, and mutual strategies and tools for curriculum development.

Teams that were strong CoPs were able to extend their work to other members of their school communities and to connect their work to school priorities. From the start, a number of the library media specialists took leadership initiative to form the teams, maintain momentum, and contribute to a change in views about the role of the librarian as curriculum partner.

Building Community Support: Online Mentoring Strategies

The use of online communication affected participation in ways both technological and social (Preece 2000). Some participants had difficulties accessing and using computers, either because of their inexperience or system difficulties at the school. One of the major barriers was lack of time. One participant noted: "We just didn't have enough time. We were so into the instruction and assessing, and revamping the lessons, that for us we felt that was more important for the kids. Our library aide posted our work online." Several participants reported that because they were oral-aural learners, it was challenging and time-consuming to read and post online.

Certain types of learning and communication were more effective face-to-face, such as modeling and demonstrations of new concepts or learning how to use new technology. The concepts and processes the participants were coping with were not always easy to express online: "It was difficult to write concisely about the project, the process, challenges and triumphs. It was easier for me to articulate about the project in person to the mentor or during the session during the break [midpoint face-to-face reunion]."

Because of the challenges of online communication, effective online mentoring strategies were critical to sustaining participation at a distance. Each month participants e-mailed individual reflection logs to the mentors and posted team reports in the online discussion space. Both logs and reports were responses to structured prompts—"prompts with a purpose," as one participant called them. The purposes of the guided reflections were to: (1) provide opportunities for individuals and teams to assess, analyze, and reflect on data related to teaching and learning; (2) provide mentoring support; and (3) encourage cross-school dialogue and critiquing.

Aware of the deficiencies of online communication compared to face-to-face, the mentors consciously used strategies that nurtured trust and strengthened their relationships with the participants. They read all messages carefully, provided feedback within 24 hours, and used a consistently positive tone. Through regular feedback, the mentors: (1) encouraged participants to collaboratively explore possibilities, methods of reasoning, and alternatives; (2) provided constructive, focused assistance; (3) gave feedback to help teams align their understandings to best practices; and (4) provided reassurance and emotional support. Examples of these mentoring strategies are provided in Table 11.2.

Building Community Support: Buddy Team Responses

Buddy teams were assigned to each other by the mentors to provide monthly team responses to team reports. This was a valuable opportunity for teams to engage with each other and provide feedback and emotional support. A number of participants noted that it was reassuring to see that other teams were facing the same problems as themselves. One library media specialist reported: "When you're the only librarian on campus, you wonder, am I doing it right? To hear from other people that they're going through the same thing, I realized I'm on track. When you send each other positive messages, it makes you want to share and want to contribute to a learning community."

Another noted: "I think being partnered with another school was good, because although all schools posted, you get so engrossed in your own project that you don't take time to read. But by being tied to another school, it forces you to take a look at what the other school learned. They may come across problems that we can make suggestions about, and they make suggestions about our work."

For some, the timing of face-to-face interactions followed by online interactions facilitated the ability to communicate online: "I would have felt uncomfortable not having met the other participants beforehand. I wouldn't know how I needed to communicate with them, how to choose my words."

The advantages of online communication were that it was convenient and "good to see what other people posted and to get feedback." However, many participants preferred face-to-face sessions. One participant noted: "Because of the time allotted and ability to have

Table 11.2.
Mentoring Strategies

Strategy 1: Encouraged participants to collaboratively explore possibilities, methods of reasoning, and alternatives.

Mentor response: "You raised some important issues in your [team] report. May I add my thoughts? You use a KWHL chart and the 'K' is a pre-assessment tool. That sounds great. What will students be asked to write down? This is where the sub-questions in kid language might help. You also asked when should the students be doing this? Wouldn't this be part of the first lesson—even before they go on the field trip? Wouldn't they also need to start the 'W' part of the chart before the trip, and keep adding to it as they come up with more questions? I think the KWHL chart is a powerful way to have the entire group see the emerging questions and the answers to these questions."

Strategy 2: Provided constructive, focused assistance.

Participant question: "I would appreciate additional insight regarding [the question web's] value because I feel I must be missing something. Is it valuable because it's an alternative to an outline? A different way of showing connections? To appeal to different learning styles?"

Mentor response: "I see it as a way of organizing the questions around a central theme. In the elementary and middle school we use it in place of an outline. Because it is more fluid, it can be adjusted at any point in the process. I always tell the kids that the question web provides a roadmap. In other words it is a visual picture of where you are going. I encourage students to add questions in response to new information. That helps them to see inquiry as an evolving process."

Strategy 3: Helped teams align their understandings to best practices.

Mentor response: "There were several things I really appreciated knowing about from your report. (1) You have the kids stretch in terms of critical thinking. You are working on causal factors in history with gr. 8 and understanding of ancient ways of knowing with gr. 7. What powerful learning experiences! (2) Graphic organizers are important tools for organizing our thinking. It is terrific that the youngsters are creating their own organizers. Could you put some examples in your workspace? It would be great for all of us. (3) You are trying to bring pieces together as teachers. With so many different mandates regarding reading and language arts, you get mired in the paperwork. Nonetheless, you can also take this as an opportunity to incorporate these literacy skills into the content areas. Good for you!"

Strategy 4: Provided reassurance and emotional support.

Mentor response: [Your partner] mentioned the 'butterflies in your tummy' feeling that everyone must be feeling about his or her presentations at the E-Conference. May I just say that you are not the only one that feels the jitters? I get them all the time when I stand before a group of adults (I am fine with the youngsters, but adults are another matter). The one thing I have discovered, however, is that most folks are sincerely interested in what I have to say because they have similar things happening at their own schools. If I begin by saying that I am a little nervous (especially if this is a new experience for me) and that what I am about to share may be experiences that they are also having in their own sites, it sends the message that I am not the 'expert.' I am a fellow teacher sharing what I know. From what you and [your partner] have divulged through your reports and logs, you have made such important discoveries—I think your enthusiasm and genuine enjoyment of working with each other will come through beautifully. [The other mentors] and I will be there to support you in any way we can."

all teams present in one location, a collegial atmosphere was created. Through facilitation and discussion, the agenda allowed us time to dialog and learn from each other." For these participants, having face-to-face sessions that effectively balanced co-reflection and action prior to engaging in online interactions was important.

The course developers learned that it was not sufficient to merely connect people by on-line communication channels. Effective strategies had to be applied to realize the value of computer-mediated communication for building a learning community. Examples included (1) familiarization with each other and the online environment in initial face-to-face sessions; (2) pairing teams in buddy teams; (3) setting specific expectations for reporting and peer feedback; and (4) responsive and supportive mentoring.

CONCLUSION

Learning as reflective members of a community of practice is an effective means of giving ourselves the growth experiences we aim to encourage in our students. The guidelines we provide in Table 11.3 are "lessons learned" from a formal course for credit, but they apply to informal school-based learning teams as well.

Leadership is a critical success factor for community participation, collaboration, and effectiveness (McGregor 2003; Snyder, Wenger, and de Sousa Briggs 2004). In the Inquiry Partnerships course, primary leadership of the group as a whole rested with the course facilitators/mentors, who planned and implemented a program of learning opportunities that provided grounding in knowledge of best practices, supported participants as they

Table 11.3.
Guidelines for Developing and Sustaining Learning in a Reflective Community of Practice

Lesson 1: Relationships in a shared practice with a vision and goals sustain the community.

Priority activities:
- Build relationships through participation.
- Negotiate a common vision for the work.
- Negotiate common goals.

Lesson 2: The three modes of participation that lead to increased involvement and deepening relationships must be supported.

Priority activities:
- Engage: Commit time, resources, and intent to stay involved.
- Imagine: Take risks with new and diverse ways of thinking.
- Align: Be accountable to vision, goals, and each other.

Lesson 3: Three creative tensions are inherent to all participation: reflection and action, the planned and the emergent, and face-to-face and online communication.

Priority activities:
- Use reflection to guide action.
- Carefully plan and adapt.
- Leverage face-to-face and online communication.

struggled with the challenges of practice, and encouraged them to grow in competence and confidence. Importantly, library media specialists often assumed a role of leadership in forming and sustaining their teams at the individual schools where trust and respect allowed strong relationships to flourish.

Reform happens when individuals and groups reform themselves, and reforms are sustained when they become part of the social consciousness of the community. By nature, social consciousness is a state of awareness arising from maturity of reflection and co-reflection within the community, not imposed from without. The vision and goals of reform are tested in practice in processes that are renewed with each testing in order to be genuine. This is the heart of practice-based professional development within communities of practice.

ACKNOWLEDGMENT

This work was partially supported by the National Science Foundation under Cooperative Agreement No. 0100393.

REFERENCES

Ball, Deborah L., and David K. Cohen. 1999. "Developing Practice, Developing Practitioners: Toward a Practice-Based Theory of Professional Education." In *Teaching As the Learning Profession: Handbook of Policy and Practice,* ed. Linda Darling-Hammond and Gary Sykes, 3–32. San Francisco: Jossey-Bass.

Barab, Sasha A., James G. MaKinster, and Rebecca Scheckler. 2003. "Designing System Dualities: Characterizing a Web-Supported Professional Development Community." *The Information Society* 19: 237–256.

Clark, Herbert, and Susan E. Brennan. 1991. "Grounding in Communication." In *Perspectives on Socially Shared Cognition,* ed. Lauren B. Resnick, John M. Levine, and Stephanie D. Teasley, 127–149. Washington, DC: American Psychological Association.

Dewey, John. 1897. "My Pedagogic Creed." *The School Journal* 54, no. 3: 77–80.

Dufour, Richard, and Robert Eaker. 1998. *Professional Learning Communities at Work: Best Practices for Enhancing Student Achievement.* Alexandria, VA: Association for Supervision and Curriculum Development.

Grossman, Pam, Sam Wineburg, and Stephen Woolworth. 2000. "Analysis of Teacher Community." Occasional paper. Center for the Study of Teaching and Policy, University of Washington. http://depts.washington.edu/ctpmail/Study17.html (accessed May 22, 2006).

Lave, Jean, and Etienne Wenger. 1991. *Situated Learning: Legitimate Peripheral Participation.* Cambridge: Cambridge University Press.

Levin, Barbara B. 2003. *Case Studies of Teacher Development: An In-Depth Look at How Thinking about Pedagogy Develops over Time.* Mahwah, NJ: Lawrence Erlbaum.

McGregor, Joy. 2003. "Collaboration and Leadership." In *Curriculum Connections through the Library,* ed. Barbara K. Stripling and Sandra Hughes-Hassell, 199–219. Westport, CT: Libraries Unlimited.

National Council for the Accreditation of Teacher Education (NCATE). 2001. *Standards for Professional Development Schools.* Washington DC: National Council for the Accreditation of Teacher Education.

Osterman, Karen F., and Robert B. Kottkamp. 1993. *Reflective Practice for Educators: Improving Schooling through Professional Development.* Newbury Park, CA: Sage.

Preece, Jenny 2000. *Online Communities: Designing Usability and Supporting Sociability.* Chichester, West Sussex, England: John Wiley and Sons.

Robb, Laura. 2000. *Redefining Staff Development: A Collaborative Model for Teachers and Administrators.* Portsmouth, NH: Heinemann.

Schön, Donald A. 1983. *The Reflective Practitioner.* New York: Basic Books.

Snyder, William M., Etienne Wenger, and Xavier de Sousa Briggs. 2004. "Communities of Practice in Government: Leveraging Knowledge for Performance." *The Public Manager* 32, no. 4: 17–21.

Spraker, Jean. 2003. *Teacher Teaming in Relation to Student Performance: Findings from the Literature.* Portland, OR: Northwest Regional Educational Laboratory. http://www.nwrel.org/re-eng/products/TeacherTeaming.pdf (accessed August 22, 2003).

Wenger, Etienne. 1998. *Communities of Practice: Learning, Meaning, and Identity.* Cambridge, UK: Cambridge University Press.

Wenger, Etienne, Richard McDermott, and William M. Snyder. 2002. *Cultivating Communities of Practice.* Cambridge, MA: Harvard Business School Press.

York-Barr, Jennifer, William A. Sommers, Gail S. Ghere, and Jo Montie. 2006. *Reflective Practice to Improve Schools: An Action Guide for Educators.* 2nd ed. Thousand Oaks, CA: Corwin.

Index

Abilock, Debbie, 30
Achievement Alliance, 25
Action research, 161–63, 166, 168,
   170–71, 176
Adequate Yearly Progress (AYP), 22, 26–29
Afflerbach, Peter, 100, 104
Agosto, Denise E., 147–48, 152
Allport, Gordon W., 164
Almost a Woman (Santiago), 152
American Association of School Librarians
   (AASL), 30, 67, 116, 135
American Educational Research Association
   (AERA), 12
American Library Association, 24, 33
Anderson, Gary K., 162, 166
Anderson, Janna, 112
Anderson, Lorin W., 137
Annual measurable achievement objectives
   (AMAO), 27
Applebee, Arthur N., 154
Armbruster, Bonnie, 98, 100
Armstrong, Jana, 100
Asselin, Marlene, 83
Association for Educational Communications
   and Technology (AECT), 67, 135

Association for Supervision and Curriculum
   Development (ASCD), 12
Auerbach, Elsa, 82
Ayers, Edward L., 114

Ba, Harouna, 116
Bagehot, Walter, 3
Ball, Deborah L., 180–81
Banks, James A., 149
Barab, Sash A., 183
Barbara Bush Foundation, 86–87
Barnhart, June E., 155
Beaty, Janice, 82
"Being Fluent with Information Technology"
   (National Research Council), 115
Berger, Pam, 118
Bilal, Dania, 103–4
Billington, James, 57
Bishop, Ann, 64
Block, Cathy, 104
Block, Peter, 6
Bloom, Benjamin, 38, 169
Bond, Meg, 162
Booher-Jennings, Jennifer, 26, 27
Books for Kids, 87–88

About the Editors and Contributors

DENISE E. AGOSTO is an assistant professor in the College of Information Science and Technology at Drexel University, where she teaches graduate courses in children's resources, public library service, information resources and services, social and professional aspects of information service, and qualitative research methods. Her research interests include multicultural resources for children and teens, public library services, and youth information-seeking behaviors. She has published more than 50 articles, book chapters, and encyclopedia entries on these topics.

PAM BERGER, a library and educational technology consultant, is publisher and editor of *Information Searcher,* a newsletter focusing on the Internet in schools and author of *Internet for Active Learners: Curriculum Strategies for K–12* (ALA Editions). Ms. Berger is an adjunct faculty member at Syracuse University School of Information Studies and is coordinator of the Syracuse University NYC PLUS Program. She has published articles in *School Library Journal, Multimedia Schools, Technology and Learning, CD-ROM Professional, Family PC, PSLA Learning and Media, Information, Processing and Management,* and *American Libraries.* Berger's blog, Infosearcher, at http://www.infosearcher.com, offers updates on new resources, strategies, and tips on using the Internet effectively in the teaching and learning process.

Her recent work includes school and public library development initiatives, university research projects and project assessment including New York City Department of Education, Library REACH Program; Libraries for the Future, National Equal Access Program in Arizona, Massachusetts, New York and Pennsylvania; Improving Literacy through School Libraries, Department of Education Federal Grant.

ELIZABETH DOBLER is an assistant professor of reading and language arts at Emporia State University. She teaches preservice and experienced teachers in both face-to-face and online formats. Prior to her position at the university, she was a classroom teacher for 13 years at the elementary and middle school levels. Dr. Dobler's research interests and experiences focus on understanding the processes used for reading on the Web. Throughout this research, she has worked closely with classroom teachers, library media specialists, and instructional technology specialists.

CAROL A. GORDON is an associate professor in the School of Communication, Information and Library Studies at Rutgers, The State University of New Jersey, and the director of research for the Center for International Scholarship in School Libraries. She has served as a school library media specialist and library administrator in elementary, middle school, high school, and academic libraries in public and private schools. She holds an MS degree from City University of New York, an MLS from Western Michigan University and an EdD from Boston University. She is the author of *Information Literacy in Action* and co-authored *Privacy in the 21st Century* as well as numerous journal articles. She has served on the executive board and executive committee of the American Association of School Librarians and is past president of the New England Educational Media Association. Her consulting and presentations extend to Africa, Asia, and Europe, as well as the United States. Her current research focuses on adolescent information searching behavior, the impact of school libraries on student learning, the development and testing of guided inquiry methodologies, and the application of Bayesian statistics and the Theory of E.

VIOLET HARADA is a professor of library and information science in the Department of Information and Computer Sciences at the University of Hawaii at Manoa. She has been a secondary teacher, curriculum writer, elementary school librarian, and state specialist with the Hawaii Department of Education before joining the University of Hawaii teaching faculty. In addition to her teaching duties, she coordinates the school library specialization for the Library and Information Science Graduate Program. Her major areas of research involve inquiry-based approaches to information seeking and use and on the study of teacher and librarian collaborative partnerships. She examines how K–12 students learn best and teaching practices that help students achieve their learning goals. She works closely with school librarians and teachers to bring these "best practices" into classrooms and school libraries. She has published articles and books on these topics and is a frequent speaker at state, national, and international conferences.

SANDRA HUGHES-HASSELL is an associate professor in the School of Information and Library Science at the University of North Carolina at Chapel Hill. In her 25-year career she has also been an elementary school teacher, a school library media specialist, and director of the Philadelphia Library Power Project. In her current research she focuses on resources and services to youth and the instructional role of the information specialist. She has experience as both an editor and author. Her most recent book, co-authored with Jacqueline C. Mancall, is entitled *Collection Management for Youth: Meeting the Needs of Learners* (ALA, 2005). She has published numerous articles, book chapters, and training manuals.

BONNIE MACKEY is an assistant professor in early childhood education at the University of Houston-Clear Lake. She has taught elementary students for several years and currently teaches reading development in young children at both the undergraduate and graduate levels. Dr. Mackey earned her doctorate in curriculum and instruction with a concentration in language, literacy and culture from Texas A & M University in College Station, Texas. She is the co-author of the book, *Collaborating for Real Literacy: Librarian, Teacher and Principal,* published by Linworth in 2004. Dr. Mackey has presented at many state, national, and international conferences and has served as a consultant for balanced literacy programs in Texas schools.

MARY JO NOONAN is a professor of special education at the University of Hawaii at Manoa. She coordinates the Graduate Program for Teaching Students with Severe Disabilities and the Ph.D. in Education Program, Exceptionalities Specialization. She has been the principal investigator of several early childhood special education grants as well as teacher education and leadership training grants. She has worked extensively as a consultant throughout the Pacific Basin region. Recent publications are in the areas of Native Hawaiians and special education, and early childhood special education inclusion. In 2006 she co-authored the text, *Young Children with Disabilities in Natural Environments: Methods and Procedures* with Paul H. Brookes Publishing Company.

MARJORIE PAPPAS is a freelance virtual library science professor, writer, and consultant. She is currently a part-time virtual instructor for the Professional Development Studies program at Rutgers University, teaching foundations and curriculum courses. Her previous university affiliations include Eastern Kentucky University, The University of Northern Iowa, and Wright State University (OH). Since becoming a freelance virtual professor she has taught for Drexel University, the University of Georgia, the University of Hawaii, and Indiana University at Indianapolis. Marjorie writes for *School Library Media Activities Monthly* and *Knowledge Quest,* focusing on information literacy, inquiry learning, digital libraries, and distance learning. She is on the editorial board of *Knowledge Quest.* She is the co-author of the Pathways to Knowledge® process model and Pathways to Knowledge® and Inquiry Learning (LU, 2002). Her current writing and presentations are typically focused on information literacy, inquiry learning, assessment, and digital libraries. She is the lead facilitator for the AASL Teaching and Learning Community, a virtual professional community.

SHARON PITCHER is an associate professor in the Department of Educational Technology and Literacy at Towson University in Maryland. She teaches graduate level reading courses. Dr. Pitcher has her doctorate in literacy from the University of Maryland in curriculum and instruction with a concentration in literacy. She was a reading specialist for over 20 years working both in schools and with adult literacy. She developed a family literacy program for Baltimore County Public Schools in Maryland, which she supervised for seven years. She is the co-author of the book, *Collaborating for Real Literacy: Librarian, Teacher, Principal,* published by Linworth, has presented at many national and international conferences, and is a professional development consultant in many schools in the Baltimore area.

BARBARA K. STRIPLING has had a 30-year career in education as a classroom teacher in Colorado and North Carolina, a K–12 library media specialist in Arkansas, a Library Power director in Tennessee, a school district director of instructional services in Arkansas, and director of library programs at New Visions for Public Schools, a local education fund in New York City. She is currently director of library services for the New York City Department of Education. She has written or edited numerous books and articles, including her latest, *Curriculum Connections through the Library: Principles and Practice* (Libraries Unlimited, 2003), co-edited with Sandra Hughes-Hassell. She is a former AASL president and a former member of the ALA Executive Board.

DANIEL SUTHERS is presently associate professor in the department of Information and Computer Sciences at the University of Hawaii at Manoa, where he directs the Laboratory for Interactive Learning Technologies (http://lilt.ics.hawaii.edu) and co-directs Hawaii Networked Learning Communities (http://hnlc.org). His research is generally concerned with technology-supported collaborative learning and online learning communities, with applications to K–12, university, and professional development contexts. His current focus is on technology affordances for intersubjective meaning-making. Dr. Suthers obtained his Bachelor of Fine Arts (1979) from Kansas City Art Institute, studied psychology at the graduate level at Northern Arizona University, 1982–1985, and then earned M.S. (1988) and Ph.D. (1993) degrees in computer science from the University of Massachusetts. Subsequently he worked at the Learning Research and Development Center of the University of Pittsburgh before coming to the University of Hawaii.

ROSS J. TODD is associate professor in the School of Communication, Information and Library Studies at Rutgers, The State University of New Jersey. He is director of the Center for International Scholarship in School Libraries (CISSL) at Rutgers University. CISSL fosters the transformative role of school libraries in twenty-first-century schools, their integral role in the learning fabric of schools, and their role in ongoing school improvement and reform. His primary teaching and research interests focus on adolescent information seeking and use. The research is multifaceted, and includes: understanding how children learn and build new knowledge from information, how school librarians and classroom teachers can more effectively empower student learning and demonstrate student achievement through evidence-based approaches, and how the development of constructivist learning approaches lead to deep learning. He has published more than 120 papers and book chapters and is an invited speaker at many international conferences, most recently in Scotland, the Netherlands, Philippines, Croatia and Australia.

JOYCE YUKAWA, assistant professor in the graduate program in library and information science at the College of St. Catherine, focuses her teaching and research on three critical areas at the intersection of librarianship, education, and technology: critical reflection, community, and professional development. Her ideas of professional development through critical reflection in community are based on the core element of awareness of self and problems in context. Critical reflection enables heightened awareness that can lead to transformations in perspective. She is particularly interested in how such transformations are supported and sustained as collective wisdom through online learning using social software. Prior to joining the College of St. Catherine, she had a career as a librarian and teacher of English to speakers of other languages in educational organizations and public and special libraries in the United States, Japan, Singapore, and the Philippines. She received her masters in library science from the University of Michigan and her doctorate in communication and information sciences from the University of Hawaii.